D1616435

ALAN
WATTS

DAVID STUART

CHILTON BOOK COMPANY • RADNOR, PENNSYLVANIA

For Helga Berliner

Published in Radnor, Pa., by Chilton Book Company
and simultaneously in Don Mills, Ont., Canada
by Thomas Nelson & Sons, Ltd.

Manufactured in the United States of America

Design by Arlene Putterman

LIBRARY OF CONGRESS CATALOGING IN PUBLICATION DATA

____

Alan Watts.

1. Watts, Alan Wilson, 1915-1973.
B945.W324H69 1976 1971 [B] 75-40066
ISBN 0-8019-5965-9

ACKNOWLEDGMENTS

The author wishes to thank John Murray (Publishers) Limited for permission to reprint extracts from *The Legacy of Asia,* and to thank Thames and Hudson Ltd. of London and Vanguard Press of New York for permission to quote from *Myth and Ritual in Christianity.*

CONTENTS

FOREWORD

Late in the 1950s there burst upon America from the west coast a new breath of air—a combination of the sweet smells of summer flowers, incense, marijuana, and stale wine. And wafted on this air came a new and sometimes indefinable set of mores and moral practices. A new generation of Americans had weighed the old, found it wanting in a sense never before seen on the American shore, and in rejecting the old ways of the generation above thirty-five, had turned to a freedom that the older people called license, but which was to spread and flourish until by the 1970s almost all that the flower children and Beatniks had advocated was generally accepted: from love beads to marijuana. Yes, even though the weed was still illegal in the 1970s, and its use sometimes severely punished by Authority, the attempt to stamp it out was no more effective than the attempt to do away with liquor in the 1920s.

In this mélange of odors and ideas there were a handful of leaders—poets, musicians, artists, writers. These were people who had thrown off the old for their own reasons and embraced the new, and then led the flower children in a search for something to replace the intense materialism of the "ticky-tacky box" society of the United States. And high among the leaders of this new society, foremost among the gurus who would convert the youth to new ideas about religion and philosophy, was a slender, youth-oriented Englishman by the name of Alan Wilson Watts—one of the first in America to affect the Christ-beard, to wear sandals and an old kimono, to be an advocate of free love and free wine and free spirit, and NOW—which he called Zen Buddhism. His primary forum for his ideas was writing—and the podium of the university. The well-heeled student bodies of the American universities had by this time become the principal source of income of people on the lecture circuit, and Alan Watts soon was moving around from Berkeley to Eugene to Ithaca to Cambridge to Princeton and New Haven and Stanford and back to Berkeley again, picking up lecture fees in four figures from the colleges and universities, and giving his message of Love and Now. Those were fine and attractive words to youth troubled by War and the Bomb—and thousands upon thousands of these youth began to buy the Watts books to try to understand what this erudite man was communicating about the Eastern world and how it could be adapted to the West. For that was Alan Watts' primary message above all else—that Zen and other avenues of Eastern thought were not assimilable only by Orientals as most Westerners (East is East and West is West and never the twain . . .) had believed for a hundred years or more.

Besides this, Alan Watts brought his message of love. Love was okay, he said. And by love he meant sexual love, and homosexual love, and love between man and nature—all kinds of love. Some detractors seem to believe that Watts did more to destroy home and mother than any other philosopher of the times. Perhaps. *But he never did destroy them for himself.* This contradiction is one of the facets of Alan Watts' character that was so fascinating; although he advocated free love, it was always adultery, because in all his thirty-odd years in America, Alan Watts was never unmarried for more than a few weeks at a time. He married three times—although he deplored formal marriage in his writings and his speeches.

This was an anomaly—like his hatred for suburbia, although he continued to live in suburbia most of his life. And where there is anomaly and conflict, there is interest. That's why the works of Alan Watts, the popularizer, continue to be so interesting after his death and have supplanted his personality, if not his influence.

Alan Watts wrote an autobiography. That book is as revealing in what it did not say as in what it did say. For Alan Watts was an exceedingly complex man, who showed only one side of his character to his adoring public. Beneath the free man, the Zen teacher, the tranquil, quiet philosopher who had it seemed, mastered the arts of living, there lived a tortured soul who was never quite at peace with himself, and who went through life regretting at least two youthful decisions that were to haunt him all the way: his first marriage, and his decision to leave his native England on the brink of war. He compounded it by becoming an Episcopal priest, and then deserting—nay, being forced out of—the fold.

This biography and study of the work of Alan W. Watts was conceived with the idea that no man is his own best student. Several times during the course of the research, friends of Mr. Watts suggested that his own writing was so voluminous and personal that he needed no biographer. Perhaps that is true, but the Watts of his friends is not necessarily the Watts of the world, and even among his friends he was seen in different ways. Indeed, as Alan Watts would have put it himself, his life, which occurred in the past, was seen through the present lives of every one of his friends, and each one's present was a different one at the time. So my Alan Watts is not their Alan Watts and will not be another's Alan Watts.

There could be many biographies, for he was a multifaceted man, and I have chosen to deal with him and his work as it hit the American scene. I am grateful to the librarians at Yale University libraries for a good deal of material and the use of many of Mr. Watts' books. Various people at Pantheon books were helpful. Jean Burden was extremely kind and made several suggestions. Maud Oakes gave me some information. Elsa Gidlow directed me to a number of points of research. Abe Mellinkoff of the San Francisco *Chronicle* made available to me the newspaper's voluminous files on Watts and gave me a bearing on him. Eugene Exman, Watts' editor at the publishing house then called Harper and Brothers, was kind enough to submit to a long interview by telephone, and later added more information about the Watts of one period. Officials of Northwestern University were helpful in providing names of various Watts acquaintances, and Dr. Bergen Evans, professor and television personality, wrote me about Watts.

I am also grateful to Paul McGuire of Pantheon Books for information about Watts' last book. Tim Seldes of the Russell &

Volkening Literary Agency told me of Watt's plans for a novel. Howard Sandum, Chief of Communications for the Lutheran Church in America, told me of experiences of his with Watts.

Russell H. Matthias of Chicago wrote me a letter that dispelled one misapprehension under which I was laboring. Patti Key of the Bookworks on Nantucket secured any number of Watts' works for me. Christine Carter, the astrologer of Nantucket, provided me with Watts' horoscope and much other valuable information and insight.

Margaret West of Paris gave a tremendous amount of useful information about Alan Watts at several stages of his career. So did John Cage, who knew Watts for a long time. Joseph Campbell, a very dear friend of Alan's, gave me a brief insight into the depth of their relationship.

For all his voluminous acquaintance, Watts was a hard man to track down because of the peripatetic nature of his friends (the people of the counterculture move readily) and because of the sense of loss that many of them felt, which made it hard for them to put their emotions into words. Jean Burden was specific about this—"just where do you begin?" she wrote me. And that, of course, was the problem of the biographer which I tried to solve.

One evening early in 1975 on Nantucket as I was writing this book about Alan Watts, there came to dinner at our house a young reporter for the New Bedford newspaper. He pried and poked about my mental furniture for half the evening, attempted to engage me in argument about local affairs "to get a rise," and at the end of the evening made a statement typical of his age, his time, and his craft:

"I don't know whether or not I like you," he said.

It is the kind of question that could be raised only by a person of the Western world, and probably only by an American. It is the kind of question that Alan Watts spent his lifetime obliviating; it represents the supreme personal ego of Western civilization as opposed to the Way, the Tao, that Alan Watts followed for nearly 58 years. For almost from the beginning of life even the very young Watts had a feeling of being at one with his universe. His universe extended beyond the bounds of Chislehurst, the village in which he was born in the dawn hours of January 6, 1915. Watts' universe extended beyond the bounds of Kent, that pleasant south-eastern county of England, rolling down to the hills and cliffs of Dover, with its thatched houses and its bricks and tudor stucco.

The question posed by my young reporter would never have occurred, even to a juvenile Watts, any more than the question of whether his environment "liked" him; because of a combination of circumstances, Alan Wilson Watts came into a quiet world and grew up surrounded by the factors—even complaisances—that make possible the establishment of a philosophy by the very young. Not that Alan Watts was to become a great philosopher. If any Western Philosopher with a capital P has ever said so, the remark has gone unnoticed. No follower of the Way—Zen or Tao as it might be called—would ever think in such terms, for there is no competition in the achievement of the Way. The prime achievement of Alan Watts did bring him publicity, notoriety, and the emoluments of the good life in his later years. In the terms of American success, it brought him fame and fortune, at least in moderate amounts, and in the United States the kind of success that passes for greatness: he became a celebrity. Knowing the uses of such fame, he composed a lengthy and impressive biography of himself for *Who's Who in America.* He wrote widely, he established a free-wheeling school of Asian studies. He spoke well and in a manner that appealed to youth. Since he lived in a youth oriented culture at a time when there was enough exposure in America to bring an interest in Asian thought, Watts found himself in the right place at the right time for a man of his ideas and accomplishments. It was as if he was part of the Tao, or the Tao determined all these seemingly chance conjunctions of circumstance. Alan Watts, a middleclass Englishman-American who never visited the East until his mature years, became the principal instructor of young America in the mysteries of Zen and Oriental intellectualism. His teaching flourished because of the natural interest occasioned by so many young Americans having casually rubbed against Orientalism in Vietnam and Japan and other Far Eastern places. The opportunity might have died, however, had not the right man been there at the right time to seize upon it. And more than Aldous Huxley or Richard Alpert (Baba Ram Dass) or any of the others, Watts in his writing and his lecturing seized the [illegible]n of young America. His contribution to the Tao, his [illegible]he Western concept of greatness, lies in his incredible [illegible]ranslate the mysteries of the East into terms understandable and acceptable to the consciousness-seeking youth of the twentieth century. For that, Alan Watts will not soon be forgotten. Most of his original hardcover books are long out of print, but the paperbacks continue to sell in the many thousands; nearly every American bookstore in 1975 carried at least one or two Watts titles in paper and the book establishments that appeal to the youth were bound to stock half a dozen or more. In those terms, Watts must be ranked among the most successful of authors, and temporarily at least among the more enduring. Only if the Youth Culture becomes disoriented by depression, would the Watts popularity decline suddenly. Finally, his works and reputation will decline as new interpreters of the ageless truths emerge to put the imprimatur of a new age on the Tao and to translate it into words and concepts of a new time. But until then, Watts will live through a body of work that has a very high vitality.

Alan Watts became a public instructor at the age of twenty, in 1935, with publication of *The Spirit of Zen.* As a schoolboy he had also written another work, *Myth and Ritual in Christianity,* but the Zen book was the important one. In it and through it the young Watts found his own way.

Time and circumstance, these were the dictators of Watts' emergence on the rim of the wheel of life. Looking at that life from the standpoint of the appropriate, one could scarcely do better in the Western world of the twentieth century than to choose a sleepy Kent village in England in which to grow up. Laurance W. Watts, the father, was an English middleclass business man, neither rich nor poor, in the tire and later motor trade. His mother was a retired school teacher whose subjects had been physical education and home economics, but whose interests were rococo in an Oriental fashion. She had taught in a school for the children of missionaries, and was used to seeing examples of Oriental art and culture about her. She brought to her marriage an unusual (for an Englishwoman) appreciation of Orientalism and Oriental art. She had, by being an Englishwoman of country stock, a deep-seated love of land and nature, which translated itself, for the young Alan, into gardening and long walks and the identification of things around him.

In his autobiography, *In My Own Way,* Alan Watts tells of life in this country village. It was mother-oriented in a way, because Watts' father's life was in the city. The impression Alan leaves is that of a skinny, weed-like boy growing toward puberty, hopelessly in love with the prettiest girl in the local village school, who spurned him because of his buck teeth and the lower social position of the Wattses. For she lived in a manor house on the edge of the village, and the Watts family lived in a cottage. They were not even up to the standards of the vicar, socially.

Out of this all, in a male-oriented Western society, came a youth who would make his own way, helped largely by women across the uncomfortable spots. He would be the recipient of a balanced English public school education, which held that its ministrations were all that were necessary to see a man through life, culturally speaking. And that was the contribution of his society. As for the rest, it was the making of Watts himself, as he travelled along the Way.

Find All
Secret Messages!

- Harry
Potter

CHAPTER ONE

THE WAY

In the last years he was drinking heavily. Those who had known him in the early days would scarcely recognize him now, beardless, scrawny of neck, bad teeth showing black, and his dissolution giving the appearance of a Third Street San Francisco bum. He lived in a tiny cottage on the side of Mt. Tamalpais and part of the time in a disused ferryboat in Sausalito. He had married three times and only the last time even remotely satisfactorily. To old friends he gave the appearance of a frustrated, cynical, aging man. This was the Alan Watts of the early 1970s—one of the most contradictory and most exciting figures of his age, a pied piper of the youth of America in the 1960s, grown suddenly old.

Having spent a lifetime defying the Western tradition—and trying in his own way to ameliorate it with the wisdom of the East to find a modern philosophy for a declining West which suddenly awakened to problems of power, energy, ecology and a strange diffidence of the young—Alan Watts suddenly seemed to have dried up. He was reduced to self-serving repetition for the most part, and his living was earned largely by the exposition of the things he had been saying for 20 years. But the trouble in the beginning of the 1970s was that fewer people were listening; and as the guru of Zen Buddhism he had largely been replaced by younger men who had taken the trouble to go to Japan and other Buddhist places and study at the sources of the Eastern knowledge.

That is not to say that what Alan Watts had contributed to the study of Eastern philosophy was not valid. When he began his writings there were virtually no other Westerners who could define Zen, let alone discourse on the subject. But such was the change in the world in 30 years that by the end of his life there were many Westerners better versed than he. With the exception of his autobiography, the books of his last few years lacked the purpose and shocking power that had gone before. One of his most pretentious, *Erotic Spirituality* (1971), with photos by Eliot Elisofon, was obviously a publishing venture far more than an extension of Alan Watts' personality. This book, about the Indian temple at Konarak, was Eliot Elisofon's book; he was the journalist who had visited the great holy place many a time. Alan Watts had not even been to the Far East before he was into middle age; his *Vision of Konarak*, as the text of the book was called, was a rehash of a great deal that he had said before in other books in other ways, and his first excursion into yoga.

No, these were not Alan Watts' best years. Nor was he a very happy man. John Cage, his artist friend of earlier days, now declared that Watts had "no or little aesthetic sense" and lamented the heavy drinking he had come to in the last years. At a seminar in Big Sur, a participant wondered why Alan Watts appeared to have a dreadful hangover and looked as though he was about to collapse—if only he could find a convenient gutter.

He was, at the end of the 60s and beginning of the 70s going backward in his life—clinging to the past. He made up with John Cage—with whom he had quarreled over Cage's interpretation of Zen in the 1950s. He proposed that they work together. Cage always liked him—the bright eyes, the quick smile, the ready, witty conversation. But Cage had his own way, and Alan's personal habits had then become so irregular that Cage found it inadvisable to pick up the offer.

Although he had recently married, in the winter of 1968 he sat down and wrote a letter to a girl he had taught in college 20 years before, lamenting the fact that he had not married *her.** This girl saw him a few months later and was overwhelmed at the change in the man who had been her teacher and spiritual advisor.

Alan Watts went home that year to visit his only real person of attachment in the British Isles, his father, who in his nineties seemed to still have a vigor that Alan Watts had lost along the way. Alan was ego-ridden, and yet somehow pathetic about it—he bragged to his friends about his international reputation and yet in an almost humble way he recited the writings *about* him in Paris *Match* and other important world publications. By the standards he had come to adopt for himself, he had "made it big" in every way. He had enough income to do as he pleased, he had fathered seven children, plus another born to his first wife that he did not accept as his own. He had largely kept up with the enthusiasms of his youth and with many of the people. But somehow they had passed him by, and he was not really content to sit on his mountain top and contemplate the universe as had all his spiritual forbears.

There were moments: When Alan and his third wife Jean Froman Watts came to England, there was a roundup of old acquaintances in a hotel suite at the Charing Cross Hotel. Friends saw for a bit the old Alan "blazing eyed and roaring with delight." He had the beard again, a grizzled beard this time, and it improved appearances no end. Friends were astounded to hear him calling his ninety-two-year-old father "Daddy"—and he seemed sunk in the past. They all went to the famous Simpsons-on-the-Strand—Alan could easily afford the luxury with the prosperity that had come to him in the last decade in America—but there he seemed to lose control of the show, something that would never have happened a few years earlier. He was no longer the guru,

* This was Margaret Jacobson West, whose relationship to Watts is explored fully later in the book. "If I ever made a serious mistake in my life," he wrote her in December 1968, "it happened around 1950. It was simply that I failed to ask you to marry me. . . .

advising all comers with an absolute sense of surety how they should live their lives. He seemed unsure; even the Zen that had carried him through so much for so long seemed no longer to stick out either in his conversation or in his manner.

And that was Alan Watts at the end. Let us look at him at the beginning and in the middle.

孩 

CHAPTER TWO

CHILDHOOD

It was a warm and comfortable little village, and the boy who studied his grammar and nature and his math and Latin and languages was very observing. He seemed to inhale all about him. Every one and every thing had a character. Half a century later he was able to reconstruct with a sharp eye and a fine pen the looks of the bathroom of the cottage in which he had grown up down here in the county of Kent. The romanticism of time had not dimmed his able memory.

There is a kind of sensitivity to nature quite common among country people of England, not nearly so often seen in America—a learning and an appreciation of nature for its own sake. An American farmer will know the look and feel and smell of all his grains and grasses, and he will know a redwinged blackbird from a crow, but his ornithological attitudes might stop just about there. Whereas a sensitive English boy of a village would be likely to be able to easily identify a half dozen ferns and even relatively rare songbirds; such knowledge on the part of his American counterpart would be unusual enough to occasion a Merit Badge. The young weed named Alan Watts grew so, seeing what was around him, and living at a pace slow enough to permit such indulgence. After all, he was born in 1915, and while there was war on, by the time he began sitting up and taking a look about the world outside the house, that war was over, and the world he emerged into was basking in the security of having defeated the Wicked Hun. The inflation of the 1920s was not yet a serious threat. The depression of the 1930s was yet to begin haunting the villages of England.

So the boy grew, inquisitive, loving nature, admiring what he saw around him, not knowing that all these qualities he displayed at so early an age would come together later to enable him to translate another world into terms that his contemporaries could understand.

As a boy he played at childish games, and he did his share of aping his elders by conducting full funerals for animals he found dead along the pathways of his village. He was a solitary boy, and he did not care for gang games; nor did he much like tennis, or any organized activity.

But he saw and he knew the people who counted in the village—the local chemist, and the lady who ran the sweet shop, and the village green grocer and the rector of the Anglican church who wore a priest's round hat and a cassock and round collar on his daily peregrinations to visit the sick and aged.

Young Alan was lucky in time and place: his parents stayed put and his boyhood was spent roaming an open countryside. (There was, for example, an acre plot behind the cottage where he lived, and that gave the Wattses place to play and garden, and even to keep rabbits during one period when the senior Watts decided it would be a profitable and useful enterprise.)

His father potted about, indulging in such hobbies as entomology, which was a proper gentleman's pursuit in the 1920s. Tagging along, Alan learned a great deal about bugs and other assets of England's natural scene. These facets of nature lore never left him, although his pursuit of them changed drastically as he matured. But he had friends, and he learned to smoke cigarettes and indulge in other forbidden pleasures out beneath the trees beyond the edges of the village. Initiated, he initiated others into such sinful delights.

Watts' mother was a collector of Oriental furniture and Oriental art in a small way, and so the boy grew up among brass trays with Sanskrit inscriptions, Chinese vases decorated with calligraphy, and the smells of sandalwood and lacquer. He was a little old for A. A. Milne—the Pooh books were published in the mid-twenties after Alan Watts had reached the ripe old age of ten. But he was not too old for Rudyard Kipling's tales of adventure in India—and it was *British India* in a time when "Empire" was still a meaningful word.

He was also "bitten" at about the age of ten by Sax Rohmer, the inventor of the master Oriental villain Fu Manchu. The adventures of the wispy bearded, Mandarin-gowned Fu appeared regularly in British magazines, and delighted adult and older child alike. From these tales of beautiful maidens and wicked doings in Limehouse and Canton, Alan Watts could almost smell the ginseng and the powdered deer's horn and the incense when the postman came. Later he would attribute the beginnings of his love for Orientalia to the Fu Manchu adventures.

Early on, the Watts family decided that Alan had the inquisitive nature and sensitivity to make of himself a scholar. Would he be lawyer, doctor or churchman?—it made no difference. With the respect for education of the middleclass Englishman, and the possibility of it that existed for those who could afford a public school education—Alan Watts could be destined for the guaranteed high income of a middleclass world that was not so easily reached through trade.

The Watts autobiography is especially delightful in the exploration of this middleclass childhood, in the wonderful rememberings of a time when there was leisure in the world and of prayers, and constipation, and patent medicines and girls.

Several important factors which influenced Watts' later life appeared in his childhood. First was the undoubted love of nature that his surroundings and his family engendered. It is quite possible for a country youngster to go through a boyhood in completely rural surroundings and remember nothing but stinks—the stinks of the chicken house, or the piggery, or the cow barns. And that boy, with that attitude, is likely to immerse himself in the nauseous gases of the city and remain there forever, retreating no further than suburbia. But it is also possible for a country boy to retain the country without sacrificing an iota of his ambition to explore the world to its fullest—and that is the kind of person that Alan Watts became. Love of nature, that was one attribute Kent and his family gave him. Hatred of priggishness and Christian prayers—that was another. Very early, Alan began to question the prayers he learned by rote, which painted good Christians as dreadful dullards, and heaven as the most boring place in the cosmos—either heaven was the most boring place or his childhood bedroom was; Alan's bedroom was to him a functional place for sleeping and being sick in.

Much of this learning and observing and living in the world of sight and sound and smell occurred during Alan Watts' first seven-and-a-half years. Usually he had a nanny or a governess to take care of his needs and watch his bowels.

But, at seven-and-a-half years old, as was the fashion in middleclass English homes, he was sent off to boarding school "to make a man of him." What it did with most Britons was to create the stiff upper lip of British fiction, to turn honest and reasonable little boys with normal emotions into hardshell crabs, or homosexuals, or both, to inculcate in them either a tremendous hardiness and love for cold showers and wool shirts without undershirts, or an absolute hatred of both, a hatred which could include cricket and rowing. At seven-and-a-half, Alan Watts left the last nanny and went off to St. Hugh's School. He went out then to be alone in that same sense that British boys were always alone thereafter.

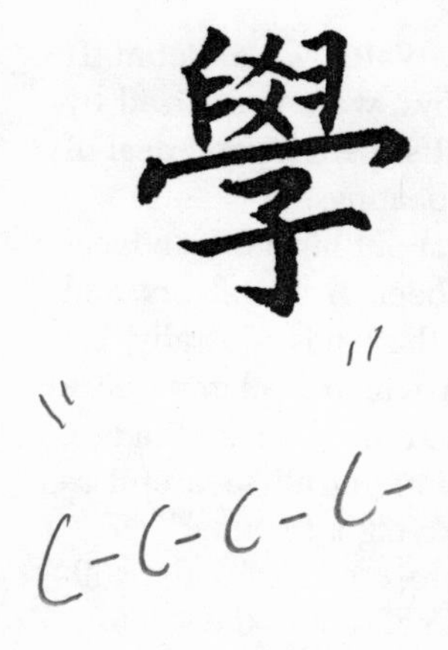

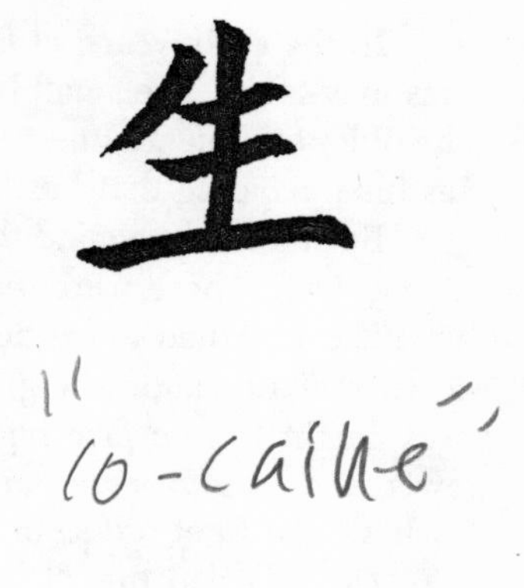

CHAPTER THREE

THE STUDENT

There is nearly everything to be said against the "public school" form of education, unless the purpose is to create a class of Spartans for the purpose of carrying out wars in far-off places. Few who spend their years in boarding schools—particularly, those who enter before the age of puberty, fail to be deeply affected by the experience. For boarding school, no matter what the parents and guardians *say*, is a means of fobbing off the humanizing processes of life and education of the young on a third party. It may relieve the parents. It may even be necessary, and in the case of orphans, it is almost inevitable. But the result is the dehumanization and even the "bestializing" of small boys. They become gangsters or victims, one or the other.

In the early years, at St. Hugh's, Alan Watts was a victim. It was inevitable. The small boys, the new boys, were brutalized by the older and bigger ones. And so Alan Watts spent a good deal of his time avoiding that bestiality and those beatings.

But there were good things to be said about his public education as well. There were masters who had been army officers, and who had travelled to exotic places such as the lands of Araby. He learned mathematics, a species of French which he later swore was taught from a joke book, for he learned all about old ladies, owls, and *la plume de ma tante*, and nothing at all so useful as "where can I get a decent meal without paying a fortune?"

He regarded the study of history as propaganda for the still-vigorous empire. He learned Latin and some classics—the smattering of knowledge that passes for culture in the West.

He learned sport well enough to hate even more most organized games, and this feeling extended in later life even to parlor games such as bridge and Monopoly. He was good enough and athletic enough to make the rugby team at St. Hugh's, but when he went on to his next school he lost interest in that sport and turned to others.

St. Hugh's covered the years 1923–1928. He was beaten for pranks, some of them childish and some more serious. He and a companion spent a great deal of time tramping in the woods on clement days, or riding bicycles through the lanes and fields around the school. In 1928, his further education was a matter of concern. The year was a bad one for the British economy, and the Watts family resources were somewhat strained to keep Alan in school. The next school up, for older boys, was likely to be more expensive.

Alan Watts solved that problem, however, by winning a scholarship to King's School, Canterbury, and went there in autumn, 1928. St. Hugh's had been close to home, and Alan's wanderings there were always within reasonable distance of the two-story brick cottage and the fields and village he had known since boyhood. But King's School was something else again. It was one of the oldest public schools in England, a cloistered, dank place, which supposedly went back to the sixth century, *anno domini*. Pupils, students, masters and the churchmen of Canterbury cathedral were set off from the city of Canterbury by walls, and, of course, much more than that. For they were important people in a squalid industrial place; Canterbury was the seat of the Church of England, and the Archbishop was the English Pope, ever since the days of Henry VIII. The Archbishop lived in lordly splendor, and the Dean of the Cathedral only slightly less. Pleasing and studious boys were sometimes entertained within the rich precincts of these apartments, and in time Watts made himself pleasant and proved bright enough to be included among that number.

What the biographer looks for in the life of his subject are the threads and pieces that seem to have a meaning in the direction of life that would follow. The concept—even the whole idea of biography—could be challenged by a serious student of the Tao or Zen, who could say with fine justification that all this tracing is rot: it was meant to be and that is why it was, and is, and will be.

Still, chancing that kind of criticism, let it be noted that at St. Hugh's and much more at Canterbury school, the young Alan Watts acquired distastes that were to last him all his adult life. They included:

Drabness of the spirit.

Boiled beef, boiled cabbage, boiled almost anything.

Drabness of dress. Also nonfunctionality, which meant boaters and starched wing collars.

Homosexuality. It lay bubbling just beneath the surface. (Watt's views may later have changed.)

Cruelty.

Regimentation.

He also acquired in these early years certain characteristics; some of the spirit, and some of surroundings:

Love of color.

Love of movement.

Love of love.

Interest in things Asian.

Understanding of the educational process.

That latter acquisition perhaps requires some exposition; the young Watts was admirably fitted to become a serious scholar in history or law or languages or the church. He had a bright and inquiring mind, and both mother and father had encouraged him in intellectual pursuits. He was not only a bug collector, as are many boys at an early age, but in the days at home, the days at St. Hugh's, and the long vacations at Canterbury, Watts accompanied his father and a local squire in insect-hunting expeditions. Then he chloroformed and mounted his specimens, identified, and kept them in cases. It was all scientific.

As for his literary education, by school's end he knew considerable Latin, a little Greek, enough French to get by in a literary way, much more than he admitted to in his joking.

His mother had presented him with a little prayer book in Chinese ideograms at an early age, which kindled an interest in that language, and he began what was to become a life-long if desultory study of the written language of the Middle Flowery Kingdom. In later life he was to profess "being half-miseducated in the manner described by George Bernard Shaw." Perhaps. But by the standards of the world around him, before he left Canterbury, young Watts was as well-educated as most public school boys. And the purpose of the public school in those days was to prepare young men for life. Only serious students, churchmen, and potential lawyers joined the idle rich at the big universities. Some went to Sandhurst or directly into regiments or the navy. Many went into business firms to serve an apprenticeship and then end up in "The City," with cottages in Kent or Sussex. Watts' education prepared him for any of these courses.

No matter his various acquisitions—he had an acquisitive mind. How many youngsters read the *Encyclopaedia Britannica* starting with A? A few, certainly—Alan Watts was not a lonely genius, but he did open his eyes wide and his ears and his nose and mouth, to savor the world about him. He enjoyed the processes of education. That ambience of his is important, because, along with a love for women and an enjoyment of pure and simple sensuality, it became the guiding factor in Watts' life.

Watts' experiences until 1928 were characteristically English, but the first year at Canterbury brought many changes. The boy had reached puberty, and was straining at the family bonds as boys will do, seeking new experiences, losing the awe of the parental gods.

Now he came under the tutelage of a local character, Francis Croshaw, who affected the youth so much that in his autobiography Watts described Croshaw as his first guru or personal teacher.

Croshaw and his wife were people of fashion: to them bedrooms were places to live and lounge, not just to sleep; food was to be enjoyed and not just eaten; wine was to be drunk and not just to make you drunk; clothes were to please you, not just to cover you. Croshaw smoked big black Burma cheroots and wore a Moroccan dressing gown around the house and drove a two-seater roadster. The Croshaws had two houses—an amazing luxury in those times. One house was in Chislehurst, and at this one they brought Alan Watts into the careless luxury where people read French novels. The second house was near Rye in the sand dunes of the sea, and because he was a friend of young Ivan Croshaw, Watts was asked along to the house and taught to drink French wines and eat with gusto. Better than that in the long summer vacation of 1929, Watts accompanied the Croshaws to France. They went to Saint-Malo. Here Alan was introduced to European cafes and cafe and street life—entirely foreign to a middleclass English boy of the roast beef and trifle education. They went to good restaurants and ate artichokes and snails and delicious meat concoctions that would have been thrown out in the garbage at home. They went to the races and to wine shops and Watts learned about wine and cheese and bread—matters on which his own parents were as woefully uneducated as most middleclass Englishmen.

They spent some weeks near Cap Breton, and the artful Croshaw took them to a bullfight in the Basque country, to the gambling tables of Biarritz, and to a performance of jai alai or pelota in the Pyrenees. By the end of that holiday, Alan Watts had the beginnings of an education that would last him all his life—in the arts of living the good life.

The impressions of that summer were indelible and deep. And in the fall came another happenstance that would direct him: in a bookshop in Canterbury he came across a book on ghosts by Lafcadio Hearn. At least that is what he took it to be, and having a young boy's interest in things ghostly, and having explored all the local ghost stories of the cathedral and the bounds of Canterbury *ecclesiastica*, he became interested in Japanese ghosts.

So Hearn had him. Hearn taught Watts to appreciate the lightness, airiness, and love of form and simplicity that is peculiarly Japanese. This appreciation furthered Watts' already awakened interest in things Oriental.

Alan, now fourteen, brought to his observation of Orientalia a sympathy that was quite unusual in a Western youth who'd never been specifically tutored thus.

School, poking about in the library and in the bookstalls, and learning comparative religion occupied much of Alan Watts' energies in this year of 1929–1930 that was so devastating to the outside world. In the short vacations he went home and borrowed books from Croshaw's extensive library of exotica. He was reading Hearn's *Gleanings in Buddha Fields*, and he borrowed Edmond Holmes' *Creed of Buddha*, in which he found a pamphlet about Buddhism. In it, he discovered that in London there existed a Buddhist Lodge, a real link with the Eastern wisdom.

All this exciting information came to Watts a-tumble, but before the year was out, he had immersed himself in the philosophy of the East and discovered that the concept of nirvana, of a constant universe, was precisely what he expected the world to be all about—and that the world was not full of deadly Trinities, dull Virgin Marys, wriggly cherubs, and sexless Angels.

At this point, Watts rejected Christianity, and the concept of the God-the-Father, God-the-Son, and God-the-Holy Ghost that is the rock of the Church. He did not believe it. He did believe what the Eastern religions add up to—that the universe exists, and is orderly, and that everything one can see and taste and hear and smell, and perhaps a great deal more besides, exists in that universe and has its explainable place in it; but there is no need for explanation nor is explanation possible, because understanding is reached by becoming at one with that universe, and understanding is total participation in the universe.

Watts tried these ideas out on English friends. His school pals were dismayed but properly respectful of one who had chosen "The Way." His friend the elder Croshaw was sympathetic and interested in the boy's ideas. Friends and relations of Croshaw had various reactions—but none of them was the shock that Watts could have expected from one of the proper English middleclass or the churchmen who surrounded and supervised his education. It was possible for the prelacy to accept almost any number of deviations from the religious norm—even down to almost downright agnosticism. But they certainly could not stomach the pantheism that Watt's approach to life now demanded. It would be like chanting a witch doctor's exorcisms during the mass.

But steadily, as he progressed through the forms of Canterbury School, Watts was delving further into the Oriental mysteries and becoming more captivated each month.

Out of Holmes' book, he extracted the pamphlet that had been tucked away there, and discovered it was a study of the work of the London Buddhist Lodge, by Christmas Humphreys, the director. Watts wrote Humphreys, soon had an answer, contrived a visit to London, and found himself a new guru. Francis Croshaw had played out his role in Watts' life, if his lessons were not forgotten.

In 1930 Watts came to London, where Humphreys led him into reading the works of D. T. Suzuki, the master of Zen. On his own he began to investigate other profound studies of the mysteries, and the athletic practice of yoga. He read Swami Vivekananda, and practiced deep-breathing exercises—the first move into yoga. He picked up the word and concept of karma, which means fate and man's irresistible move to conform to his own nature. He was, by this time, thoroughly entranced with the study of Eastern religion, and would remain so the rest of his life.

More than most young men, Alan Watts had opportunity to compare the studies he was making as part of his education with his private world. He went to church services regularly. He advanced in standing in the school to the point where he was brought into the "brotherly" aspects. That is, he was chosen to do such things as represent the Canterbury School at a national conference on religion at Hayward's Heath, Surrey, a meeting which was led by the Archbishop of York—a stout churchman with round collar and belly to match, whose laugh came rumbling up out of that proud substance to ring for yards and reverberate about the walls of any room. Here Watts was in the presence of the most socially and religiously advanced, amiable type of Anglican clergyman. And Watts was impressed.

But he was equally impressed with his nocturnal and sybaritic meanderings into the city bookstalls and the mysteries of the East.

Ivan Croshaw was still Watts' close friend, even if the young man had moved beyond the kind of sensual awakening he had received from the elder Croshaw. The two of them managed to get into London from time to time, and wandered about in the town, where Watts picked up more of Vivekananda's work, including the specific instructional manual *Raja Yoga.* Secretly, in his dormitory room on the top floor of the school, looking out over the gray stone buildings, he practiced the exercises that were not forbidden only because nobody in authority had the slightest suspicion that *anyone* would every bring that foreign Eastern stuff into the sacred premises. And when Watts came down with the "flu" and was hustled off to the infirmary for several weeks of recuperation, he worked over his yoga at the expense of his school exercises. Caesar and Tacitus lost, and the Buddha won.

School holidays in 1930 and 1931 consisted of getting to London as quickly as possible and having as much to do with the Buddhist Lodge and Christmas Humphreys as was possible. Here Alan met many exotic people, some of them Russian exiles. And since Humphreys loved the ballet and the opera, these new delights were opened for Watts, and he learned to admire the Russian life style, too. He was opening his eyes wider and searching more diligently, for now he was studying several aspects of Oriental religion—southern- or India-Ceylon-based Buddhism, and the northern or Zen-Tao way. He was, he called himself, "a shaman" on his own way in a religious jungle. One thing he had decided—he could not pursue the vocation of Anglican churchman because he did not believe.

And this matter was to become important in 1932, because he completed his early formal education that year. He did very well—and was head boy at Canterbury in his senior form. By this time he had published a booklet on Zen. It has since disappeared into the maw of history—a loss that brought Watts considerable pleasure in the last years of his life, for it apparently was a juvenile effort. But he was also writing serious articles under the direction of Christmas Humphreys. And at King's School, Watts had quite a following—although subterranean—and several of the boys he knew persisted for a time in their association with Buddhism after they left.

Watts departed in the winter of 1932, a term before the end of the school year. He would not be a churchman—he might otherwise have secured support from the church for higher education. He was a senior prefect, captain of his house, and a leader of his sixth form.

And yet his thinking was definitely not that of a middleclass young English gentleman of the 1930s. When it came time to write senior essays for those who would have church support in going on, Watts refused to conform to the proper way of doing things and wrote an essay the authorities found out of tone and out of character for a student.

Perhaps it was inevitable. The Tao would hold it so. At fifteen Watts was a declared Buddhist. He was really ashamed of the culture in which he had grown up. Sexually, he was white-hot and itching to lose a virginity that had become a great burden—with no opportunity at all outside of holiday to perform heterosexual exercises, although more opportunity than the masters could possibly imagine for other activity. One of his handful of really good friends was turfed out of the school for taking a long walk in the woods with the daughter of a local greengrocer—and apparently not at all because her father complained. Sex—and especially illicit sex—was something to be practiced by the youth at every available opportunity (their view) and never to be heard about (world view) and to be considered most dangerous (female view).

Alan Watts' paternal grandfather was a professional photographer, and that did not much appeal to Alan. His Uncle Harry ran a Woods' tobacconists' shop on Queen Victoria street in the city. But there was no place in the tobacco world for Alan except as a confirmed smoker who had begun at thirteen, even though tobacco smoking was then regarded by authority with the same opprobrium as marijuana smoking was to be regarded by a later generation of authority.

In the cold and dreary winter of 1932 there were few places in the London scene for a bright young native Buddhist. He might go to Hyde Park and talk his head off—even appearing in *dhoti* or kimono or yellow robes if he so chose. But he most certainly would not earn enough from that to pay the rent and feed the gas meter.

Laurence Watts did the very best thing he could for his son, not having the money to send him off to Oxford to complete his education. He gave him sound advice about life, and the need for self-education. He accompanied his son to sessions at the Buddhist Lodge and guided by a sense of orderliness, became that group's treasurer. And—he found a place in his own organization for his son to have a temporary job, soliciting funds for the London hospitals. With Alan's presence and his wonderful gift of gab—for he was a dark, slender young man who carried a furled umbrella and wore tweeds or dark suits with the flair of "a gentleman"—he could impress hard-hearted business people and soft dowagers.

And thus, with a job, and the trains that ran from Chislehurst to London, and the right to live at home and eat at the family board, and sleep in his old bed, Alan Watts descended upon London in the winter of 1932. As he put it himself, he did not feel burdened by poverty or the lack of the higher educational facilities. He was reading for himself, and he was ready to face the world. Ready?—the truth was he could hardly wait.

照 

CHAPTER FOUR

THE EDUCATION

"You look with friendly eyes upon fellow humans, and much of your effort may be directed toward the welfare of others." So read the horoscope of Alan Watts that Nantucket astrologist Christine Carter drew—based on only the facts that Watts had himself revealed to the world in his autobiography.

Writing in 1972, Watts gave the necessary details:

He was born at Rowan Tree Cottage in Holbrook Lane, in the village of Chislehurst, Kent, almost due south of Greenwich, on the morning of January 6, 1915, at about 20 minutes after six, with the sun in Capricorn, conjuncted with Mars and Mercury, and in trine to a moon in Virgo, with Sagittarius rising, and under bombardment in the midst of the First World War.

Watts had, in effect, invited astrologers to map his life; he had wanted that and he had had it done for him before. He was a believer, he said so in an article in the June, 1941, issue of *Horoscope*, the leading American astrology magazine, in which he indicated that astrology was a valid part of the Way—"thus the horoscope relates you to the universe, giving you and it one and the same map. . . . All horoscopes, as maps of the universe, are equally good because they are all whole. . . . "

And other astrologers, writing about Watts, referred back to that Sagittarius symbol, and said they could have predicted he would be a person connected with religion:

"Self-expression, success—all important. . . .

"Enthusiastic energy, contagious and inspiring to others. . . .

"Personal magnetism very strong. . . . "

This was the seventeen-year-old who thrust himself out into the world of London, entering that city's life, without causing a single tremor in the foggy early months of 1932.

Under adjurations from his old teachers, and from his father, and above all from Christmas Humphreys, Alan Watts was reading as much as if, indeed, he had gone off to Oxford to be tutored and pass. He was reading Lafcadio Hearn, and Lionel Fuechtwanger, Anatole France, Havelock Ellis, Bernard Shaw, and Robert Graves—who had suddenly spurted into popularity after a long writing career. He was also reading others: Keyserling, and Nietzsche.

And above all he was reading the Orientalists who were at King's School: Vivekananda, Lao Tzu, the *Upanishads*, the *Bhagavad Gita*, the *Diamond Sutra*, and D.T. Suzuki.

Of them all, Suzuki was to have the most lasting effect on Watts. He worked at collecting funds for the hospitals each weekday, and then repaired to the tall house on the dreary street in Pimlico, where he mounted the stairs and was transported into another world—the Orient. For this was Toby Humphreys' house. Here were the sights and smells of the Orient, enhanced and preserved by the thinker and his wife Eileen.

The library interested Alan Watts most. The Humphreys lent him books and guided his interests, and introduced him to a concerned and serious bookseller. This person was Nigel Watson, who with his father John Watson, ran a bookstore at Cecil Court on Charing Cross Road. It was a store specializing in the mysteries, and while most of the material was occult and much of it rather frothy, the collection on Far Eastern philosophy and religion was regarded then as the finest in London. Here the budding Buddhist went to secure his stones of faith.

Through the bookshop, which was also a gossip parlor for the odd people who frequented the shelves, Alan Watts met Dmitrije Mitrinović from Yugoslavia, who lived near the British Museum in the Bloomsbury district of London; who wore formal clothes most of the time, a cutaway coat, bowler hat, and striped trousers. The young Watts was so impressed by this Balkan guru that he aped his dress and began carrying a stick. Mitrinović knew about the mysteries of the East, and he took a liking to the young Englishman and began inviting him to parties and places of amusement.

There was gaiety in these meetings, for as Alan Watts was learning religion and philosophy, he was also learning the taste of beef stroganoff, and chicken paprikash, and *dolmades* and other dishes of southeastern Europe. His education was broadened in a number of ways; he learned to drink slivovitz and ouzo, and he began to gain an appreciation of liqueurs to match the initiation into wines given him by Francis Croshaw.

Now, working in London, travelling on the trains, and listening to his arcane friends discourse on matters that often were beyond his ken, Alan Watts was judging his society, and finding it culturally lacking. He thought of England as "diseased with religion." He was familiar with all the rites—he had carried the train of the new Archbishop of Canterbury in the investment procession, and he had discussed matters of religion with bishops before he was seventeen. So he knew what he was rejecting, and why: he was ashamed of a civilization that fostered violence and thrived on repression. For himself he wanted something brighter and more promising.

One must not for a moment forget that Alan Watts was one of the great lovers of life of the twentieth century. From his earliest days, the free life beckoned, and he was forever in search of experience and adventure.

The "enthusiastic" energy forecast in his horoscope was

there, and it showed itself in his relations with the Buddhist Lodge people and in his newfound friends.

He already recognized in himself the showman that he was to become, and his foppish dress was a part of it. Mitrinović taught him about the ways of the occult lovers, and he adopted incense and other trappings. Yet he did not reject the useful and the attractive of the English culture.

He had other characteristics in his personality: a strong personal magnetism that caused men of forty and fifty to tolerate a teenager was his greatest gift of the moment. But he was not content simply to be tolerated. He had already written his Zen pamphlet and now he demolished Christianity with *Myth and Ritual in Christianity,* an expose of the foundings and practices of the church that justified his own rejection—at least in his young mind. Now, he wanted more. He wanted to exert an authority and leadership far beyond his tender years. He did not beat about the bush. As he studied the enlightenments and the roads of the Eastern philosophers, he determined that he would gain the respect of his elders by writing. He began to contribute to the Buddhist magazine published by Christmas Humphreys and to work on a book on Zen.

Mitrinović was a mysterious person who somehow always seemed to have money. He carried crisp new five-pound notes about with him and paid for daily expenditures with them. He was driven about in a limousine manned by a chauffeur. He kept his expensively furnished flat, and invited his followers to come to him—usually about 11 o'clock at night. It was a devilishly late hour for a young man bound by the schedule of southbound trains. The last possible train left Charing Cross Station shortly before midnight. By that time Mitrinović's place became alive; Alan Watts had to take the choice of begging for digs or losing out on his education. He tried it both ways, and once was even driven home in the early hours by his mentor's chauffeur.

One might expect that the way of the true Oriental philosopher would be first to acquire the necessary mental furniture. Alan Watts had part of that. He possessed a very real knowledge of the Protestant Episcopal, or Church of England, both high and low. But as for the rest, he knew no Sanskrit, with which to study the Indian mysteries, nor Chinese, with which to undertake the reading of Lao Tzu and Chuang-Tzu, the greatest of the Taoists. His reading of the analects of Confucius was in English. His reading of Lao Tzu was in French, in the Julien translation of 1848. Not knowing the languages, Chinese or Japanese, he had to rely on the translations. Then and forever after, he took the position that knowing the languages or visiting the countries was unimportant—that he could master the mysteries in his own tongues and his own way. This attitude confounded some members of the philosophical community and kept him from being taken seriously in the most surly of academic quarters. But it also delighted those of America and other lands who wanted to understand something of the mysteries and tranquilities of the East, but were not prepared to spend four or five years learning languages to do so.

The economic depression and the worsening political climate of the 1930s brought about a number of demands for social change, and Alan Watts was soon involved deeply in one of them, a movement called New Britain. It was led by Mitrinović. The concept was basically socialist-egalitarian with strong technological overtones. Private capital would be reduced in power and the state would assume responsibility for productivity. In fact, much of what Mitrinović, Ezra Pound and that crowd suggested was accomplished in the years after 1945 by the socialist-minded labor government of Britain, although in a different way and without the psychological overtones of the New Britain movement.

To Alan Watts the delight of it all was that he was taken seriously and allowed to do a number of odd jobs that would have fallen to more experienced hands had there been enough of them. His principal function in the New Britain movement was to review books for the magazines *New Britain* and *The Eleventh Hour.* This gave him a readership, and a cachet, and a certain power as well as opportunity to read the books.

The horoscope of Christine Carter saw an Alan Watts who would ever relentlessly pursue his ambitious goals—and the goal of the moment was self-education and self-gratification. The education was supplied bountifully by his mentors and his reading. The self-gratification was harder to come by, for not having a place in London to entertain a young lady, and having no desire to pay for what should be bountifully available in a broad and enlightened world, Alan Watts was restlessly searching for romance. There were girls, and they were willing to kiss and hug and see how things came out, but there was also the dratted 11:55 to Chislehurst that hung over all attempts at *amour*, and many was the night that he broke from an embrace to spring unlovingly and unloved for the train station.

The New Britain movement was failing in the refusal of British social and political parties to amalgamate and pay attention to the dreamers. For one thing, they wanted to stop Hitler when he marched into the Rhineland and began the systematic destruction of the Versailles treaty. The governors of Britain were too deeply immersed in their frenzied finance and economic worries to pay heed.

With his star rising, his handsome face and form, and his bright inquiring mind, Alan Watts might well have gone far in politics. He was a good listener, not yet a great talker, but he was already showing the signs: his elders had confidence in him. And had he become political in his ambitions he could have risen far. Or he might have become a journalist; Fleet Street was a busy place and welcomed bright young men with poking minds.

Curiosity he had aplenty. He investigated typefaces and toyed with the idea of designing a typeface of his own. He changed his style of handwriting from the oval penmanship he had learned to the far more artistic and readable Italian Chancery script, printed with a special broadpointed pen. He went to Japanese places and learned to appreciate Japanese food and various arts of defense and skills of exercise, such as judo and kendo.

For two years he learned. Mitrinović taught him the skills of the orator and the polemicist, and he learned to organize and control a public meeting.

But as Watts watched the tremendous outlay of energy of Mitrinović and his friends going to waste in a dry and unfertile English intellectual soil, he lost his taste for politics, and decided he would never again engage in the political functions. He would seek his livelihood in other arenas, and he would spend his energies more specifically in correlating the unsystematic and confusing writings of various experts on the subject of Buddhism. Here was an almost untouched field. The major authority on Buddhism who wrote in English, Alan Watts discovered through Christmas Humphreys, was D.T. Suzuki, the Japanese scholar. Soon Watts knew as much about Suzuki's approach as anyone in England, and he was encouraged by Humphreys to begin putting it down in writing. In this fashion then, Alan Watts wrote his first book of real importance: *The Spirit of Zen.* In the evenings for a month he sat down in his room and wrote. The result was a small book that purported to explain Zen.

John Murray Ltd., publishers of London, were persuaded that the work had intellectual merit, and that there was a need for such a book in a relatively new field of interest for Westerners. Murray decided to publish and brought the book out in a hardcover edition in 1935. Alan Watts, author, was just twenty years old.

As Alan's father said on the latter's ninety-second birthday, when he was considering his son's remarkable career, "Alan has always known precisely what he was going to do, even as a child."

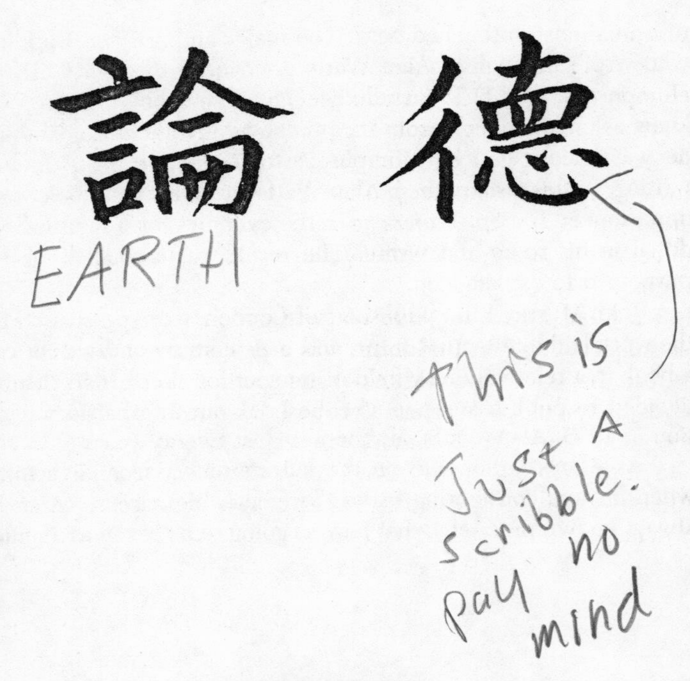

CHAPTER FIVE

ABOUT ZEN

D.T. Suzuki was one of the first informed men to write in English about Zen Buddhism, which flowered so spectacularly in Japan, in terms of its origins and close association with the Tao of Lao Tzu and his followers. He pointed out that when Mahayana Buddhism was first introduced into China it was not very successful because the people resented all the new ways that interfered with their old. The concept of monastery life did not appeal to the Chinese, and the new belief seemed a threat to ancestor worship which was the underlying rock of Chinese philosophical and religious practice.

What Alan Watts set out to do in *The Spirit of Zen* was to explain Suzuki, and thus create a new climate of interest in English-speaking readers. The book was titled fully: *The Spirit of Zen; A Way of Life, Work, and Art in the Far East.*

The Spirit of Zen was dedicated to Christmas Humphreys, Watts' encourager, mentor, and guru in the study of Buddhism. Writing from Bromley, in Kent, in December of 1935, Watts introduced his own work with profuse thanks to Professor Suzuki and an adjuration to his readers to read the work and then to turn immediately to Suzuki's three-volume work, *Essays in Zen Buddhism.*

It was not hard for Alan Watts to write a thorough treatise on his subject. For Zen Buddhism was a new study and a new concept to the Western world. As Watts counted, until 1914 the only work on Zen in any Western European language was Kaiten Nukariya's *Religion of the Samurai.* The first volume of Suzuki's *Essays* was not published until 1927. Thus by the time that Alan Watts entered the Buddhist scene, the last of Suzuki's works was only a few months old, and Watts was one of the first knowledgeable Westerners in the field. This was important to the book and to the life of Alan Watts.

Watts made no special claims for Zen as "the" way of enlightenment. He did point out at the beginning of his book that many Westerners—and he certainly was speaking for Alan Watts—were tired of the old religious experiences and ready for something new. He likened Zen and the other religions to paths up the side of a mountain—the others circling and winding around the mountain and around again, while Zen thrust its way straight up to the top.

There was a certain amount of pretentiousness—and a bit confusing it was too—in his quotation of the French from Wieger to illustrate the Asian. But this could be put down to the youthful peccadillos of the writer attempting to impress his reader. He did establish the confines within which he would speak to the reader, and he nobly obeyed his self-injunction:

> *. . . anyone who attempts to write about Zen has to encounter unusual difficulties; he can never explain, he can only indicate; he can only go on setting problems and giving hints which at best can bring the reader tantalizingly nearer to the truth . . .*

Watts wrote of the frustration of attempting any fixed definition, for he found that Zen could not be put into any existing "ism." He admitted that the Zen masters had a thorough disregard for logic. They were wont to illustrate their wisdom by fables with elusive meanings.

One of Master Wu Tsu's favorites concerned a monk who came to a master and asked for instruction in Zen. The master asked if the monk had eaten breakfast. Receiving an affirmative reply, the master directed the monk to wash his bowls. And thus, as a result of this conversation, the monk became enlightened.

Madness? Watts wondered, as well one might.

Or what was the point of Master Wu Tsu posing the problem of the cow trying to go through a window. The cow's legs, horns, and head go through. The tail does not. Why not?

This Zen lore, Watts warned, should not persuade against accepting the fact that Zen had a tremendous influence in the total culture of the Far East, which has long been underestimated.

Watts attributed the uniqueness of much of Oriental artistic achievements to Zen as a way of life. Yet, of course, here he overstated his case—one does not understand Chinese and Japanese art solely because one understands Zen—and it is possible to have a fine artistic appreciation of Oriental art, even calligraphy, without the slightest interest in Zen. Many Chinese artists have found it to be so. But Alan Watts was only twenty years old when he wrote those lines—that fact must never be forgotten in reading *The Spirit of Zen.* Already, at twenty, he had read enough and talked enough and tried enough aspects of the Oriental way to understand more of what he was approaching than the great majority of his readers.

Watts began his study of the origins of Zen with a careful warning that the reader must not expect to become enlightened by learning what it was about. Here Watts showed the peculiar genius that was to make him the popularizer of Zen in America and to a lesser extent in England. Watts would be to the Eastern philosophies what Isaac Asimov would be to the sciences: the translator into the terms of the masses.

And for a glimpse of his method note this:

One could, Watts explained, study the great works of the Eastern masters for a lifetime without finding any blinding visions or the calm of enlightenment. And then, to make his point absolutely clear, Watts borrowed a notion from Dr. Trigant Burrow, a well-known philosophical scholar: to expect to learn from a description of the subject was like a hungry man expecting to be satisfied by reading a restaurant menu. Here is an instance of Watts knowing how to wrap up an argument in a popular phrase, and to pictorialize complicated matters so that they seemed to become clear to the average reader.

Suzuki had said much the same in his own writings and in the prefaces to such important works as James Legge's English translation of *The Texts of Taoism.* But Suzuki spoke in the language of the scholar. When he wrote about Zen and Taoism, he had so much to say, and the ideas chased each other across the page so quickly, that the average reader ended up numb and confused. Here is his description of Zen:

> *As to Zen philosophy, it has enough of Taoism: mysticism, transcendentalism, unworldliness, a certain antinominalistic and anarchistic tendency, all of which are closely woven into the background of high-flown Indian speculation. What, however, is the most distinctly characteristic hallmark of Zen is its insistence on the awakening of* pratyāmajñā. Pratyamajna *(Sanskrit) is an inner perception, deeply reaching the core of one's being (*hsin *or* hridaya.*) This corresponds to Chuang Tzu's "mindfasting" or "mind-forgetting" or "clear as the morning" (chao-che). In Chuang Tzu, however, this experience is more or less casually treated, while in Zen it is the most essential discipline. Modern Japanese Zen has achieved great development around this point.*

It was no wonder, then, that Christmas Humphreys and others of the Buddhist Lodge of London saw the need for interpretation of Zen and Suzuki by a Westerner. Alan Watts did not know it as he wrote this book, but he had found his niche in life.

In discussing the origins of Zen, Watts explained Buddha's motivations and his actions in a few flowing sentences. Gautama, the prince who became the Buddha or Enlightened One, was never one to claim that his *dharma* or doctrine was the enlightenment. It was the Way, it concerned itself with enlightenment. And that is all he would ever say when others questioned.

What happened to Buddhists is much of what happened to

other religionists: form became more important than content, and they lost their way, seeking in the form the content. That, said Watts, was where Zen took a new road, revering the Buddha but not mistaking him or his belongings for what they sought, which was their own enlightenment. And the secret was to go beyond words or deeds or ideas, to the essence of life itself. Conceivably, then, a Zen follower could achieve a kind of enlightenment in observing the falling of the snow. Insight was all; all else was nothing.

Zen is a Japanese word. Its Chinese character Ch'a refers to Buddhist or Taoist ritual, with heavy overtones of repentence and remorse. The concept, of which Ch'a may be a transliteration, was the Sanskrit meditation in conjunction with the search for enlightenment—or the proposition of "being at one with the universe."

Watts did not reveal his childhood experiences in his first major book. The fact is that he had not yet achieved the loose, chatty style that was so revealing and so captivating of younger readers and audiences in a later day. His work was a sort of scholastic exercise, not footnoted well, and with some strange references to works not listed in his bibliography. Yet among the books on Eastern religions it stood out brightly because it was clearly written and the concepts did not depend on immersion either in a musty library or a monastery.

There is simple history here in this first book. Watts tells the story of the coming of Zen: it seems that the historians of the subject believe satori was achieved by Gautama at that moment under the fig tree when he declared himself enlightened. This was the fifth century, before Christ.

At that time, Gautama's followers began to hand down the whole of Buddhism, until the principal disciple 28 times removed from the begging bowl and robe of the original Buddha was Bodidharma. He lived in the sixth century A.D.—or 1,100 years after Gautama. Bodidharma brought Buddhism to China. Meanwhile, Buddhism was splitting into two major sects: Mahayana and Hinayana. The Mahayana was sent to China, and to Tibet and eventually to Japan. Hinayana settled in southern India, in Burma, and in Ceylon, Siam, and other fringe areas. The differences between the two types of Buddhism came about because of the writings of followers of Buddha in two different languages. Some wrote in Pali. Some wrote in Sanskrit. Scholars dispute whether the Pali versions were older than the Sanskrit—and here originated the split. The known fact is that nothing was written down until 150 years after the death of Gautama, the Buddha. The writings in Pali that were handed down concerned themselves largely with the conduct of Buddhist monks. Those who followed the Pali version then quarreled with the Sanskrit believers, and the Pali followers refused to accept anything pertaining to Buddhism that was not in Pali. Therefore they became a group of monks with rigid forms of worship and rigid ideas. This was the Hinayana belief, or road, which has attracted the people of the south. The Buddhism that went to China, and combined with Taoism to become Zen, was much more flexible—metaphysical, Watts called it—and the Mahayana version became split into many different concepts, taking from the lands and people. For example, the Lamaist Buddhism of Tibet is quite formalized and centers around the monasteries. The Lamaism of North China, (which has its own high lama as opposed to the Dalai Lama) is different. The Buddhism of Korea differs. And Zen, the form that went to Japan, has become the most free-wheeling of all.

In this little book on Zen, Alan Watts exposed the beliefs he had espoused himself at this time. During the King's School years, while still studying the principles and rituals of Christianity, he had decided that the Zen way was his way. And since his explanation is vital to understanding the man who was growing out of the boy, some attention must be paid his ideas.

Watts felt that both Hinayana and Mahayana Buddhism had a common basis, in that both professed that the individual seeking to isolate himself into a retreat to resist outside forces was living in a delusion. There was no escape, for man cannot escape, or isolate from life. What was the self?

As Watts declared, the Buddha did not answer that question, but he taught his followers that man would discover the answer only when he stopped identifying himself with his person and when he stopped resisting the external world.

The Buddha said that all living things were in unity, and he demanded that his followers replace hostility by divine compassion (karuna) and that having done so they would achieve nirvana, the end of suffering and the condition of bliss.

The Hinayana belief was that there was rebirth or reincarnation. Death was no escape from suffering, it was merely a temporary rest, before attainment of the final enlightenment.

Zen departed from this view, for as Watts pointed out, few Zen Buddhists were literal (as the southerners certainly were) about the doctrine of rebirth. And here, Alan Watts stated the philosophy.

It was difficult to believe in rebirth, for rebirth was based on the concept that an ego survives indefinitely, that the person who is here now was the person who was here 10 minutes ago.

Watts continued the book with a study of the two forms of Buddhist belief. He rejected Hinayana because of its negative belief that nirvana gave a soul release, and that was the end.

But the Bodhisattva, or practitioner of Mahayana Buddhism, was not so satisfied. He believed he could not enjoy eternal happiness in a universe filled with suffering. All life was a part of himself, and he was a part of all life. That was the eternal Self. So as long as there was a single creature on earth which was unenlightened and not sharing happiness, the Bodhisattva could not accept his own happiness. Thus, the Bodhisattva achieves nirvana after many lives and much suffering, like the Hinayana practitioner—but the Bodhisattva then rejects nirvana and continues to strive for the happiness of others.

One of the factors Watts found most appealing in Zen was the non-intellectuality of it, its clearing away of the debris and constructions of scholarship, or the intellectual concepts, definitions, and speculations.

Watts tried, in his writing, to show that the Buddha was everything and nothing, all at once, or any single thing the questioner wished to contemplate at the moment.

Those who believed in Buddha found wisdom which could only be transmitted to someone prepared to receive it, and then it was a wisdom which could not be put into any intellectual formula. Only those who wanted it enough that they were prepared to give anything for it could understand. To others it was nonsense.

There are many tales about Oriental philosophers, and some of them are so obscure as to be difficult for a Westerner to conceive or to relate to life. But some are beyond nation or concept, deeply imbedded in humanity.

Watts told of Chuang Tzu, who was one of the fathers of Zen, an exponent of the ideas of Lao Tzu—one of the great philosophers of Asia. One day, just after Chuang Tzu's wife had died, a disciple came upon the old man at home, singing and beating time on a pot, when he had expected to find Chuang Tzu dressed in the white of mourning, wailing as was the custom.

He demanded to know why the philosopher was behaving in so unseemly a manner. Not to shed a tear over the dead woman's body was bad enough. But to make merry and sing and shout when she lay dead, was that not blasphemy and disrespect of the dead?

No, the bereaved husband said. His wife had died and he felt the loss. Yet she had lived before her death as the woman who had been his wife. Now she was dead, passing from one aspect to another, like the seasons go from summer, to autumn, to winter, to spring. If he were to weep and cry he would show his ignorance of those laws.

Watts traced the development of Buddhism in China, through the Tao period, through five Zen patriarchs, ending with Hui Neng, who supervised the last transitions of the idea from its Indian beginnings to a Chinese base. He was so important a figure that the collection of his sayings is called the Sutra of the Sixth Patriarch, although the word sutra usually was reserved for the sayings of the Buddha as they have come down.

Hui Neng's writings told how he came to be enlightened, through adopting the proper road in a period of crisis when the faith was threatened by materialism.

So—in this manner—Alan Watts instructed his readers in the history of Zen, bringing it down to the great division of the Sung Dynasty of China, in the thirteenth century A.D. At that time an offshoot began to show great strength, and Zen lost much of its power in China. The offshoot was the branch of A-mi-to-fou, or Amitabha, and it involved the further personification of the great Buddha to bring all things and persons to nirvana in time. The followers believed that by pledging themselves to Amitabha, they would achieve rebirth in the Pure Land, a place where they were almost certain to attain enlightenment. Thus they were released from the wheel of life and rebirth.

This Pure Land Buddhism took precedence in China and also in Japan, except that in the twelfth century in Japan, Zen was adopted by the Japanese Samurai as their own religion.

Watts noted that even as he was writing (1935) many of the educated and professional people in Japan gained strength and vigor from periodic visits to Zen monasteries. He predicted an ever-expanding interest in Zen, in countries other than Japan.

Having surveyed the origins of Zen, the young instructor then considered the "secret" of Zen. Why, he asked rhetorically, would anyone want to strive to become a Buddha (Enlightened One). He proceeded then to answer, to show his belief that Zen, the striving after Buddhahood, was the direct approach to happiness.

He made the point that physical possessions are meaningless. Alan Watts learned and accepted this belief at an early age. Happiness had nothing to do with possessions. This concept was to become an important aspect of the Watts character, and one to which he would allude several times in future works.

In this book of his early writings, Alan Watts was creating—he was bringing a new dimension to Western understanding of the East by the lucidity of his prose. He clarified the Zen idea that possession of anything in life is illusory, that the concept that things shall not alter is an impossible idea. In a search to understand life, man must realize that truth cannot be defined. According to Zen, man must not try to grasp or define truth, but accept the fundamental Buddhist ideal of non-attachment.

Watts saw the Zen life as a force moving like the wind across the face of the planet, like the birds flying this way and that, unfettered, lazing about. And yet to him there was another aspect of Zen:

> *. . . Zen is not always a gentle breeze, like decadent Taoism; more than often it is a fierce gale which sweeps everything ruthlessly before it, an icy blast which penetrates to the heart of everything and passes right through to the other side. . .*

It would not be easy for a Westerner to adopt Zen, because a person from the West would not have the long years of association with general principles that have been absorbed by osmosis into Oriental, and particularly Japanese, life. For example: a novice coming to Zen would soon enough discover that Zen accepts all the good and evil in the world as parts of the nature of the Buddha, as bits of the whole of the universe.

Was this not equating sin with virtue? To a young man, bursting with life forces and eager for every experience, would not Zen be an invitation to libertinism? Watts thought not—in these early days of his adherence to the Eastern religions. He pointed out that the members of the Zen communities resorted to the most strict kind of personal discipline, in order to avoid any thoughts of libertinism. No one, said Teacher Watts, should undertake the practice of Zen without first having adapted himself to a thorough moral discipline.

In later years, Watts was twice to revise the book *The Spirit of Zen*, and he was to become aware of the anomalies in the book—of which this last concept was a large and important apparent contradiction, in the manner of Watts' own life as he lived it. In the wave of his successes, publishers kept asking to reissue the book; Watts' problem was that if he undertook to extract all the anomalies, he would have to end up rewriting the book—and never again in his life was he able to reach quite the same ability to state the case for Eastern philosophies in absolutes that he was in his twentieth year. Whatever its faults, and what qualities *The Spirit of Zen* lacked, it possessed the great enthusiasm of the new believer. Watts worked over several other portions of the book and brought the bibliography up to date twice, but he did not tamper with his own enthusiasm, and so the book remains a monument to the youthful Watts, so deeply immersed in incense and the concerns of an Eastern world whose permeation of the West had not really yet begun. By any standards of the day, Christmas Humphreys and his crowd were "far out"; it would be 20 years before the returning soldiers of World War II began to scatter an infusion of understanding of the East in America, and bring Eastern philosophy to a height in England.

Alan Watts detailed quite specifically the intellectual, spiritual, and physical demands of Zen on those who would acquire the virtues through it. He wrote of the similarity between the spirit and a garden—the spirit must be cultivated as must the garden to produce well. So moral law must be mastered in Zen before the conquest of spiritual law. And moral law could be mastered only through self-discipline. And self-discipline could be mastered only by imposed discipline. Thus came about a long period of training of the Zen student, which in fact was not unlike the training and vigils of the squires seeking knighthood in the tenth and eleventh centuries in England, France, and the Norman world. For knighthood, a Christian state of being, was much like the Samurai Zen mastery in its own way. These last are not Watts' thoughts but my own, in trying to explain what he was saying about Zen. As Watts described "the ten stages of spiritual cowherding," a series of Oriental pictures he had seen to illustrate the study of Zen, he spoke of the men hardening themselves by nightlong vigils in the cold of a Japanese winter with no fire and the stars twinkling through the broken roof. Thus did the English squires stand too in a graveyard, or in a chapel, keeping long vigils in the name of God.

These restrictions on which Watts dwelt in his little book, were to be discarded when a man's mind was thoroughly under control. The cowherding sequence came to him from Professor Suzuki's works, and the last picture shows the Zen student, now master, having adapted himself to the life, taken the discipline, become friends with the cow, and apparently having sold the cow. He is in the company of common folk and is drinking wine. So the Buddha has achieved his way, and can withstand the temptations of the world.

The Spirit of Zen is designed as an introduction for young England. It describes Zen as not just philosophy, but a religious experience. To achieve such experience, two factors are essential, the satori and the koan.

The former is the revelatory experience. It is not to be confused with the southern Buddhists' nirvana or enlightenment, for nirvana is a permanent acquisition; satori can be as changing as my own sensation of astral projection in the bedroom of a twelve-year-old boy. Watts joined Suzuki in discussing satori as a "turning over" of the mind, with the notation that it usually occurred after one had made a long and exhaustive effort to discover the meaning of Zen. The masters of various periods have tried, with only limited success, to describe satori as it came to them. It could come in the most rare ways—such as examining a pea on a plate. It could come while staring off into nothingness, in the midst of an organized Zen prayer session. And satori—the achievement of this release and enlightenment of the moment, is the reason for being of Zen.

One road to satori—the most common of those ways practiced—is the use of koan. The koan is a problem, on the face of it an impossible problem—something that cannot possibly be answered by using the normal logical processes of any society.

Watts cited such koans as the problems of determining the sound of one hand clapping, and discovering how much life there is in a worm.

He related the dilemma facing a man who kept a goose in a bottle. The goose grew and grew and the man was forced to puzzle how to release the goose unharmed without breaking the bottle.

Watts told of the man who was hanging from a branch of a tree, high above the ground, holding on only by his teeth. He was asked by one at the base of the tree to explain the nature of Zen. Should he answer and fall to his death?

The purpose of the koan is that the koan is actually to be used. It is an impossible problem, yet it must be possible because all things are possible in the universe. Therefore it must be considered, and the consideration of the problem is the work of the student of Zen. Only when the student has studied his koan for a long time, and has come to the conclusion that he knows the koan cannot be understood—then he lets it go. There is a release in this motion, depending on how much concentration the student has given. It can become satori.

Suzuki mentioned, and so did Watts, that there were some 1,700 koans, each of which could be approached by a student of Zen, and might be, according to his master. The more koans, the more the enlightenment. The more concentration, the longer the period of enlightenment.

In so writing, Watts also referred to Western religious experimenters. He described passages from William James' *Varieties of Religious Experience*. James knew of one man who had a religious experience of great depth in his inability to pray, and his final conquest of that problem.

Watts also quoted a French Protestant writer, Adolphe Monod, on an experience not unlike satori.

All this was the result of a reading program really prodigious in so young a man. Having tried yoga, having visited gurus and athletic practitioners, Watts could write with authority of the similarities between yoga and Zen. But in the end, he noted, the similarities are not so great, because the positions of yoga may be useful, but the Zen masters discourage the kind of trance that is commonly sought in advanced yoga. Rather than yoga, the Zen monasteries featured Za-Zen, which is an intensive period of meditation.

Although he had never visited a monastery, had never visited Japan, had never seen a Zen ceremony, Watts was an excellent interpreter of life in a Zen community. He devoted a whole chapter of his book to this subject, describing the dress of the monks, their cubicles, their eating and sleeping, and laced this all with a good dose of the history of the religion. He introduced his readers to Po Chang (or Hyakujo), the founder of modern Zen Buddhism and the monastic system. For while the yellow-robed brothers of the south and other Buddhists in other lands are content to beg for their living, the Zen monk works for his subsistence, chopping wood, growing vegetables, or undertaking more complex labor such as administration and government. Yet the Zen is never far from the land, for one of the precepts of Zen is to remain close to nature—in the sense of work.

Watts (who had never see one), described a meditation hall, the Semmon Dojo, and told something of the life in the monastery. Indeed he devoted many pages to the specifics of life, the manner of praying, the manner of eating, the places and manner of sleeping. The book purported to be an introduction to Zen for the Western world—and it was a very good one. The koan was described several times, and several difficult koans were given particularly elaborate treatment. The reader of Watts might not be able to come to grips with Zen practice from simply reading Watts—but he would at least have enough feeling for the Zen to decide whether or not he wanted to pursue it or use it as a matter for dinner table conversation.

And as for Watts himself, there are clues to character. For Alan Watts, having undergone the teenage "conversion" to Buddhism, as much in rebellion against his education and the flat strictures of the Church of England that he knew, was having some serious problems in adjusting his new ideas to his own circumstances and habits. If Watts had lived in Japan or China he might well have hied himself off to a monastery for a period. Such was patently impossible in the depression years in London: there were no Zen monasteries about, and the price of a steamer ticket to Tokyo was quite beyond Watts' wildest dreams. Nor did he speak any Oriental language—and while that was not a stopper, it was going to slow him down unless he continued to work in the Western languages. The problem was with him and had to be faced.

He was already facing it:

> *In conclusion, it should be made clear that not every Zen monk desires to remain for ever in a monastery. . . . the ideal of the Bodhisattva is not to remain apart from the world; it is to be in it, though not of it. . . . A man may be free to travel where he likes, but there is no place on earth where he can escape from his own Karma, and whether he lives on a mountain or in a city, he may still be the victim of an uncontrolled mind. For man's Karma travels with him, like his shadow. Indeed, it is his shadow, for it has been said, "Man stands in his own shadow and wonders why it is dark."*

Weighty words for one so young. That is what I am trying to suggest—they were weighty words, and they were facile words, much more facile than the words of Suzuki, for example, to whom every phrase set down suggested another and separate idea. Thus Suzuki's portrayal of Zen was incoherent, because of too much understanding. Young Watts, having Suzuki in English at his disposal, had no such trouble, skitting and flirting through the material. Watts appears less in the book than one might expect—Suzuki appears constantly. But by the process of converting and writing Suzuki's thoughts down, Watts was learning his subject.

He was sold on the Eastern religions, or hooked as a later generation would put it.

"The rare treasure," said the twenty-year-old author, "is the capacity to see Truth."

As such, Zen was not aimed at the mass of people, but at a handful. Neither Alan Watts nor any other could see a time when Zen would have a great appeal to the Western world.

The effects of Zen, said he, would be found in the work of certain individuals and classes, such as the Samurai of Japan. He did not expect any great social changes to come through Zen, at least not right away. The whole process of Zen, as seen by the masters, worked through small groups of people. They would learn and enlarge the grand group, but slowly, as a stone dropped into a pond sends its circles out. Thus only after thousands of years would the circle expand to reach the shore; by then the chosen few had become the whole community.

In the discussion of Zen and its place, he brought forth his own studies of judo, jujutsu, and kenjutsu or fencing. Christmas Humphreys took Alan Watts down to the Oriental sections, to Soho and the rest, and introduced him to the local teachers. Watts put on the loose jackets and trousers of the student of the manly arts, and learned. And then he wrote and compared and amalgamated the things he read and the things he did. And thus when Watts spoke of the mysteries, even though he had never spent a day in a monastery, or carried a monk's begging bowl, or spoken more than a handful of words of any of the exotic languages to which he referred—somehow the mystery came across. The Mysterious East had found a new young champion who would be heard from again and again.

CHAPTER SIX

FACETS OF THE MYSTERY

1936 was a crisis year in the life of Alan Watts, and this is what his astrologer said of him:

> *You relentlessly pursue your ambitious goals. You have inexhaustible energy; determination makes you impatient of the weaknesses of others. You may drive others, but none so hard as yourself. It may be you have found that you cannot leave the most important details to others.*

Whether that last was true or not, Alan Watts did drive himself in his twenty-first year, in many a direction.

He was still hugging and kissing any willing girls, driven by his karma. But alas, in the circles he frequented, unless they were serving girls or babysitters, there were few enough that were young and unattached.

In the business world, his father was helping him along, not quite sure what Alan wanted to undertake as a course of life. The elder Watts introduced his son to Robert Holland-Martin, Chairman of Martin's Bank, and chief of the hospital fund-raising operation. Such a man might have been useful to an ambitious Londoner in half a dozen ways—he was useful to Alan Watts because Holland-Martin presented him with a pass to a splendiferous exhibition of Chinese art brought over by cooperation between the Government of China and the Royal Academy of Arts. The centerpiece of the exhibition was a Buddha 60 feet high. That summer of 1936 Watts spent many a precious hour contemplating the Buddha and studying Chinese art forms. He was not simply trying to understand the East, he was immersing himself in Eastern life as much as a youth in the middle of London could do.

Watts continued to hang out with Mitrinović and his crowd. He still learned from John M. Watson, the bookseller who helped him with his reading. He added new friends and acquaintances to these—new dimensions to a crowded life. Through his reviewing, Watts then met Eric Graham Howe, a psychiatrist and author, who was to influence him in a number of ways. It was a time of discussion groups—little knots of intellectuals who tried to resolve the problems of society on a small scale. And at such meetings Watts met other psychiatrists including Philip Metman, the Orientalist; Frederic Spiegelberg, a refugee from Hitler; Prince Leopold von Loewenstein, a living aristocrat of the old school of gentility that no longer existed; and many other middle and upperclass persons, most of whom broadened Watts' horizons in one way or another. He was a singularly unabrasive and attractive young man. He knew how to drop artfully the fact that he was author of a serious work on Zen, yet not make a fool of himself over it, particularly in front of people who were truly important.

In his own way, Alan Watts was important too. He had been given much of the responsibility for the editorial management of the Buddhist Lodge's journal. Thus he was able to offer something to the participants at Eric Graham Howe's salons. He could publish their more esoteric ideas.

That is how Watts got to know Spiegelberg well for a time. Watts heard Spiegelberg talking about his own religious experiences and ideas, and out of it came an article in the Buddhist journal on "The Religion of Non-Religion," which Watts characterized as a kind of atheism with God as a central figure. Spiegelberg had all that Watts envied at that moment: he had studied philosophy and psychology with Jung, he had been a disciple of Zimmer and Hauser. He knew Sanskrit, and could quote from the Asian religious masters. These were the kinds of knowledge to which Watts aspired, and in his own way he began pursuit of them; he learned some Chinese characters, and some Japanese adaptations of them.

So the seances with Eric Graham Howe and his friends gave as much to Watts' life as did the meetings with the Russian and Balkan emigré crowd. In fact, Howe was to have a more important effect on Watts' life, indirectly, than nearly anyone but Toby Humphreys. He was to introduce Watts to Krishnamurti, the guru.

Krishnamurti was a fabulous character in the London of the 1930s. Years before he had become the hero of the Theosophical Society, a semi-religious sect that sprang up in India at the end of World War I. He had been given castles and palaces by the rich and told that he represented the second coming of Christ, that he *was* Christ. Krishnamurti denied this, and refused the castles—and came to England, and travelled to America, lived on the fat of the land, supported by his wealthy followers in a style to which he had not been accustomed in India.

So the coming of Krishnamurti was an event in the world in which Alan Watts now lived.

That evening, after Howe had called him, Alan Watts was privileged to be one of the serious persons who sat at the guru's feet and listened to him lecture about philosophy. Watts was taken with Krishnamurti, and he was fascinated, obviously, by a man who turned down offers of God-dom and castles in Spain, yet managed so well. For always in Alan Watts there was a touch of the charlatan—or perhaps it would be more charitable to call it the showman. Any showman would stand in awe of Krishnamurti, who had merely to gesture and one of his wealthy friends would deliver a new Rolls Royce.

So began a year filled with excitement for the young student of exotica. It was a time of deep misgiving in Britain, with Hitler arming across the channel, and Mussolini waving his sword down south and in Africa, and the desperate deadly struggle taking place in Spain. Such times seem to arouse hope in the hopeless, and a spirit of religious exaltation in the optimistic, and a good deal of experimentation. Thus in Britain that year were assembled a number of Oriental religionists, chief of whom, from Watts' point of view, was his idol D.T. Suzuki, whose works had formed the backbone of *The Spirit of Zen.* Alan Watts must have met Suzuki with mixed emotions, because he had borrowed so freely from the master, and might wonder if it had also been frivolously.

Suzuki's main reason for being in London was to attend a World Congress of Faiths assembled there. This was red meat for Christmas Humphreys, Dmitrije Mitrinović, and Alan Watts. They moved among some of the most prominent religious characters of the times.

Suzuki was all-important in the development of Alan Watts as a religious person. For Watts was peripatetic—quite apart from his youth he was unable to sit still for long. His whole life is a symphony in movement. Conformity to the typical Zen Buddhist practices would have been impossible for him. As he wrote in his autobiography in that characteristic iconoclastic, popular way, he never could bear the "uptight" school of Zen buddhists, who seemed to think that Zen was a matter of "sitting on your ass for interminable hours."

Suzuki agreed. Not in those terms. But he agreed. He was a radical departure from the usual Zen Buddhist, and in Japan he was sometimes referred to with bitterness and dislike as the traitor who had popularized Zen Buddhism and threatened its ruination by bringing it to the attention of the masses.

Suzuki's attitudes were Alan's cup of tea. The English student had neither the training in Chinese, Japanese, or the Indian philosophies to attack Zen in the traditional manner. The middle of the 1930s was hardly the time to raise the money to spend several years in Japan sitting in a monastery, learning—even if Alan Watts had the pshychological makeup to accept such a regimen. Suzuki gave him an out. Suzuki and Krishnamurti together gave Watts the groundstrokes of a philosophical game of his own. Krishnamurti's basic philosophy was much more akin to the Tibetan Buddhist idea than Suzuki's but both ideas served. Krishnamurti held that man was on the wheel, that there was absolutely nothing he could do to alter himself. Therefore he might as well relax, and relaxing and accepting the fact that he was but a small part of the universe, but very definitely a part, he might find enlightenment and happiness.

This philosophy, carried out in a kind of Aristotelian dialogue with those who claimed to be his disciples, suited Alan Watts to a T. It obviated all the difficult studies and disciplines. But it was not Zen Buddhism. Now along came Suzuki, all critical of the practice of Zen in Japan, and even suggesting that it would be good if the monasteries burned down.

From the pair of them, Alan Watts learned that he could be what he said he was—it was as simple as that.

In this strange and rarified circle, Alan Watts had already become a personage. Master Suzuki was invited to deliver a paper at the University of London. And he did. It was an argument against the usual criticism of the Far Eastern religions: that they were negative and fatalistic, and had nothing to do with life on Earth. To lead the discussion after the paper, the authorities chose Alan Watts, one of the editors of the Buddhist journal, and author of what was by then a major British work on Zen. Watts, at twenty-one, was an important figure in his own way.

From this conference, from his exercises in judo and Japanese fencing and his discussions with Mitrinović, and his tutoring under Christmas Humphreys, Alan Watts conceived the idea of a new book to explain to Britons the philosophies of East and West. This was the area that troubled thoughtful churchmen: could ever there be a meeting of East and West, given such totally different approaches to life? In the 1970s such questions do not seem so important. Westerners have had 40 years of close observation of the Eastern world, and they have discovered merits and fruits of Eastern philosophy. Easterners, on the other hand, have come to the West in droves to study and absorb, and many of the nations which have furthered the philosophies of the East, now struggle with the technocratic problems of industrial society.

But then, in 1936, these problems were very real, and a matter of grave concern to interested churchmen and people of a philosophical turn of mind. Buddhism, Zen Buddhism, Hinayana Buddhism—these were new words understood by only a handful in Britain, with trappings of mystery and intrigue about them.

Alan Watts' answer was *The Legacy of Asia and Western Man, A Study of the Middle Way*. Presumptuous? Indeed it was, and in later years Watts indicted his own work as "another somewhat immature book." He was, of course, speaking at this later date from the prestigious peak of hindsight. It could not have been so bad; *The Spirit of Zen* had good reviews, at least from Christmas Humphreys, and Humphreys was the guiding spirit of Buddhism in Britain. This new book, however, was more presumptuous in a different way. Watts could trade now on a certain cachet as an aficionado, if not a master, of Zen. From that vantage point he would survey and compare. It was not fakery—at least not conscious fakery. Alan Watts was deeply immersed in the mysteries. He was still associating with Mitrinović and his crowd, and had lately been initiated into a secret society of Mitrinović's called the Wild Woodbines. Watts had also found a willing young woman (who remained unnamed in his autobiography) and was enjoying his life to the utmost. He had not yet discovered all the pleasures but he was coming right along.

For more than three years, Alan Watts had been reading, reading, reading, in English and French, to investigate Eastern thought. As bookseller John Watson reminded him, there was a long way to go. By 1936, Watson estimated that there were some 2,000 books on Buddhism alone, *published in English*. There were twice as many in French and German. The bibliography of Alan Watts' new book must be immense; it was, and he called attention to it in the opening phrases of his introduction. His attempt was to sort through the interpretations and the materials, and to stack the Eastern ideas up against the Western traditions, garnering from the East what could be reaped—at least reaped by a twenty-one-year-old author poised on the dizzy heights.

This concept had come to him with the Congress of World Faiths. Alan Watts was deeply involved with that body. After his leading of the discussion of Suzuki's lecture, he became more so, and was elected to the council, and later to the executive committee of the organization. Of course, a book must come from all this; what other way did so young a man have of holding his cachet?

And he chose well. The line he was pursuing was not pretentious—no one was going to be able to hang him as passing himself off as the great philosopher. His was the pseudo-humble approach, a fake naiveté that could hardly be faulted except by a determined cynic. In the circles in which Alan Watts moved, there were few of these, so even the aggressive Watts was forgiven much.

His horoscope showed a youth straining with ambition, hard-driving and pressing, wanting independence in every way, and finding it hard to come by. He was certainly ready to do anything—run errands for Christmas Humphreys and stay up half the night listening to Mitrinović and his friends. "Always in motion, mentally or physically, or emotionally. . ." That is what the stars said of him.

Others said other things. Mitrinović said to him one day that he loved him (spiritually) but he did not like him (personally). Watts was shy, and pushed harder because of it. But he was moving. That was what was important, and the new book showed how fast and how far.

Understand that Watts' book dealt with burning issues of the religious world of the day, that he did know more about Eastern philosophy and religions than half the professors of England, that he was attending the series of lectures being given that year in London by Carl Gustav Jung, and that Watts was also studying yoga and his Japanese friend's work.

His book was addressed to three varieties of people: the Christian who wanted to relate his own faith to others; the "new psychologists"—the disciples of Freud, Jung, and Adler who believed they had found a new religion that would displace the old; and the lovers of Asia and things Asian who would pay little attention to things Western.

From the beginning of this book, Watts used all that had occurred in his own young life. He addressed himself to his fellows, those persons who had achieved much and little. As Watts as a boy had embraced Anglo-Catholicism, and then discarded it, Watts the young man spoke to the thoughtful person who felt "uncertain of his roots."

Here was Alan Watts, in his young years, in 1936, exhibiting the problems that would vex a whole generation. Perhaps that is why, when the time came, Alan Watts would appeal to the flower children, and then to the negative or "other" culture that youth tried to impose on society.

What was Alan Watts learning? In his own university, with teachers Humphreys, and Mitrinović, and Watson, Jung, and Suzuki and the rest, his early books could be regarded as theses, indicating his degree of intellectual pretension and attainment.

In his new book, author Watts quoted and paraphrased prodigiously. Here was a trick of the trade that would never leave Watts—he would become adept at name dropping and would maintain that useful habit. It was a part of his patina; even in his autobiography he wrote of such people as Professor Bergen Evans of Northwestern University (and television fame) as if they were old friends—when the fact was that Evans had encountered Watts but once in his life, at a dinner party, and not even an arcane one, where the only words they exchanged were a few of what Evans called "commonplace remarks."

There was nothing commonplace about Alan Watts' new book. For its time it was an exciting study of a new subject—at least new to the majority. The *Church Times* called it "witty and perverse"—perverse, of course, because it treated English Christianity as no better than the worship of Kali.

Jung, said Watts, was moving with Freud along separate lines, to achieve some of the philosophical ideas that the thinkers of the East had developed centuries earlier. Freud, said Watts, was developing ideas better expressed in the Tantra and the cult of Kali. Jung's "discoveries" could already be found in Buddhism, Taoism, and Vedanta.

Alan Watts had a way of tantalizing a reader. Speaking of Jung, he could knock him down with a feather, show the Watts erudition, and allow even the most strait-laced parson of the Church of England room for some quiet erotic imaginings. Jung and the other new psychologists were fine, said Watts, because they presented conclusions not unlike those of Buddhism and Taoism in forms better suited for the Western mind. But on the other hand it was unfortunate that Jung and Freud did not know enough of Tantra and Kali (as Watts indicated he certainly did) to avoid the deadly dangers of these imbalanced cults. For Freud taught that life's goal is death, and death is the re-entry into the womb of the mother. That philosophy, said Watts, had been the excuse for some of the most savage and "depraved" rites in the Asian religious underlay.

No wonder the churchmen called the book perverse. It was downright wicked in suggesting prurient ideas to the faithful. It could also have been called sly and suggestive. It was all Watts. It was important Watts for any who would understand the evolution of his personal philosophy.

In his clear way—for he was from the outset a fine tribute to the quality of English prose taught at the public schools he had attended—Watts discoursed on the fundamental problem of a staggering Christian faith: the need for a renaissance of popular faith in the church. Watts suggested that it might be possible for the church to embrace these new ideas from psychology and the East. What was needed was a bit of imagination, he implied.

He said many things that were true and important, as well as things that were racy and breeches-rising:

Marxism and Fascism: the purely rational ordering of life is nothing but social determinism.

Humanism—it has already shown its bankruptcy.

Sometimes he came a cropper. On Art: realism provides the height of rational art; futurism is the inevitable result.

And as for the will: it was not the *I* that willed but the profundity of the mind, in which the satyr and the divine nature of God were to be found.

There was one for the clergy—wicked indeed. Imagine Canon Dawson, the Rector of St. Nicholas Church, in his round Anglo-Catholic hat scurrying over to Coffins grocery in Chislehurst, and then off to visit the sick, *like a satyr!*

What the good canon and all others should do is study Jung and the unconscious, and those Asian religions, so they could understand the Christian allegory in a new and more satisfactory way.

Alan Watts now regarded the Christianity in which he had been raised as one of the ways to find the truth. It was not his way—he had abandoned it as cold, cruel, and hopelessly oldfashioned. Here in London in 1936 he was in the height of religious fashion, surrounded, he was quite certain, by the wave of the future, and he was going to be a part of that wave.

He was not going to quarrel with Canon Dawson or any other. He had achieved his own outlook in his study of the wisdom of Asia.

> *The theologies of Brahmanism and Mahayana Buddhism are regarded in all the important texts as subordinate to the practical technique of spiritual development, and they insist not that a man should believe in a set of theological propositions but that he should tread a path.*

That idea summed up Watts' own feelings of the time, the serious feelings.

But he could not avoid the little sly digs that the reviewer for the *Church Times* caught; an example: "So far as the religions of Asia as a whole are concerned this catholicity can hardly be called intentional. . . ."

How wicked, how baiting of the Christians. For Watts knew there was no catholicity in any sense of the word in the Asian religions, and the reviewer conjured up that phrase out of sly perversity; a young man on an ego trip, having his fling with the churchmen who had beset him (some beating his bottom) in those years of cold water education.

There followed then, interesting descriptions of various Eastern religions, of the kinds of yoga, of Taoism and its derivation into Zen, of Shinto, with copious quotations from the many works he had read on these subjects.

To the Anglican churchman the discussions of the Eastern mysteries could be of interest, even as simple curiosities. But oh, how it hurt when Watts took after the church:

> *However shallow we may find the interpretations which the Catholic church has placed upon its ancient symbols. . . .*

What kind of reaction could the author expect to that, from a bishop?

Or this just after:

> *In the doctrines of the Fall of Man, the Incarnation, the Immaculate Conception, the Atonement, the Resurrection and*

the Trinity we may see mere mythology, mere relics of paganism, of no significance to an age of scientific understanding . . . from the standpoint of meaning it does not matter whether Christianity is a development of Paganism, an offshoot of the Wisdom Religion, or a purely independent growth. These are historical and not psychological questions.

My, how the teeth of the bishops must have gnashed as the young Buddhist roasted them for their fuddyduddyism. He took the church apart and put it back together again in a way that would be meaningful to a young man of the 1930s.

To Hell with Original Sin. Everyone knew it was rejected by modern rationalism. Much more to the point, would it not be, to follow the Tao—if one is in perfect accord with the Way, the question of good and evil does not arise.

And he leaped into an excursion in Brahmanism to show the Western churchmen what they had to learn; "If we would find the technique which Christianity lacks in its present form, we must turn to Asia for further knowledge of The Middle Way."

But wisely, Alan Watts stuck largely to what he knew: Christianity in which he had been immersed as a boy, and Buddhism, into which he had thrust himself as a youth. He drew his examples from his reading. Occasionally he overcited. (He said himself later that he never could read German, yet a number of German works are there in the footnotes.) But is that so great a sin? Let the first scholar who has not practiced a little fakery of his own cast the stone.

There was more than fakery to Alan Watts.

Coming to the essence of his comparative arguments, Watts arrived at the study of enlightenment, and he quoted several scholars on the subject. He went to the Waley translation of the Tao te Ching:

The man of highest power does not reveal himself as a possessor of power.

Therefore he keeps his power.

The man of inferior power cannot rid himself of the appearance of power.

Therefore he is, in truth, without power.

Then, Alan Watts rendered the thought a different way, translating into the Adlerian concept then popular, and using Parker's translation of that passage:

> *The highest Grace makes no pose of Grace, and for this reason really is Grace; whilst the lower quality of Grace may never divest itself of Grace, and yet never feels like true Grace.*

Having done so much, Alan Watts did more. He went back to the original Chinese, to translate word for word.

> *High Tê not Tê and thus has Tê, low Tê not lose Te and thus no Tê.*

It makes sense. Chinese has no articles and verb forms are much simpler than English. What is indicative here is that in 1936, Alan Watts was either already embarked on the study of Chinese, and he knew enough of the conformation of the language to be able to pick out the characters, or at least he knew a Chinese scholar who could do this for him, and he could understand the result. It is no mean accomplishment.

Tê, in the above, generally speaking means the enlightenment or state of grace to be desired.

Later Watts would develop more spectacular techniques of presenting the wisdom of the East, and the mysteries that went with it. But for a young man given the time and the low state of the arts of Orientalism in the Western world, he was doing well.

He could not refrain from bringing in some items from left field: a page of dissertation on Japanese fencing was not really needed in this book. But Japanese fencing was one of Watts' enthusiasms; fortunately in dealing with mysteries and religions, almost anything Eastern could be related to anything else. One cannot escape the feeling that he was strutting his knowledge a little here, but understandably: he could or should have known that his central argument would offend a great number of Christian theologians, and he had best cover himself with all the expertise at hand.

Summing it all up, Alan Watts argued that his whole study had been to bring people to the Middle Way, and how Christianity could and should discard some of its historical trappings (virgin birth, Trinity, original sin) and move to the study of enlightenment of the Easterners. His own proclivities came through at the end:

> *We devoted a chapter to Zen, and it seems that this is a subject which must be approached in a different way from any other Eastern cult. For it is not specifically Eastern and does not use the alien terms and forms of exotic faiths but the language of ordinary life. In substance it appears to be the pure religious experience, apart from any creed, and in form the pure everyday experience common to all men, apart from any nation or race. As the supreme vision of the mystic which no words can describe, Zen is found all over the world. But as a specific cult it comes nearer than any other to the bedrock of religion, because it points uncompromisingly to our ordinary experience of life, telling us to find there what others seek in the distant realms of philosophy and symbolism. Ideas and symbols are necessary, for their study is like the Prodigal's journey into a far country. In the end we return to the home from which we started, but it comes before our eyes in a new light, and Zen is just this returning home. It begins where philosophy ends, just as historically it represents the fulfillment of Buddhism. To avoid any prejudice or misunderstanding, it is best to remove it from its Chinese associations, to forge the label Zen, to return to our own relivision (sic), and consider this: that between the greatest height of spirituality and the most ordinary things in the world there is no division. We shall study every philosophy, search through all the scriptures, consult every teacher, and practice all spiritual exercises until our minds are swollen with the whole wisdom of the world. But in the end we shall return to the surprising fact that we walk, eat, sleep, feel, and breathe, that whether we are deep in thought or idly passing the time of day, we are alive. And when we can know just that to be the supreme experience of religion we shall know the final secret and join in the laughter of the gods. For the gods are laughing at themselves.*

After that came eight pages of bibliography and 10 pages of glossary. It was an impressive display.

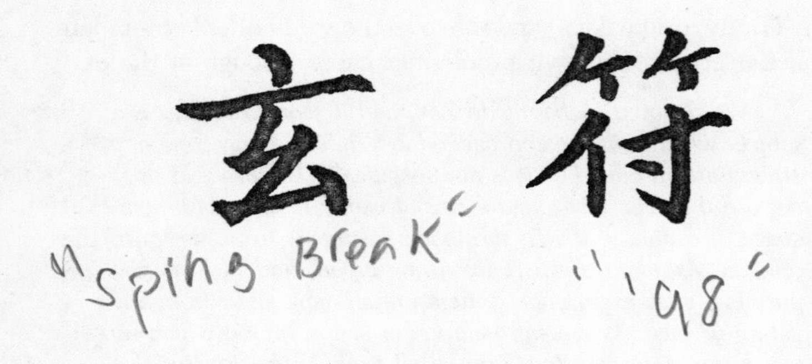

CHAPTER SEVEN

MYSTERIOUS CHARM

"As much as you desire freedom," wrote Alan Watts' astrologer, "you have probably taken on more burdens than is average."

How true those words were of the twenty-two-year-old Watts in 1937. He was still working in London, and living in Chislehurst, although he did not come home every night now that he had a girl in the city. He was deeply involved in the harum-scarum doings of the Wild Woodbines, whose rites were rooted in sexual symbolism and alcohol. Alcohol was bad for Alan Watts, or so said his astrologer. He seemed to think it was quite good for him, and the flush of face and disappearance of problems made him continue to so believe. The Wild Woodbines were wild—and from this point on Alan would have association with groups of free spirits who played and fornicated and drank all night. It was tremendously important to Alan Watts that he was attracted to women by the score.

"Your very intense nature and aura of power probably turn on the ladies," wrote his astrologer. "Part of your success may be due to your adroit handling of them."

There is an interesting point to be made here: the Nantucket astrologer, Christine Carter, did not know whose horoscope she was casting when she began, and when she had finished she did not have any ready association with the name Alan Watts. But when she was told something about him, she sent her original notes, in which she had deleted, for the sake of grace, the above portion as well as another—a discussion of Alan Watts' high ideals and his many love affairs.

"I will argue for the Sagittarius trait of having such high ideals that it is not 'horniness' but a true search and expectation of the next 'love' as really living up to the humanly impossible ideals."

So there was Alan Watts, immersed with his religious friends and with others whose interests were more physical. But in the end, the Buddhist Lodge seemed to take ascendance over the purely sensual. One of the traits of Alan Watts' character was that though he admitted to sensuality with ease and a trace of pride, there was more to all his relationships than that. It is easy to put him down as sensualist and showman. It is also unfair. Had he not been sensualist, he might never have been repelled by the stern dictates of his Christian God of youth, and attracted by the freedom of Suzuki's Taoist-Zen. Had he not been showman, he would have been unable to get his ideas across with such skill as he was already doing after two books, both taken seriously in theosophical and metaphysical circles. His second, *The Legacy of Asia,* even found its way across the sea and into such esteemed libraries as that of Yale University.

So Alan Watts was a person to be taken seriously, and he *was* taken seriously. As an executive member of the Congress of Faiths, Watts was active in the planning for that organization's second British meeting in the summer of 1937 at Balliol College of Oxford University. He made more acquaintances there, and spent many hours drinking and talking about women and song as well.

In 1937 Watts' lady love was Eleanor Everett—rich, attractive, American, and on the loose in Europe. She had come to London to study music. Her mother was a Buddhist enthusiast, and the pair met through Christmas Humphreys and his wife at the Buddhist Lodge. There Ruth Everett, the mother, discoursed on the wonders she had seen in Japan (they had just returned from those crystal islands). Young Alan Watts, whose finances stopped any aspirations he had to go there, was enchanted by the mother's experiences and the daughter's beauty. As he said, it took him just about a week to fall hopelessly in love.

Then, after that week, Mother went home to Chicago, leaving Eleanor and Alan to amuse one another while Eleanor studied piano. She also began to study the arts of love with her enthusiastic worshipper.

Now what attracted Watts to this girl? She was short, and exceedingly young. She had not even lost her baby fat yet—and it was apparent that when she grew older she would be a plump, matronly type of woman. Well, that was precisely the type of woman that Alan's mother had been—a games mistress in an English boarding school, all ruddy cheeks and running water. So that was certainly a part of it, in addition to the obvious matter of youthful libido and the first real opportunity to express it.

They went to concerts, and symphonies and ballets, and a new section of the world, the world of music, was opened to the admiring ears of Alan Watts.

The fact was that Eleanor knew much that Alan did not know. She had *visited* a Zen monastery in Japan, with her mother, and had been virtually adopted for a time by Nanshinken, a famous Zen master at the monastery of Nanzenji. She was fifteen that year (before she met Watts) and she had practical experience that he must have envied. But he had the gift of gab and the way of expression. They were young and it was time for love in London. So the affair went well; she sensed what he knew from reading, concerning Zen and many other matters. She began to make a few changes in Watts—not that he needed much encouragement. He sported a moustache. That went. He dressed with the severity of a parson, in grays and blacks—she persuaded him to buy sports clothes (which were very sporty indeed in the London of Savile Row).

Watts gives Eleanor credit for bringing him his first important personal religious experience. They had been meditating at the Lodge that evening and were walking back to her place. He was worrying about the eternal present, which had been the koan of the day. She remarked, very simply, that the present was simply a continuum—and suddenly a great weight was lifted from Watts' mind, and for the next week, he said, he floated through life having enjoyed his first satori.

The cynical will say it was love, sex, and self-hypnotism. Perhaps. That is a decision that every reader will have to make for himself.

Others, like Margaret Jacobson, who knew him so well that he late in life lamented not having made love to her, have said that "somewhere in his life something went terribly wrong," and she suspected that from the beginning Watts was "whistling in the dark" in his books and his religious searchings. "He really did not believe in what he preached," she said.

But what Margaret Jacobson was talking about was a later phase—the Watts who exposed himself so fully to the world of Asia was not a case-hardened man, not a cynic in any way. Indeed one of the most refreshing aspects of his early writings is his sincerity of search; the scholastic deficiencies were more than overcome by the enthusiasm with which the young student of the East approached his subject.

He was deeply moved. If there was any feeling before that he had run out his string with the Buddhist approach, it was resolved on the occasion of the satori.

But Watts was at loose ends, there was no question about that. He did not possess the educational credentials to take a chair in Eastern studies at any of the big universities; it was not a time when non-academics were welcomed for their knowledge rather than their degrees. There was no place where he could earn the money to support a wife, unless he went into journalism—not a notoriously high-paying profession in the 1930s.

The religious business was not good. Adolf Hitler had seen to that; he and Benito Mussolini were terrorizing all Europe. This was the year that Neville Chamberlain became Prime Minister and appeasement was in the air. The Japanese attacked China and the whole Far Eastern picture changed. Zen, associated with Japan, became far less popular than it had been.

To a young and still basically conservative middleclass Englishman, love and sex added up to marriage. When Watts posed the question of support, Eleanor laughed it off, because she had plenty of money. Here came a crisis in their relationship. Watts chose the easy way. His apologia is unknown, but he permitted the elder Everetts to pay his way to Chicago. They were going for Christmas, so Edward Warren Everett could look him over.

Watts did not explain further. But he did say that he was not loath to leave Britain at the time. He saw little for himself in his homeland. His avocation was really religious and philosophical writing and talking. It was all he had, except for that experience as a fund raiser. The Chamberlain appeasement policy was most certainly going to lead to war, one way or the other. He was sure of that. He had no desire to fight in anybody's war—he simply detested the idea of shooting at and carving up people. No matter how the Japanese twisted Zen and Shinto to make it conform to their warlike ideas (all the world under one roof—a Japanese roof) basically the philosophies of Asia were peaceable and gave the right of life to animals and plants. As Watts had pointed out in his second book, the Asians never had a religious war to match the Wars of the Roses or any of the other slaughter sessions of Christian against Christian, to say nothing of Christian against Moslem—or Western infidels and Christians against Jew.

So the problem was resolved in a few discussions. Alan and Eleanor travelled to Southampton and boarded the *Bremen.* On the voyage across they ate themselves silly, and Alan began to sample and appreciate wines in a manner that his limited budget previously had prevented. New York, a week later, was merely a stopping point of canyons, so he called them, and the great sprawling concourses at Grand Central. They got aboard the Commodore Vanderbilt, one of the luxury overnight trains to Chicago in those days. They ate in a comfortable dining car, on white linen with warm shining silver and scrubbed china, and they amused themselves by watching the Christmas lights of the towns and villages.

Watts passed through the portals of La Salle Street Station, into a chauffeur-driven limousine, and into a life of luxury such as he had never known. For the Everetts were rich Americans, and once they had accepted this young man of Eleanor's there was no trouble at all. Alan exerted his best British manners and his finest charm—both were impressive and Warren Everett took to him quickly. Soon Alan had the older man talking about his own experiences (with women) and those lesser conquests (other businessmen).

The young people's war was won without a battle. Watts did not like most of the Everett family—but a meal ticket is a meal ticket and he *was* in love with the daughter. So he stomached the insipid relations and Chicago. He liked the young folk who gathered around the Everett household, and they seemed to like him. All went well.

The holidays over, the family approval given, Eleanor and Alan went back to England on the *Bremen.* Watts could not remember quite why. But they did, and were married in London a la Church of England because staunch middleclass morality forbade a Buddhist ceremony even though both were professing Buddhists at the time. Watts was not then the man he would become, obviously. So it was an Anglican ceremony at the Parish Church in Earl's Court.

The life of luxury was on. They moved into an expensive flat on the west side of Courtfield Gardens—a duplex in fact. But this was now 1938, Anthony Eden had resigned as foreign minister in a dispute with Chamberlain. Austria was annexed without a whimper to Hitler's ugly Third Reich.

Watts and Eleanor talked about the crisis. His vision was unclouded—he saw war coming certainly. He did not wish to be a part of it. He had undergone a certain amount of military training at King's School, and he had not enjoyed the experience. Further he had failed to achieve a scholarship and this could be counted upon to almost assure Watts a role as private in the front rank of whatever dirty detail was upcoming. He was a pacifist to boot. And yet how could one be a pacifist if war broke out and Britain was invaded? The thing to do was get out in time, he said, and that is what he did, on the money of the Everetts.

But Alan Watts did not do this without compunction. Forever after there was an air of apology about him when he described to friends his reasons for leaving his native England on the brink of war. Margaret Jacobson said that in many ways she felt a cardinal explanation of Alan Watts' character could be found in this decision of his to sit out the war rather than fight with his countrymen. He was to have a guilty conscience for the rest of his life. "The fact that he mentions not a word about Hitler, Nazism, World War II in his autobiography says volumes." (That was a criticism later to be shared by Thomas Lask of the *New York Times*—who could not understand how Watts could be so determinedly nonpolitical as never to consider a political or "social" question on the large screen of history.)

Ms. Jacobson felt this decision of Watts' was to dominate all his life, more as he grew older:

> *The older he got the more he must have realized that he acted cravenly, and on that point, no doubt a lot of Englishmen, even the most enlightened, would have agreed. What would Malcolm Muggeridge think of a smart ass kid holing it up in a New York drawing room while he and Grahame Green and others just as good sweated out the war in the Blitz or in Godforsaken places like Lourenço Marques . . .?*

Should Watts be criticized for escaping a war he did not want for a cause in which he did not believe? It is hard to judge Alan Watts by nationalist standards, for he had no such allegiance in his heart. He was an opportunist, but then most of us are to some degree. He was also a practicing Buddhist (although the Christian marriage ceremony tells much about *that*), and—most important—with the coming of the war he would have no way of making a living even if he was not called into service for his country.

Whatever the morals of it, he left England, and he and Eleanor set up in a big, expensive (by the standard of the times) apartment on 87th Street and Riverside Drive in New York City. Mama Everett arranged it all—Ruth had decided to live in New York to be near her current guru—and perhaps to be far away from Warren Everett. So the young couple settled in right next door to Mother, and Watts began thinking about what he was going to do with his life.

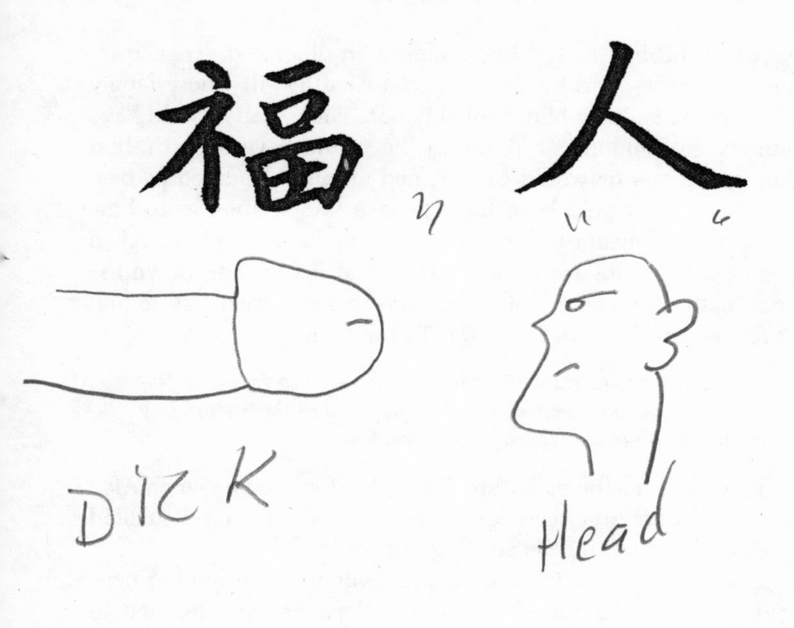

CHAPTER EIGHT

THE MEANING OF HAPPINESS

One must accept at face value and as truth Alan Watts' considerable soul-searching as he left his homeland on the brink of war. No man does that without realizing the consequences; it is a type of desertion and if he ever tries to retrace his steps there will be unpleasantness and punishments because of it. Yet Watts did not believe in war. On the other hand, as he stated himself in the inner debate, he was not a total pacifist. Had he been caught in France by the Germans, it is quite probable that he would have ended up in the underground resistance movement. He was a rebel against authority and the establishment, and the overlay of Asian culture on him made it easier to give up all that had gone before and set out on a new tack. The interesting question is whether he would have done this had he not been offered an unlimited expense account as it were—had he not married a wealthy girl whose family was willing to support him. Probably not. Then Watts would have continued in London as a Buddhist; he would have been drafted when war came, or would have joined an ambulance corps or a labor force. He would have had to make the decision as to how much principle meant to him, and probably he would have taken the easy way. There are Asian writings that lead a man down the garden path. Zen can certainly be used to argue for pacifism and also for least resistance. From the Tao te Ching:

> *All efforts made with a purpose are sure to fail. The Nature of the Tao necessitates their doing so, and the uncertainty of things and events teaches the same lesson.*

It could, then, be called the line of least resistance when Alan Watts set out for America with his new wife. Or it could be called opportunism, pacifism, the starry glitter of love.

Immediately, Watts gave himself over to an orgy of Americanizing. He was introduced to cocktail parties and learned to drink like a Madison Avenue advertising account executive. He discovered American ice cream and all its variations: milk shakes, malted milks, and dozens of varieties of ice cream. By his own testimony he must have sampled every one of the permutations of the ice cream sundae; gobs of ice cream topped with ladlesful of goo, plopped with maraschino cherries, dusted with crumbled nuts and splashed with snorkling whipped cream.

Alan and Eleanor's first child, Joan, was born in the middle of November, 1938. Those interested in the dates of such things would have their cattiest hopes well realized: the marriage occurred in April, 1938, and the child was born seven months later. If asked, Watts would have been inclined to tell his questioner to go to hell in a perfectly pleasant way. And what if Alan Watts had conformed to the normal 1930 mores about love and marriage and the birth of children? He would never have become Alan Watts. And whatever he was doing in New York, he *was* becoming the Alan Watts who would be one of the heroes of the American counterculture of the 1960s. The child being born out of wedlock would probably have been more than Eleanor could stand. That implication comes through in Watts' autobiography—at least he says he cannot quite remember how he came to get married as he did. That suggests that in no way was Watts in control of that situation, but he was yielding to the forces of love, moneybags, and the residue of an English middleclass conscience.

It would be easier, of course, to second-guess all this if Watts had later given up marriage. He paid no attention to the bonds and obligations, but he did not give up the institution. He was a more complicated person than he sometimes seems to be. To a youngster of the 1970s he might appear largely hero—the St. George struggling against the dragons of old age, fuddyduddyism, and a cruel and heartless capitalistic society gone wrong with militaristic tendencies and mass hysteria. To a middle-aged businessman, he would appear to be a libertine, a professional charlatan. So it all depended on where *you* were at when you encountered Watts. Look at the poses for the painter:

> *Ardent young Buddhist. Forsakes all to escape horrors of decadent Europe and seek the new world.*
>
> *Fortune hunter. Seduces sixteen-year-old child. Makes her pregnant. Lives off her income. Marries her only when the pregnancy forces it.*
>
> *Adventurer. Shrewdly estimates his chances of success and survival in a coming war, given his economic potential and hopes. Moves to new field.*
>
> *Philosopher. Is excited by sights and sounds and smells of the new world. Has great hope for a new kind of life and knows that other gurus and students of the mysteries have found happiness here.*

There are parts of all these figures in the real Alan Watts. When Joan was born she was an object of fond interest. In all there would be seven children born of Watts' marriages, and overall, by his own middleclass standards he was a terrible father. Of course he justified it. As time went on he justified everything. But in the beginning he was just a young man feeling the new world about him, unfortunately burdened with a loving, demanding wife of a well-endowed, middleclass, middlewestern family—which tells a very great deal about Eleanor Everett Watts, and about her mother and father. Images out of Babbitt appear, not to encompass Watts, but to dance about the apparition of Eleanor in her smugly comfortable Riverside Drive apartment, living next door to Mama, and wondering when and what her young foreign husband was ever going to do for a living.

Nor was Eleanor alone. Mama wondered too; for the rich are just like anybody else about their money except that they confront situations that could not possibly face the less than rich. But then television character Archie Bunker somehow managed to get himself saddled with a non-working student of a son-in-law. And there were overtones of Bunkerism on the upper floors of the Park Crescent Hotel on Riverside drive, where the two families lived.

Again—oversimplification. Mama Everett was almost totally occupied with her Zen master, Sokei-an Sasaki, who had a small walkup temple on 74th Street. She was certainly not a Mrs. Archie Bunker. But she was a middlewestern American and so was Eleanor. She was also a serious student of Zen, who mastered language and Chinese and Japanese poetry.

There is a key to Alan Watts in his attitude toward his mother-in-law. He respected her. It comes through his writings that he liked her—as much as he ever liked anyone but Alan Watts. He admired her taste—she was a collector of Orientalia as well as a student, and later opened a museum-temple on East 65th Street. He did not admire her method. She was what he called a "footnoter," a person who valued scholarship for its own sake. And for some reason, probably through early rejection, Alan Watts detested the American Oriental Society. In his writings over the years he probably had more evil to say of that organization than any other body of men. Although he was a person of enthusiasms, not hates, he hated the American Oriental Society.

In the months of 1938, just after the Wattses came to America, Alan's knowledge of Zen was not nearly so profound as his writings on Orientalia would have one believe. Zen was his medium—he so professed. But he knew very little about it, virtually no Japanese, and his Chinese was most sketchy. He had digested Suzuki, but he had no use for Za-Zen (sitting on your ass) and he only now learned something about it from Ruth Everett, his mother-in-law.

But he soaked up Orientalia like a sponge. Through Mrs. Everett, he had the opportunity to learn because she was studying with Master Sasaki and together they were translating one of the important sutras into English. Sasaki and Mrs. Everett spent a great deal of time together, on long drives in the country, at the temple, in Mrs. Everett's apartment among her books, and Alan Watts was free to come and go. He questioned Sasaki. He questioned Mrs. Everett. He learned.

One thing Watts learned from Sasaki was style. They were not unalike, those two. Sasaki had come to America as a disciple of a guru named Shaku Sokatsu. He was a bright man—he must have been to survive in an alien culture as artist and story writer. He was also a wood carver. Then he discovered that one could earn a living teaching what he had practiced—Zen. So he shaved his head, and wore the proper garments, and garnered incense and sweet-smelling woods and established himself a walkup temple—something like a storefront church of a later day for those priests who were digging it where it was. The walkup church or temple of the 1930s and 1940s had an aura of its own.

Or perhaps it is overstating the case to say that Watts learned style from Sasaki. Watts already had style, he had the grace and manners of the middleclass English, which are overwhelming to a certain type of American. What Sasaki and Zen taught Alan Watts, with a large assist from the Everett women, was to take it easy, to doff the starched collar and the umbrella and put on the Hawaiian shirt. In fact, Eleanor even taught Alan the hula, and it was a mark of his personality that he studied it, not only from the dancing point of view, but from the point of view of grace and release as well.

Watts was also impressed with the trappings—the brown and brocade robes, the incense and candles. He had been impressed similarly with the high church services of the Anglo-Catholic church at home in Chislehurst. He would always be impressed by incense and bells and chimes, gongs and drums and the full play of the senses in celebration of religion.

He was also much impressed by Sasaki, an earthy humorous man. Suzuki had been more the scholar; Sasaki was the practitioner of Zen. And from Sasaki came to Watts a great revelation: there need be no sense of sin in anything. Life was one great harmony of the universe. One cast himself wholly into life, grasped it to him, and watched it with eager eyes, smelled with inviting nose, heard with welcoming ears, touched with ready fingers. What a philosophy for a hedonist! Watts knew that it was for him.

After some weeks of idleness, Alan Watts decided he had to do something to justify his existence. The idea of getting a job made him quail; he had none of the educational apparatus that one needed for the kind of job he could do. America was stuffier than Britain by far in the matter of college degrees; form has always enveloped and overwhelmed content in American colleges and universities. It was unthinkable that he go into *business*—although another sensitive young Englishman who aspired to be a poet was doing just that and would later become a millionaire advertising man. He was David Ogilvie: Rolls Royce, the Hathaway shirt man with the patch.

And besides, Alan did not *have to* have a job. That was the secret of it all. He had an understanding wife and an understanding mother-in-law, and his father-in-law was off in Chicago.

Watts did not have the Buddhist Lodge to lean on now, but he no longer needed it. He had advanced beyond that. His two books for John Murray of London gave him a certain cachet. His association with the World Council of Faiths could be cited as intellectual armor. And he had friends, and ways.

One friend he found in New York was Professor Frederick Spiegelberg, a German, who was now teaching at Union Theological Seminary. Watts could not aspire to a seminary job—wrong religion, lack of credentials. But Spiegelberg could help him and did. The older man put the younger in touch with the Jung Club of New York, and the members of that organization invited him to give a speech on psychological matters. Having attended all the Jung lectures in London was a lucky thing—although Watts would have found another road had it not been Jung. That got him started. He used the Club's mailing list thereafter, and he made friends with the owners of an occult bookshop in the East Sixties, who helped him more. Soon he was giving seminars, talking to small groups, usually in some apartment in the city. He moved his classes several times, and each time to larger and more luxurious quarters. He began with half a dozen students, but as his reputation grew by word of mouth, so did his clientele.

For the fact was that Alan Watts had so early in life found precisely the metier for which he was cut out. Later he would call himself a religious entertainer. He was that. He certainly appealed to the one who sought a new way, or a new look at the world about him. For no matter his subject, he made it seem reasonable, pleasant, and understandable.

"Everything seemed so simple," said one woman who attended some of his speeches.

For one reason—Alan Watts put a lot of work into every public appearance, and a seminar with five or six people was to him a public appearance. He had the perfectionism of a showman. He wrote his lectures, then he delivered them—he did not read them. He had them mimeographed, and he worked over them. He collected, and adduced and deduced—and in the process he turned lectures into a book.

One of those who came to the seminars was Eugene Exman, then religious editor of Harper and Brothers publishing house, of New York. Exman was brought by Eva Lewis Smith, a social worker and one of Watts' regulars. Exman came, and when he left he had to admit to Miss Smith that he was impressed. What impressed him was the presence and the lucidity of the lecture. As an editor will do, he asked Watts why he did not put it all together for a book and Watts was only too eager to oblige. Not long afterward, Eugene Exman received the manuscript of a book from Watts called *The Meaning of Happiness; the Quest for Freedom of the Spirit in Modern Psychology & the Wisdom of the East.*

Eugene Exman closed the door to his office, and began to read.

He liked what he read, and in the spring of 1940 the book was published by Harper's. Watts later complained that it came on the world just as Hitler hit France, and that no one wanted to read about happiness at such an unhappy time. Exman remembered it differently.

"It had more than modest success," he said. "It was a real success and sold a lot of copies."

Watts was already a happy man. He had no regrets, no hangups, no fears, and no worries. In a way he was the ideal of the man who marries a rich wife, not because he intends to live off her money, but because it is nice to have that backstop so that one might forge ahead without financial worry. A philosopher, like any other kind of writer, lives in a state of suspended financial animation. To Watts at this point in life, it did not matter.

The Meaning of Happiness tells much about the Alan Watts of 1939 and 1940. First, it shows him moving away from the constant citation of the work of others—as though he were afraid to come out on his own. Having eschewed forever the scholarly road of the Orientalists, he was freed from this, and the style of *The Meaning of Happiness* is totally different from anything Watts produced before. This was not just because Watts organized the book as a series of lectures; the change was greater. Watts had learned more from Sokei-an Sasaki than anybody realized at the time.

Watts used his friends to help put the book together. One of his seminarians was Dr. Charles G. Taylor, a student of Jung and a homeopathic physician. Watts called on Taylor to help him with some difficult portions about psychology. It never hurt to have a professional backup. And it was the same with the Zen—Sasaki helped him and let him use some otherwise obscure materials that would be hard to come by.

But the rest was Watts, and a compendium of Toby Humphreys' counsel, the mysticism of Mitrinović, with perhaps a bit of the Wild Woodbines thrown in, and all the hundreds and thousands of books he had read over the past six years.

Watts' success in the book, as in his lectures, stemmed from his recognition of the growing interest of the middleclass of America in the combined mysteries: Freudian and Jungian psychology, and the Eastern philosophies. One might say that the war and its dislocations brought a profound dissatisfaction with the way things were and with the organized religion of the past. Whether or not that is cause and effect, it is what was happening.

Alan Watts addressed himself to the principle that these two forces (Jung and Asian) were important and pervasive. Of course he had made precisely this point in *The Legacy of Asia,* but now he did it with the polish of a savant. Already, if he had a regret, it was for those early works. He quite forgot that the early works had put him where he was in 1939. But now, instead of leaping into his subject he geared himself in; the introduction set up the argument and the subject, and the reason there was a need for a Middle Way between East and West.

He wrote well, for both layman and specialist alike. So said John Haynes Holmes, who reviewed the book for the *New York Herald Tribune.* "The author gets our attention on his very first page." Alan Watts had learned something about simplicity of thought and word, and tailoring the material for his audience. For although Watts was here discussing Oriental and Western thought, it was 15 pages into the text, including introductions, before he brought forth his first Orientalism, his first foreign phrase that probably would be obscure to his reader.

And soon he was deep into a philosophical turn that was to be important in his future thought and writing. He spoke of opposites in the universe—the opposites of life and death, male and female, black and white, weak and strong. Man, Watts said, felt the opposition between the self and the universe. There was the creature that was *I* and other elements that were not I. But, he cautioned, there was really no conflict, for the self could not exist "without the multitudes of selves and entities of which it is composed." He urged that, although nature seemed indifferent to the individual, man should adapt himself to nature instead of fighting it.

Watts suggested a little less preoccupation with self—he did not believe at this point in his life that he would find much acceptance. Indeed, as Alan Watts went along through his ascending popularity, he was neverendingly surprised at the acceptance he received outside the establishment, and even inside it from time to time.

And what he thought would take thousands of years to accomplish—the coming together of East and West, was certainly to be begun in his lifetime. He, from the standpoint of the recipient West, was to be more influential than anyone could know at the third quarter of the twentieth century. For he was going to become one of the shamans or gurus of the alternative society—and it would be another 10 or 15 years before it could be seen whether that society would replace the old. In the mid 1970s it seemed very much a tossup: who would triumph? The bright young Harvard school types or the shaggies from Berkeley? (with all due apologies to both stereotypes). Or would, as seemed more likely, the most useful and adaptable of the concepts of Watts and his fellow alternates be adopted and the others—some of the less socially desirable—let go?

Watts, writing in 1940, appealed to something deeply troubled in the American soul with his book on happiness. It was hard to be happy in a world gone mad with war. Norman Vincent Peale knew that. So did Dale Carnegie. The rage for self-improvement and the search for tranquility and happiness in a dreadfully unstable world occupied many a man, but the men in the pulpits, generally speaking, were not meeting the needs of the people.

Alan Watts sensed all this. His exaggerated feelings about the decay of modern Christianity were shared by thousands of Western church goers, many of whom still maintained the fiction of belief, but who, in increasing numbers, were deserting the ranks of the churches. In the West, and particularly America, religion had deserted the people, it no longer met their needs. The high and growing divorce rate showed there was something wrong with the concept of marriage.

Watts could deal with such subjects as "the fear of fear" and did so. There was plenty of fear in America—Franklin Roosevelt had recognized it in his first inaugural address with his famous adage. But eight years later the depression mentality had not been wiped out, and it had been given new strength with the war in Europe.

The trouble with man, or one of his dilemmas, said Alan Watts, was that he had chosen to isolate himself from nature. This complaint could not be levelled at the Buddhist, or many another Asian thinker. It was aimed at Westerners with their amazing and frightening technologies that were capable of raising buildings a thousand feet in the air, and yet whose morality permitted destroying a whole forest in a few months.

But Western man, said Alan Watts, was committing the greatest wrong of all in his refusal to live at one with nature. Westerners spoke of the conquest of this and the conquest of that. Another 20 years would go by before Americans lost their taste for conquests of various kinds. In 1939 and 1940, as Watts wrote, they still thought in those terms. He was 20 years ahead of his time—that is what Eugene Exman found so refreshing in the book.

Watts emphasized that man should not seek to master, but rather seek "union instead of isolation." What was needed was a change of attitude and without that change, only unhappiness could result.

That same kind of unhappiness, said Watts, did not exist in Asia. It was the disease of modern Western man, and it could be traced back to the Catholic philosophy of the Middle Ages. Christianity differs from many other religions, and particularly Eastern ones, in giving an immortal soul *only to man*, and setting up the rest of all living things for man's use.

Such a view was not shared by Buddhists or Hindus or others. The result of this difference was that it more and more caused man to consider God anthropomorphic—in man's image—although most prelates said it the other way. So God took on more and more human characteristics, while the lesser or different characteristics of animals and flowers and plants became relegated to the irrational. And the irrational became identified with the devil. So nature, instead of becoming ever more beautiful and enticing to Western man, became ever more hateful, devilish, and despicable.

There was a rebellion against this concept—the Renaissance. But out of it came Western Europeans believing that the proper study of mankind was man. Without exactly saying so much at the beginning of his book, Alan Watts opened the question—but is it? Is the proper study of mankind man? The Orientals do not think so. Man is part of nature, and because of that they observe man. But if the proper study of mankind is man, then the study of anything else is improper or at least irrelevant. And it was in this way that Alan Watts was trying to get his audiences and readers to consider the East and drop the fetters the West had imposed upon Western man.

There was a good deal of psychological history in *The Meaning of Happiness.* That was to be expected—Watts was wise to cast his arguments within the mold of the day—it made them readable and brought instant attention. He might have written a book more like *The Legacy of Asia*—the point is about the same—

but where the one was only a *succès d'estime*, the other brought him real attention, and furthermore served as the basis for a new kind of study that brought him income, since he was the guru.

He went, briefly, into Freud, and the more into Jung (he knew a lot more about the latter). But then, as usual, he was back with Lao Tzu, Chuang Tzu, and D.T. Suzuki.

Still, nothing that had gone through that bright and inquiring mind was forgotten. There was a growing feeling that his old mentor Mitrinović was a fake, along with H. P. Blavatsky, and Gurdjieff, all of whom apparently had connections in the heart of Asia with what ought to be regarded as secret sayers of the truth. The trouble was, they were a little too secret, and after the initial impact, when the Suzukis and Krishnamurtis began to surface, the Mitrinovićes lost some of their power to summon a Mercedes from a follower. But remember, we are talking about 1939 and 1940 and let no American forget Father Divine and Heaven (any number of them) Reverend Ike, or Korea's Rev. Sun if he wants to scoff at the beliefs of Western man.

One of Watts' basic arguments was against the idea of religion as a denial of life. He had already found his simple philosophy: the universe is now. All else he was to say was derivative and expository. He believed this, he had begun to live it, and he would live it more as he learned how to do so.

One prime trouble with organized religion, the religion he had known and the religion most Americans knew, was that it hated the world as it is, and mankind was not immune from that superhate. Witness original sin, with which the church saddles every one of us, willy-nilly. It is an unfair universe, as Watts would put it, that would saddle an innocent child with a sin he never committed. Even a grain of wheat is better off than that.

Of course Buddhism and Hinduism and other religions had their self-hatred and imperfections too. In Buddhism, particularly Hinayana, or southern Buddhism, the object is the mortification of the flesh, to the betterment of the soul, so that eventually the soul has no more need of the flesh, and hopefully, enlightenment is achieved. Pointing out that anti-life stance was Watts' contribution to the argument against the Easterners.

In his own way, Alan Watts was offering his adherents a philosophy of acceptance and change. Women, for example, sometimes found it impossible to consider growing old. But Watts, from the vantage point of twenty-three years, found it easy to be glib about women and age.

He said that a woman should age gracefully; if she did not understand and accept the aging process than she would be prey to unhappiness, for life was really a full-scale movement from birth to death. There were beauties in every age.

These were interesting thoughts for a twenty-three-year-old man, and some of them were his own. Much, of course, was a compendium of what he had absorbed and observed over the past six years. It is remarkable just how much he had grasped, and how easily he moved among people more than twice his age who were truly expert in their fields.

The first third of Watts' new book was devoted to trying to exorcise the demons of modern man. Then he got to the point of the use of Eastern wisdom—"something from which we can learn, but which we should be careful not to imitate."

This was an odd statement for Watts. The next was odder:

"It is unwise for a westerner to become 'converted' to Buddhism or Hinduism, as missionaries expect the 'heathen' to become converted to Christianity, for there are aspects of the Eastern religions which would be decidedly harmful for us to adopt."

Consider that statement in all its implications! For Watts—the student Watts—had converted to Buddhism. He had renounced Christianity. He had written a book in praise of Zen, and a second calling for a Middle Way, which indicated that he had no use for Christianity as it was constituted in the 1930s in England. Now, suddenly, he was backing away from total acceptance of the East.

The answer is to be found in Alan Watts' life, and particularly in what he saw happening to his wife Eleanor. She had been a child when her mother dragged her off to the Far East and the Zen Buddhists. She had been a child when she married Watts. Suddenly she was a woman with a child, and she yearned for a "normal" American life. She wanted to go back to suburbia, outside Chicago, and live in a little town with a country club and a nice church and pleasant streets and friendly neighbors.

She grew fat on the gluttonous fare that did not seem to affect Alan's weight a bit. He must have had the metabolism of a hummingbird to put away the ice cream and meals he ate—he said in his autobiography that he ate like Boies Penrose, the 350-pound Senator from Pennsylvania, who could put away a couple of dozen oysters, a two-pound steak, a chicken, with all the rolls and trimmings and vegetables, and then hope that dessert was going to be something interesting and filling.

Fat and unhappy, Eleanor began to have depressions. One day, passing by St. Patrick's Cathedral on Fifth Avenue, she stopped in to rest her overweight body, and had a vision of the Christ. It shook her. It shook Alan Watts. And it coincided with the views he was beginning to develop here in America. There was not going to be much future for a philosopher who was a Buddhist and a practitioner of Zen. There simply were not that many old ladies and matronly ladies and other curious rich people to go around. So it would behoove Alan Watts, as a practical matter, to change his ways.

This idea that Asian wisdom was a little too rich for the American blood came to Watts as he was writing *The Meaning of Happiness* and it coincided with his growing acceptance that he might be able to come to terms with Christianity. He knew the Anglican faith. He also knew that in America there was a high Episcopal group that did everything but ring in the incense and the bells.

If Watts was to come to terms with the Western world, instead of forcing the Western world to his terms as the younger Watts had hoped to do, he had to equate the religious and philosophical experiences of Eastern and Western faiths, and find common ground as a Christian.

There was a way.

Watts cautioned his readers against trying to apply Oriental standards to their own lives. They must distinguish between principles and application. *They must not imitate the Orientals.*

There it was. That was an entirely new aspect of the Wattsian philosophy. Hitherto he had encouraged imitation, now he was opposed to it. No one at the Union Theological seminary could take violent exception to that kind of thinking. A little far out for them maybe, but there had been far-out laymen and far-out priests before, and the church had survived.

Watts also had to seriously consider how he was going to make his living. He could not continue forever as he was. Or, if he did continue, knowing what he knew, he would lapse into total cynicism or, even worse, become the victim of his own mysticism. He had not the training to become a Guru, and he did not believe he was the reincarnation of one of the old masters. But he could pretend to it, and he had seen enough of charlatanry and enough of the effects he could accomplish presenting Oriental religions and philosophy, to know that he could make it go. But at what cost?

That was the question. With Eleanor so desperately unhappy, seeking guidance from priests and ministers and psychiatrists, the thought of the need for change was never far from Alan Watts' mind. It was necessary to achieve some kind of ambience that could include what he knew—the Eastern way, and the Western ministry, for had he not been an acolyte? And at the same time he must maintain his individuality and his freedom of action. The remainder of *The Meaning of Happiness* was largely devoted to the exploration of tentative ways in which he, Alan Watts, could come to terms with the different worlds that clashed within him.

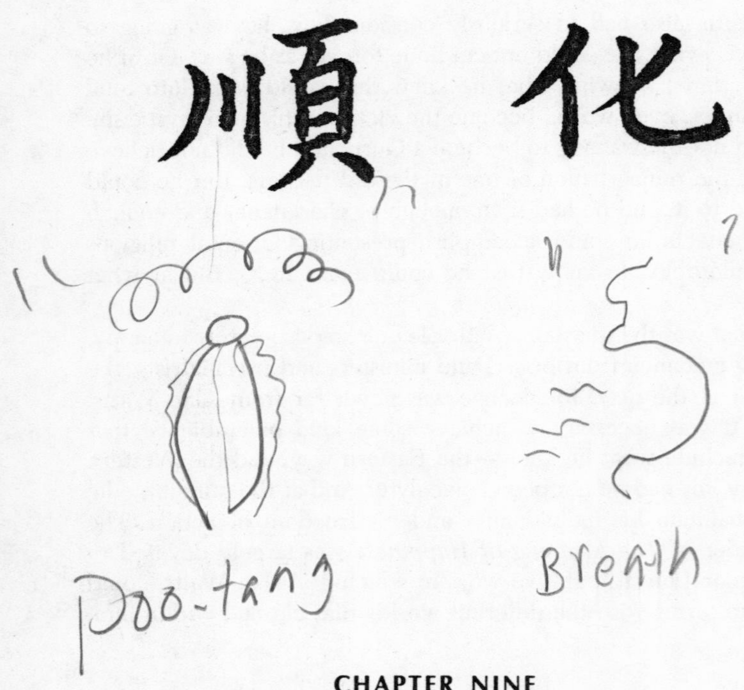

CHAPTER NINE

CIRCUMSTANCES ALTER CASES

"For regulating the human in our constitution and rendering the proper service, to the heavenly, there is nothing like moderation."

So said the Tao te Ching, and so said Alan Watts as he prepared to alter his life to put his work and his thoughts into a context that might be acceptable in America.

Watts had no conception at that time that he was going with the wave of the future. Indeed, speaking of happiness, it was not a happy time for the Watts family. Eleanor was overweight, and it was almost undoubtedly a psychosomatic disease: she was concerned about her husband, his habits, and his undoubted attraction to women all their married life. And with reason.

As Christine Carter had it, Watts was a lion with the ladies. In the first place he was an uncommonly handsome man. In the second, he dealt in the mysteries, which made him an attractive and mysterious figure. Women (and men) who interest themselves in such esoterica have time, restless imagination, and usually money to gratify whims. The combination is not unusual for the fomentation of a high degree of sexual activity.

When Watts' bedroom peregrination began is not revealed precisely in his memoirs. Quite possibly it never began at all, but was always there, this restlessness of spirit that caused him to go from one woman to another, seeking pleasure. The growing portliness of his wife, and her growth *away from* what he believed in could not have helped their marriage much either. The children continued to come along; they were the "stabilizing" factor in the marriage. There was another factor; the question of citizenship. As the spouse of a citizen, Watts had the right to live in the United States. But American immigration authorities are stuffy people, always have been, and they have looked with considerable Puritan suspicion on scandal and aliens who are unfaithful to their American wives. Morality and citizenship in America have always travelled hand in hand.

The family group provided an odd lot anyhow. Ruth Everett would later marry Sokei-an Sasaki, and still later go to Japan and become Abbess of a Zen institution. Her association with Watts would last considerably longer than her association with Eleanor and Mr. Everett.

For Alan Watts was changing, adapting himself to the new times and the new environment. For the moment at least, Zen must move to the background, and something more practical must emerge. The word Nazi, for example, appeared several times in *The Meaning of Happiness;* not even such a study could be written without consciousness of the burning of the world about him.

The Meaning of Happiness showed signs of the struggle that was taking place within Watts, to adjust to the new in a positive way. There was more Jung and less Tao in this book, and a good deal of the ins and outs of psychotherapy that had seized New York with so strong a grip.

He was sounding new notes, the relationship with Eleanor had brought him to full maturity, and he was now considering man and woman without those mysterious clouds that surround the sex thoughts of the uninitiated. New elements entered his writing. In the last half of *Happiness,* he considered masculinity. He was not masculine, in the truck driver sense or soldier sense. He had high contempt for that kind of masculinity.

He philosophized about the male-female relationship and deplored the fact that there was little understanding between husband and wife in the United States. Wives were driven to clubs and sewing circles; and manliness demanded cigar smoke and whiskey.

Perhaps his male-female relationship worry was directly connected to his own life. For he did have problems. One was about his future as family breadwinner, not that he needed the money, but he certainly needed a niche.

One option that spread before him was to become a fake like some he had known back in London. He was charitable, and probably right to consider them as victims of their own self-delusion. Having set up a system, and having hypnotized themselves into seeing their own miracles, the fakers began to believe. Watts would have understood Elmer Gantry had he then been familiar with Sinclair Lewis' hardshell preacher. Watts understood more of the world that swirled about his twenty-four years than seems possible for so young and basically inexperienced a man.

It would have been very possible to be a successful fake. He knew it. He considered it, and rejected this course. For he was an idealistic young man. Eugene Exman, the Harper's editor, found him both stimulating and sincere, and Eugene Exman was an expert on religion and philosophy and a student of the types of men who take these vocations.

Watts as philosopher had to be taken seriously.

In his philosophy, what it came down to, said Watts (and in reading him, one can not avoid the feeling that he was arguing with himself), was the matter of faith. Watts—who had admitted to no faith since the Anglicans had driven it out of him in the matter of virgin birth and original sin—now could write in all seriousness, "For the truth is simply that without faith we are forever bashing our heads against an immovable wall."

He recapitulated his own struggle a few pages later, noting the depressive atmosphere of Protestant Christianity. It was small wonder, he said, that people turned to Roman Catholicism, to Calvin, Luther, Knox, and Wesley. Or even to sun-worshipping.

But the problem for the modern in American society, he said, happened to be that Christianity was the traditional faith. What Watts wanted to do, where he saw his chance to make a contribution to the society and to live the life he wanted, was to try to bring together East and West, to interpret the wisdom of the East in light of the Christian experience.

As he wrote these things, Watts knew that circumlocution was necessary to get around the problems of trinity, virgin birth, and original sin. Yet he had hope. The Christian church could change, had been known to change, and the emergence of the Virgin Mary to the Godhead itself (there is more prayer in the Catholic circles to the Virgin than to the Holy Ghost any day of the week), gave Watts hope that he could, backed by a powerful public movement, bring about the kind of change that he saw as the salvation of the Christian religion.

He had to make compromises to achieve this condition—and he was ready. Until he had studied the religions of the East, said the changing Watts, the teaching of Christ and the symbols of Christianity had no real meaning for him. Had he studied Augustine, a Kempis and others, he now said, he would have come to the same conclusions. (Hardly).

But what Alan Watts was doing, visibly, was seeking a handle that would let him lift himself into the American theological mainstream. In the sense of his compromise, his danger also rested. For to be true to himself he had to regard as "symbols" what others in the Christian church would regard as "absolutes." And if he could sufficiently cover himself in verbosity, he might get by without anyone noticing. That is one of the virtues of theological rhetoric.

How many angels can dance on the head of a pin?
is not
so much different
from

What is the sound of one hand clapping?

Now is it?

That kind of discussion is where Alan Watts would surely shine, and his superior knowledge of the mysteries of the East would serve him well if he could avoid the unpleasantness of the theological rack on flat statements of belief.

This *crise de foi* came in the middle of *The Meaning of Happiness*. It was apparent that Alan Watts had resolved it only partly. Theoretically his argument was complete—he could make the transfer now, where he would have laughed had it been suggested to him two or three years earlier. Practically he had other problems to solve.

The last of *The Meaning of Happiness* is a digression into the historiography of Eastern religions. This posed no confrontations of faith, and it was Watts' opinion that the exposure would be useful. In fact, there was a good deal of repetition of the first two books—but this was understandable because those books were written for an English market and this latest one for an American market.

The explanation in the remainder of the book was designed to remove a false conception in the minds of Westerners about the Eastern religions. Too many in America equated flush toilets with progress, and progress with achievement and achievement with happiness. But too much of the time in America achievement equals misery, not happiness. Watts' concept here was to remove the misconception that because there were so many poor in Asia, they were also miserable, and therefore unhappy. He also needed to say that Eastern religions were not negative although they did not bow to the gods of progress.

In 1940, in an America flexing its muscles, a United States burgeoning with power and the realization that it was becoming a balance force and one of the most powerful nations in history, in spite of the recent depression—it was very hard to make people realize that activity and steel mills and two cars in every garage did not necessarily mean progress. Americans had not yet come up against the pollution factor of those cars, Pittsburgh had not yet declared the effluent of the steel mills a disaster, and no one thought Americans would ever accept the idea of a 200-mile territorial limit to protect off-shore fishing. The world in 1940 had not yet been truly threatened by man. It was true, of course, that there was a war, and that was a threat. But it was a conventional war and a conventional threat at the moment. The Blitz was just on in England; no one knew the full power of the terrible weapons that were in hand, or the weapons that would be devised in the next five years. So to take Americans out of the concept that West meant Progress and East meant Backwardness was not easy. It could not have been transmitted to the mass of American people; not until Japan had shown that a "backward" race could carry on a successful and highly technological war, would there be much respect in America for Asians.

Sympathy yes. Respect no. And respect, not sympathy, meant acceptance.

What Americans must learn to do, said this erudite English scholar of the East, is to learn to enjoy themselves. They must learn from the East. They must realize that religion was a beginning—not an end. They must develop a love of life; this was the secret of happiness.

Having shown himself the way in his writing, Alan Watts then began to explore the practical possibility of fitting himself into the American religious picture. He went to Eugene Exman, who advised him that the easiest and, for Watts, best course would probably be the adoption of the religion of the Society of Friends. Here was the most relaxed of the Christian churches in terms of the particular dogmatic problems that had driven Watts from the church. Also, as Quaker, he might rise as he wished, without all the folderol of study.

Watts rejected that idea. His experience with Quakers in England had convinced him that they were a serious and dowdy lot, not at all inclined to the joy of living that was essential to his purpose.

Looking about him he saw the American sects.

Roman Catholic. That meant seminary and celibacy. He had the awkward encumberment of a wife and two children, even if the religion had beckoned. Doctrinally speaking, there was too much of the absolute, although ritualistically speaking, there was no Christian service that appealed to him more, and all his life he had admired the church that could create so much in architectural beauty, art, and music.

The basic American Protestantism had to be rejected. The Congregationalists were the old Puritans, and much too pure. The Methodists were inclined to noise and bombast, and they hated cards and would never countenance the bawdy jokes that Alan Watts loved to tell. The Baptists, immersion or not, were out of the running for all the same reasons. The Presbyterians, while not hard of shell, were dull.

It was really very simple: Alan Watts had grown up in the Church of England. He could still remember Canon Dawson flapping about the village in his cassock, doing good and, more important, doing more or less as he pleased as long as he did not shock too many personages.

So it had to be the Protestant Episcopal Church, which is the American branch of the Church of England—at least its closest cousin. The Episcopalians had their differences but they managed to keep a semblance of unity hovering above men of such varied experience and belief as the good Dr. Oswald Taylor of Grace Church in Portland, Oregon, who believed in the trinity and original sin, and the Reverend James Pike, of San Francisco, who ended up at least believing in neither one and resigning as a Bishop of the faith. Certainly into this panoply Alan Watts could find his way and a place of happiness.

As for the book, it was doing well enough in a mild way. *The New York Times* said it was "novel and interesting." Other reviewers treated it as a work by a serious and experienced scholar. No one on record questioned its direction or the credentials of the writer: that was America. Alan Watts had written a provocative book and it had been published by an eminently respectable house. It succeeded, where a thousand other books that year failed.

Apparently Alan Watts' wife was already prepared for this momentous step of conversion. His mother-in-law paid very little attention; she was so bound up in her own life and Zen that she had little time for anything else.

The young Watts couple then began scouring Manhattan for churches, so Alan might familiarize himself with the various forms. He found them very different—there were very low churches and moderately low churches, but finally he discovered in one Manhattan church the love of pomp and ritual that had always attracted him to Roman Catholicism. And to this he came back again and again. Alan Watts was prepared for the change:

> *Now it seemed natural to me to be exuberant about religion, just as it also seemed natural and uncontradictory to be religious and at the same time to be exuberant about life, to go about our loving and eating and drinking with the innocent splendor of the flowers doing likewise. If one is going to have church and ritual of any kind, why not live it up? If I put on vestments of brocade, light candles, burn incense, and intone mysterious chants, I do not do it to fool people or to flatter God. I do it out of simple delight and fascination for the color, the stately dance, and the sense of mystery—not of the kind of mystery which can be revealed or explained, but the kind of mystery which God must be to himself. Mystery, mystic,—the Greek rueiv—the finger on the lips; mum's the word; do not spoil it with an explanation. I was not really interested in what rites and ceremonies symbolized, and still less in future results they might be supposed to achieve.*

Alan Watts intended to become a priest—and that was the word he used. It tells much, for a "low Episcopalian" hates the word priest as opposed to minister, and a high Episcopalian revels in it. The two feel strongly enough about the problem to become blood enemies, for religious brothers always strain at gnats.

Watts intended to be a priest of a type—there are many in England and some in America. I have known a number. One was the chaplain at the boarding school of one of my children, a handsome, hard-drinking, joke-cracking delight of a man who had been a captain in the British army before he took to the cloth and came to America. I never asked him why. But he was much like the young Watts must have been—a real seeker of truth who also loved vestments and ritual. He rose to become headmaster of a very fashionable school, and as far as I know he lived a very happy life.

That was Alan Watts' intention. He had no idea in the 1940s that the track he had been on originally was the one that would appeal to young America, and to some youth all over the world. There was no concept of rebellion—it did not start until the 1950s with the Beat Generation, then progressed, finally to wash itself out in the economic depression of the middle 1970s where problems of survival overcame all the residue of an overripe and too luxurious society in America.

But in a world half at war, with America nervously wondering when her turn would come, Alan Watts understood that his best chance of finding a place was in the religious community, and that he would be acceptable to the Episcopalians and they to him.

The die was cast.

司

CHAPTER TEN

PRIEST

All during this period of decision, Alan Watts and Eleanor were cutting it up in New York, where they were very welcome among the bohemians of Greenwich Village and the psychology crowd of the Upper East Side where the psychotherapists and psychiatrists kept their shingles out. They drank and they played and they sang and Watts taught the others the lesser wonders of the East, while his high-priest friends taught him how to be an Anglo-Catholic clergyman.

Of course he had to have a piece of paper that gave him the license to marry people and bury people and conduct ceremonies in an Episcopal house of God. This paper was going to be a bit more difficult to get than the approval of the high-living, laughing crowd that was attracted to Alan Watts.

In New York, that mecca of liberalism, he was soundly rebuffed by the bishop, and by the General Theological Seminary. He was advised to go somewhere and get a college degree. He was advised to study church history. Someone had told the bishop about his books—but of course the bishop had not read any of them.

The thing to do was find a bishop who would take him under his wing. The Everetts were big in the Chicago area, and had many contacts there. Luckily Bishop Wallace Edwards Conkling of Chicago was a more lenient fellow, a high church thinker himself, and through the Everetts a sort of friend of the family. That is, Eleanor knew the rector of the Episcopal church of Hinsdale, one of Chicago's poshier suburbs, and the rector was an old pal of the Bishop. With pushes and advice from his New York high church friends, Alan Watts and Eleanor and the child went off to Chicago to visit the Bishop.

Watts' love of show could not have been better pleased, for the Bishop was a real bishop. He looked like a bishop, with white hair and scarlet cassock and little fancy skullcap. Except for the color he might have been a Buddhist abbot; except for the rigging, he might have been a Roman Catholic archbishop.

The Bishop was interested. Watts was a handsome and impressive young man. The Everetts were people of substance. The educational gap did not bother the Bishop—Watts would have to do what was necessary, but the way could be paved for him.

And it was.

The family influence, and the romanticism of the whole project obviously appealed to Bishop Conkling—and it also appealed to Bishop McElwain, the Dean of Seabury-Western Theological Seminary in Evanston, Illinois, the home of Northwestern University.

So the Bishop considered. Watts had no credentials, but there were precedents, and the fine category of special student. As a special student, Watts was not, immediately at least, a candidate for the Bachelor of Divinity degree. Anything could happen from there on, Watts was made quickly enough to see.

The Bishop asked for a bibliography—of all that Watts had read on history, church history, and religion. He could not have given the twenty-six-year-old Englishman a more suitable task. For Watts could produce his three books—all with nice big bibliographies of their own, and he also wrote out a list of some 250 other works. That was impressive enough. Bishop Conkling's problem was to make it look good—to justify the decision to let Watts in—and it was not so great a request. The bibliography was honest and successful. It got Alan Watts admitted to divinity school. He and Eleanor went back to New York, packed up the apartment furniture, and moved to a house in the north end of Evanston, near Lake Michigan, with their little girl Joan and their black maid.

Alan Watts then set out to become an Episcopal priest—never a minister of the gospel but a priest.

Had the high brass of the church in New York learned what Watts was up to in his personal affairs, they would have stuttered and turned red and raised the ceilings of their naves. For Watts was an artist—he made erotic drawings of his friends. He also continued something he had begun in boarding school days, the illumination of manuscripts in the medieval style. He continued to study Chinese, particularly the calligraphy of the language, which is an art form in its own right.

Withal, he began what he called his "square" period. It befitted a divinity student to live a careful life, so the house was painted in suburbia's colors, and the new furniture was suburbia's furniture. They went to football games and bought life insurance—all very square.

In a way it must have been torture for an Englishman. It must have been worse torture for a free spirit, after the new wore off. For Chicagoland is the heart of America, and has all the wonderful homespun qualities of the heartland. Chicago to the New Yorker is like Liverpool to the Londoner, or Liverpool cum Birmingham. In those days there were not many bright spots. There were some leftover speakeasies and a few hotels that served good food, and a handful of restaurants other than the stockyards variety.

But Watts did not complain. He, a round peg, was trying to settle into his square hole. And for a while he did not slip through.

One reason he managed was his undoubted and sharp intellectual curiosity. It is often said that a good English public school education is better than most American college degrees. The

Watts case would certainly prove the point. He had not studied formally past sixth form—it had been years since he had touched a Greek lexicon, but almost immediately he found himself at the head of the class in Greek. Apparently that was not saying very much—why should it? Only a handful of American colleges and even fewer preparatory schools (and virtually no high schools) even taught Greek in the 1930s.

Very soon Watts had outdistanced the other members of the class and at the end of the first year asked and received permission to study without classes on a tutorial basis. Now he began a course of study of Christian history similar to that he had already undertaken on the mysteries of the East. He was perhaps the most thorough scholar, particularly of the mystical aspects of the faith, that had ever prowled about the libraries of the Seminary and adjoining Northwestern University.

In his perusal of the dusty tomes of the Seminary library, he came across an ancient Greek text, St. Dionysius' *Theologia Mystica*, plus a Latin translation. But the work had not been translated into English. Abetted by the authorities of the Seminary, particularly the Reverend Elmer Templeton of the Greek department, Watts translated the work into English.

It was a triumph. He had accomplished something in the Christian world of religion—and if it was obscure it satisfied Watts for two reasons. First of all it proved to him to be the equivalent of Asian mysticism—which appealed because it upheld his thesis that one could learn from the other. Second, and even more important, it was published by the Holy Cross Press of New York, which gave Watts a leg up on the ecclesiastical ladder. It was just the proper kind of thing a right-thinking, bright young Episcopal minister should be putting his mind to.

And yet ministerial candidate Alan Watts was not fooling all the people all the time, and he knew it. He was suspected by his brother students and some of the faculty of pantheism—many of the brightest flowers of the church were guilty of that sin. Had it been the days of the Inquisition he might have suffered the fate of Fra Lippo Lippi, but in the 1940s the good teachers of Evanston were not burning acolytes at the stake. Besides, by his own statement, Alan Watts had a "gift for semantic dexterity." Indeed he had—I have already indicated it in some of his comments about the mysteries—his own writings are much more indicative. They rise and fall, and if one reads them aloud they are mellifluous, but like many another clerical or philosophical or psychological tract (his have been identified as all three) sometimes they are also somniferous.

Alan Watts was a patient man, and even though he was not at all sure of his vocation, he sweated through the course, and on Ascension Day, 40 days after Easter in 1945, he was ordained a priest of the Episcopal church.

The Reverend Mr. Watts had not changed very much from the ecclesiastical student, who had not changed very much from the Zen Buddhist of London. He was thirty years old, still handsome and youthful of mien, slender and quick to smile. He loved good food and drink, sometimes too much of both, and they did not agree with Eleanor. They had more children now, and Eleanor had settled down to become what she wanted, a middlewestern suburban housewife.

At thirty Watts was troubled. He must now go out into the world of religion and make his way. He took stock.

"To be precise" he wrote later, "I am not so much a priest as a shaman."

When he said that, he meant one thing. Others of the world could take it another way. And the more pedestrian of them considered Watts to be a very strange fellow indeed, and basically unchanged from the London days. He considered shaman to be a word of approbation for one thing. A priest represented the establishment—a shaman was an individual bringing knowledge and comfort to his people. To Watts anything that linked him with nature was to be preferred to things that forced him into the molds of Western society, be it church or be it temporal.

Long before, Watts had known that he could not be soldier or even journalist. He had chosen the priesthood as the most likely form of Western occupation in which he could succeed. He was right; if all went well, he could succeed in this task. Yet how would he do as pastor of a low Episcopal church in some Godforsaken midwestern town, or even a city like Grand Rapids? The answer was obvious. He would go down the drain very quickly.

In a sense, Watts was safe. He did not have any influence in the church except that which Eleanor's connections had managed to produce through Bishop Conkling of Chicago. The chances were that he would be sent on a mission post, not necessarily to darkest Africa, although that was a possibility in the minds of the church fathers (never his).

Watts asked Bishop Conkling to turn him loose in the city of Chicago as a priest at large. What he wanted to be for the High Episcopalians was what Fulton J. Sheen became for the Roman Catholics a few years later—a priest turned loose to convert important people, to make appearances to show the church as "a concerned party" to the social problems of the day. He was to be like a battleship sent out from Britain on a tour of Asian countries, to show the flag, impress the hell out of the natives with big guns, and yet show by demeanor that the institution produced gentlemen and people worth knowing.

The new minister put it that way to his Bishop, although he had a more Wattsian role in the church in mind for himself. He intended to continue his studies of mysticism, and then wrap the church around them. In a later day it would be called bringing "relevancy" to the church, and good pastors everywhere would worry about this problem; some would do things like start boarding houses and saloons on church property. It would be all the rage—not precisely what Alan Watts had in mind perhaps, but that kind of thing.

But not in 1945. The war was just over in Europe. It had not yet ended in the Far East. The boys who came home were not interested in rebelling against much of anything—they wanted to get married, to get jobs, or to get back to school and finish interrupted educations. Nor was the youth of the country the marked target for the church. In 1945 there were whickerings of difficulty, but the fathers did not know how deep was the trouble into which they were falling by years of inattention to the changing mores and changing needs of a society. The children of the twenties had grown up watching their fathers and mothers drink bathtub gin; the children of the thirties had seen their dads drinking very bad 3.2 beer and liquor when they could afford it. The children of the forties were not really beginning to grow up yet. So the rumbles of trouble were yet to come.

Thus even though Bishop Conkling was a genial and liberal prelate, he could not justify turning Alan Watts loose on Chicago without a parish. But recognizing the special qualities of his young priest, the Bishop did the best thing that he could for him—he assigned him to the mission at Northwestern University. He was to be the Episcopal Chaplain of the University. This gave the Watts family a run-down house called Canterbury House, in the middle of the campus, next door to the Seminary. It gave them very little money, but Eleanor still had some, and by this time Alan Watts had cultivated some rich friends. They helped with expenses to put the house into shape. Watts and his wife and volunteers cleaned up the house, Eleanor decorated it until its whole character was changed from filth and shabby gentility to minor splendor. They had a small chapel dedicated to Canterbury's Thomas à Becket (which explained the name Canterbury House), and the Reverend Mr. Watts had the use of the huge Seminary chapel on Sundays.

It was as if, in those first days of his arrival in America, he had gone into the confectionary and sat down to be served a dozen variegated ice cream sundaes.

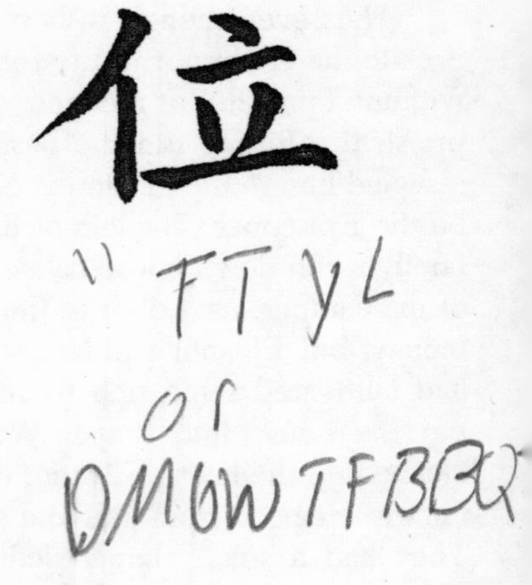

CHAPTER ELEVEN

OCCUPYING THE THRONE

In a way he was the priest, in a way he was the king, given control over the kingdom of the minds of all these youths and attachés and teachers at Northwestern University. It was not a temporal kingdom, but in his bailiwick he had the sense of influence of a bishop—and why not. He was an important personage, the young who came to him were either believers in what he had to offer, or they would have liked to be believers, or at the very least they accepted him as an unusual priest, partly because he was English, partly because he looked so young and innocent.

Watts had a heady freedom to practice the kind of religion he wished—to experiment as much as he liked, to follow his bent and bring East and West together in the Middle Way that he had begun describing in the very first book on Zen, 10 years before.

Perhaps the fathers of the church should have paid him more heed than they did. For, knowing what he wanted to do, Watts set out with joy and great spirit to do so. He loved music—he had been much impressed by the medieval chants and music of the Roman Catholic church. Therefore, he would have good music in his chapel; to get it he enlisted the aid of the Northwestern School of Music. The challenge appealed to young musicians of the school, and presto, he had music, Gregorian chants, and whatever else he wished. Even experimental music. He had choirs and instrumentalists and composers at his beck in a way that few ministers anywhere could so command.

The campus everywhere has a grapevine as sure and quick as the Bamboo Telegraph of Asia, and almost immediately the word was out on Northwestern campus that something was happening over on Sheridan Road at the Episcopal chapel. I mean *happening.* Watts did just what he wanted to do, he dug up a version of the high church mass that was of questionable legality perhaps under canon law, but might slip by. It was gorgeous, full of vestments and candles and high drama and good music. The Reverend Mr. Watts amazed everyone by keeping his sermons down to 15 minutes and he talked about things that *counted:* either how a young couple might find happiness, or the mysteries of Asia in relation to Western man. Interesting things. Not the dried up dandelion chaff of the past.

The joy of Watts in life, and the hope in Watts of achieving his end was bursting forth in these first months. He consulted with his students and banned all "corny hymns." He brought the high drama of liturgy and costume to his church. He tried his best to remove the God of guilt from his chapel, and substitute the God of love and joy who was his own. It worked beautifully, he had the Episcopal students of the college chanting his praises and wondering what was to come next, and he had strangers, from in college and out, coming to see the show.

For that is what it was, of course. The Watts who loved to put on vestments was primarily a showman. Not that he did not know his theology—he could spout it with the best of them. Not that he did not know the canon law. He had studied it carefully.

But the trouble was, and it soon became apparent, that there was no real place outside of the one he occupied for a minister of

Watts' stripe. It would have demanded a change in the church or a change in Watts to make it work on the long haul. Watts was changing—all men change and he changed constantly—but he kept coming back to the same grain of his truth that had kept him moving since the days at King's School—the hard core of the Christian faith must be tempered, and the mysteries brought forth, so that the God-power was put in perspective. Otherwise, Watts and the church were going to part.

It was not apparent to him. It was apparent to Dean Alden Kelley of the Seminary, who told other students that Watts was not long for Christianity. Dean Kelley was a wise man, he observed Watts, and he had no open objection to what he was doing. God knew and so did everyone else, that the church needed change, and if this pleasant, bright-eyed young Englishman could deliver it, someone was going to have to consider it seriously.

For the first time in the history of the Seminary, that place became a center of university activity. It was said there was a perennial bull session to be found in the chapel, at the Reverend Watts' house, or someplace around there, usually with Father Watts in attendance. He was joyous and easy with the students, he was young enough to let them associate themselves with him, rather than associating himself with the voice of authority. He was an active seeker of acolytes and initiation into the mysteries. He gave courses in instruction to the candidates for confirmation. Eleanor revelled in her life as wife of the parson—although it was far more than that. She gave teas at the house, and she paid the liquor bill when teas became cocktail parties. For Father Watts was "with it" and that could be seen at half a glance.

The acid test of Watts' ministry was the friends he made among the students, and he made scores of them. They liked him—and students do not *like* that many professors. They felt he knew their problems and could relate to their sense of the universe. In many ways, these youngsters just back from the wars, or having come up through the war years, were lost in the same way that Alan Watts had been lost back in 1932 when he moved so hurriedly out of preparatory school upon learning that he was not going to get the coveted scholarship to Oxford. The world on which he was thrust, the world of British depression, was cold and hard and offered only oddments of future. He had to carve his own—and to cap it all, there he was at the sage age of seventeen, a man without a God because he had forsaken the one given him at birth.

So Watts did understand, and he knew that if the Episcopal brand of Christianity was to be made palatable to his young people it had to *relate* to their lives. A little pomp covered many things—and that was not bad either.

To add to his dignity, Watts grew a beard. He had that long thin face, the aquiline nose and deep-set eyes so often attributed as being common among Jews and not so common among Englishmen. His friends told him he looked like Jesus. That was not bad, either. But the goings-on? He and Eleanor and a student named John Gouldin made a sort of triumvirate for a time.

They went cruising out on garbage raids in Eleanor's huge black Packard. Alan drove, while John kept an eye out for useful trash, such as a cast-off saucepan that could be transformed into a clock, or a doll that could be painted and used as an idol. They hijinked with air rifles and fencing and stuffing fishnet floats with matchheads as explosives. John also was in the choir.

Watts played God at Northwestern, and took other stances of which his church was unaware. One of his students at Northwestern was Margaret Jacobson, a middlewestern beauty, who enrolled in the course in religious instruction he set up in his first year as Chaplain.

"I marvelled at his ability to clarify the most abstruse metaphysical concepts," she said in a letter years later. "He would frequently use an elegantly simple pen sketch or a Zen master story to put across this or that point. In such a way I was introduced to Zen before more than a handful of Americans had ever heard the word, much less knew what it was. . . ."

Because she was pretty, thoughtful and active on the campus, Margaret Jacobson became one of the central group around Alan Watts in this important period of her life.

"At the time, Emerson Harris and Bob Morse and I formed a sort of triad. Em, at this point, fancied himself in love with me (he was always falling in love), and I fancied myself in love with Bob (I was always falling in love, too). Bob was a big handsome fellow, with the face of a Buddha, at once enigmatic, serene, and merry. Em, alas, suffered from having a big hooked nose, a big hooked chin which rose to meet the nose, a growth of yellow woolly hair, and about 30 pounds too much weight. . . ."

This was Margaret's freshman year.

But like so many students she knew, she was torn between "that religious awakening which frequently takes place at that time" and the social life of the campus. "One half of me wanted to be a leftwing egghead, practicing the chic rituals of Sunday morning, the other half wanted to be pretty, average, and much dated. . . ."

And like so many of those others who picked up the religious fever in freshman year, by sophomore year she was out of it.

". . . the group of idolatrous students who clustered around Alan were *not* fraternity and therefore *not* to my taste. They also looked like a lot of neurotic misfits, which no doubt they were."

So after that first year, Margaret Jacobson drifted away from the religious enclave for a time, although she continued to observe religious feasts.

Still, for the very young and some who stuck with him, Alan's was the most exciting game on the campus. And if the staid Episcopal fathers elsewhere had heeded what was occurring here at Evanston, the history of the Protestant Episcopal church might have shown a swift increase in youth membership, rather than the steady, dismal decline that came in the 1950s and 1960s.

The years 1946 and 1947 were fine productive years, and the future looked bright. Alan Watts needed a certain amount of seclusion for his own work, for his meditation and consideration of his plans, and for his writing. For he was always writing something, a sermon, a piece for the college paper, an article for one of the religious journals. He was forever a man in motion, a thoughtful man on the move.

All this action kept him young. As his astrologer put it:

"Capricorns often seem to start out mature beyond their years and get younger and enjoy life more with the years. . . ."

She certainly hit the nail on the head, as far as Alan Watts was concerned. He worried less about the universe, now having found a place in it for himself. He loved parties, and Canterbury House was one continual fête of one kind or another—sometimes tea and cakes, sometimes hard liquor, sometimes beer, sometimes nothing at all but intoxicating conversation or music. There was a joy of life there that was unsurpassed on the campus.

But there was also a witch in the closet. After Alan Watts had gotten well settled in at Evanston, he could look with a certain pride upon his accomplishments; modest perhaps, but bringing the young into the fold was like the parable of the sheep, and any minister could take satisfaction from such basic work.

Then out of the closet stepped this witch, not a malignant spirit, but a gentle lady from Chicagoland, the mother of one of his most promising, young, hell-raising, psalm-singing students.

"Don't you realize, Father Watts," she said, more plaintively than in anger, "that you are just a decoy? The religion you are giving these young people is not the religion of Saint Luke's and Saint Mark's here in town, and from what I can see it isn't the religion of the Episcopal church anywhere. They're going to feel very lost when they leave Northwestern."

Knowing what he knew about his stretching of the bounds of canon law, Father Watts was prepared for storms of bombast. He could have argued a bishop to a fare-thee-well over what he was doing and its relevance to church history. He was ready for trouble from that side. But now he was disarmed. What the lady said was so obviously from the heart. Father Watts was preparing his young flock to enter a fold that did not exist, and was unlikely to exist without the most severe volcanic eruptions within the church. Who thought that Father Taylor off in Portland was going to change his ways after all these years; he would not even have the church carpeted for fear of becoming too worldly.

So there was a crack in the structure that Alan Watts was building, and immediately when the lady spoke up, he perceived her remarks as simple truth.

Time went by, and he worried about the problem. There were two ways to approach it: one was to continue precisely what he was doing, and as he continued to succeed—which he certainly was also doing—he could point with pride and view with alarm in church publications. All the while acolytes of Wattsism would be infiltrating the church world from the Seminary at Evanston. He had more than a few either passing out, or just in the middle of the works.

Keeping going, depending on time, relying on the support of the liberal and lenient Bishop Conkling who had appointed him, he could wage the good fight, and in time, when his Jesus-beard had grown white, he might emerge as the saviour of the church, the man who had brought relevance to Episcopalianism in America.

Or he could quit and walk away.

Watts was not the quitting kind, but he was troubled. And his troubles continued. Most of them were internal, but they were goaded by outside watchers.

Dean Kelley of the Seminary warned Father Watts one day: his standards were too high, he put on too good a representation of the church, and his students were never going to find that degree of color and exuberance when they went out into the general Episcopal world.

It was another blow, and Father Watts again knew in his heart that the crack was widening, even though his successes were many. Looking back later he recalled Richard Adams, who came out of the Navy to go to the Seminary, and became a priest. And Robert Platman, who graduated from the Seminary to eventually take a fine parish on Long Island. And Robert Morse, who would became chaplain of Episcopal students at the University of California at Berkeley.

That was part of the positive.

The other part was internal. By various mental maneuvers over the period of his seminarianism, the Reverend Mr. Watts had managed to reconcile his gaudy beliefs relative to Asian philosophy with the church and its history. He was so good a student that he could find half-forgotten, rare, and obscure sources, undeniably Christian, whose views he shared.

Not that he had completely accepted Christianity. In his studies he had lost the contempt he felt for the Christian religion when he opted to be a Buddhist at the age of fifteen.

Now, he had changed.

He was not about to disavow his Buddhist sympathies, but felt that he "could almost completely accept the Christianity of, say, Etienne Gilson or Evelyn Underhill."

To put it another way, when he had entered the Seminary he had submerged his truths. That is not to say that he had become cynical and was ready to trade his soul for a profession. But the pressure was definitely on from Eleanor and her family, and he was so busy resisting the impetus to become a faker that he found it easy to persuade himself that he could reconcile his own beliefs with Christian doctrine.

And perhaps he could. The church authorities were giving him time. Dean Kelley was gentle in his admonitions; there was no threat in them. The Bishop was not on his back. He was certainly encountering less flack in his flight through Christian doctrine than Father Hewlitt Johnson, "the Red Dean of Canterbury," whom he had known and who was to become the terror of the Episcopal world in the 1950s with his profession that Christianity was not so far removed from communism, and that maybe the English-speaking powers were doing more harm than good with their *weltpolitik*. Churchmen who challenged politicians were always in trouble, particularly when they did so on moral grounds. As long as Father Watts had the sense to stay out of politics—and he showed no interest whatsoever—he had time.

He was trying to become a solid Christian. He had even converted from the Buddhist forms of meditation, from the consideration of koans to reciting the Divine Office from the Breviary. He went to confession. He followed the precepts of an enlightened Anglican monk. He tried, and he tried.

But he had his difficulties with prayer. His problem was basic and philosophical: the Christian is concerned with *self* and the relations of that self above all other things, with a God that created him in his image. The Asian philosophies to which Watts leaned were concerned with the *one-ness* of things. The meeting of the two concepts was hard, perhaps it was impossible. Alan Watts did not think it was at all impossible in 1946. In 1947 he tried very hard to be a good Christian in the doctrinal sense. In the teaching sense, he was very effective; in the ritualistic and decorative sense, he was superb.

But the nagging continued.

Thus worried, he entered 1947.

謙德

CHAPTER TWELVE

HUMBLE SERVANT OF GOD

The chapter title indicates one of Alan Watts' deep personal worries in 1947, as he was writing another book. He was trying to get into what he called "a Christian frame of mind" and he found it hard. There was one hope: he discovered among the dusty tomes of the basement library a book by a seventeenth century Jesuit priest named J.P. Caussade. As Watts described the book after reading, it offered him what he needed. *Abandonment to the Divine Providence* had obviously been composed by a man as troubled as himself. Its central theme was the need to yield to the eternal now, which was the presence of God.

With this release it was not hard to justify the same kind of approach to the verities that he had practiced during the years of avowed Buddhism and which he had tried to erase by the use of private Christian prayers in recent months. He tried the concept out in *Holy Cross,* the religious magazine and was pleased enough with it to work it up more fully in his new book, *Behold the Spirit,* which he completed in February, 1947.

When the book was finished Watts sent it off to Eugene Exman, his publisher in New York. Over the years he and Exman had kept in touch, for the religious editor was truly impressed with the novelty and sincerity and apparent good sense of *The Meaning of Happiness* and the sales had been such that he need have no reservations about recommending another book to his management. Back in the New York period Exman had thought enough of Alan Watts and his work to send him manuscripts to read for his comments and recommendations. He had been particularly careful to send a manuscript by another public lecturer of note, Rubio Mosely. When Exman found that Mosely had done all he could to meet objections to it, he sent the manuscript off to Watts for editing and rewriting. Watts did the job, he was paid $200 for it, but when it came back Exman was still dissatisfied. Watts might be a good thinker, but he was not an editor, obviously, or his mind was turned elsewhere. This had all happened during the summer of 1940 when Alan and Eleanor Watts were vacationing from the city in Connecticut. In fact, however, Exman ended up publishing the Watts version of the book, because time was growing short, and the book did well enough.

Watts then had no strikes against him with Exman or Harper's—which is a prefatory note to saying it was a shock when the publishing house turned Watts down.

"When I did that, of course," said Exman years later, "I rejected Watts, and thus we lost an author." As it turned out, Harper's lost an author who would have been worth many hundreds of thousands of dollars to them.

But Exman turned the book down because he did not like the direction in which Alan Watts was going or what he had to say. There was nothing much of the controversial, exciting Watts in *Behold the Spirit.* All the old pizzazz had disappeared.

Watts opened *Behold the Spirit* with the charge that the Christian church itself was responsible for the vast hunger of the spirit because it did not satisfy that hunger.

Why not?

Because the church was showing no signs of spiritual life. In other words, it was dying in its institutionalism.

The truth, said Watts, was that the church was dead, and what he called the best minds of the church admitted it and deplored it.

These were very strong charges. Many people believed they were true, but most churchmen were not about to make them; it was as if a bastion of the Democratic party were suddenly to declare that the whole American political process had outlived its usefulness and we should go over to anarchism.

He would be heard, but he might be stoned out of the party.

With the Watts theological argument it was a different matter, because very early in the book it was apparent that he was going to fight this battle on the Christian grounds, citing Christian sources and not his Orientals, to make his points. In the past seven years since his last book, Watts had read widely in Christian theology to the end that he now could talk with as much erudition about Thomas Aquinas, Pascal, Rom Landau, Meister Eickhardt, Garrigou-Lagrange, and Reinhold Niebuhr, as he used to do about Suzuki, Jung, and Chuang Tzu. Now, in fact, he could talk about both—but he opened the book with his charge of the death of the church in a very Christian manner, using Scripture and the old mystics to prove his points.

In the beginning, Watts addressed himself to a truth: the decline of the church.

> *There is an abundance of rather unprofitable literature by both Christian and non-Christian writers bewailing, grumbling, or pointing scorn at the deadness of the church and the general decline of religion of whatever sort. For the most part the constructive side of this literature is merely so much sermonizing and exhortation to "return" to the beliefs and practice of certain things which the Church knows well enough should be believed and practiced but cannot find the heart for them. . . .*

Then he began taking on the doctrinaire:

The fact was, he said, that religion had to be mystical to be useful, and the mysticism had been exorcised from the Christian church. That was most of what was wrong. The attackers associated mysticism with trances, hermits, and negative conceptions of God, with blanking out one's mind—in other words with what he had in his preministerial days called "sitting on one's ass." But there was not any of that earthy, interesting language with the human concepts that there had been in the earlier discussions of the Middle Way.

In fact, Watts seemed to have been lulled into a new dullness. By the standards of theological writing in English about Christianity, it was not an over-dull book, and if one read closely, it was bound to reveal a good deal about its author, if not so much new about the church. For the fact was that Alan Watts was using this book—and so much is obvious from his life—to try to put the round peg in the square hole, and find the proper place for himself in the Christian community, so that he could remain within it.

He knew one thing: he was a mystic. He knew another: he was now a practitioner of Christianity and entitled to be a theologian. He *belonged* to a priesthood, courtesy of the four years in the Seminary. The title *Reverend* let him speak out, and he was entitled to an answer from his peers.

So he did speak out. He started with a good strong right cross: the essence of mystical religion is the consciousness of union with God.

There, the traditionalists could make anything of that they wanted to.

A bit further on, Watts posed the burning issue of the day: granted that the church was in decline, what was there to be done? And then he had the temerity to answer the question in his own way. He urged that Christianity be explained in terms understandable to the modern mind. He called

> *. . . for an improved worship as to the nature of which both Catholic and Protestant liturgical reformers are in considerable agreement; and, more important than all, for saints, for Christians of deep faith and moral heroism who will do more for God, for man, and for the Church than any number of thinkers, teachers, and liturgists. . . .*

The reader who knew what Watts had been up to with his bells and candles and fancy dress, and the super-services that called up every device ever permitted in an Episcopal church, could understand that Watts was calling, in the language of the clergy, for what he was doing himself so successfully in Evanston.

And of course he was right. If the church wanted the young, then the authorities had better make the church a place of interest to the young. Watts was writing in 1947. It would be *15 years* before Episcopal ministers would discover "soul music" and pop art as part of the natural curriculum of youth—and religion. The Episcopal Kent School in Connecticut would invite banjo players to participate in the services. Staid old St. Paul's School in New Hampshire would cut back the dogma, popularize the mass—and finally very nearly give up religion altogether because it was either that or the school might fail.

Watts foresaw all this in 1947, and he was working against it—giving very dearly of himself as religionist, to try to bring his young people to an appreciation of God. To him that meant a tranquil NOW universe—so much of his philosophy was very clear. But as he groped about, trying to correlate all he had learned of East and West and put it into an argument that could lead the way for the salvation of the church—and this meant his own salvation *in* the church—Watts began to stumble.

Then followed pages upon pages of theosophical discussion, lightened only by subheads such as *Thesis, Antithesis, Crisis, Synthesis,* pat headings: *The Epoch of the Spirit, the Gift of Union,* and truly learned and labored footnotes.

It was dreadful stuff—but there was a reason for it. When the doctor is giving the little child an unusually strong and personally obnoxious medicine, he has learned to coat it with cherry syrup, or something equally orally obfuscatory.

So what was Watts doing?

He was saying that the church had better get off its collective ass and dummy up about what young people would dig, what was the in thing and way out and what was strictly square. Watts was telling the church to get moving—get moving, buddy, before you get run off the street.

Three pages later we see Watts beginning to answer his own questions, to shine the light that would lead the church out of its darkness and into the center of the new world.

. . . Mahayana Buddhism . . . Sankhara's Advaita Vedanta . . . the Zen synthesis of Taoism, Confucianism and Buddhism. . . .

Those are familiar terms to readers of the earlier Watts. Now in 1947, they were joined on the page with Plotinus . . . St. Augustine . . . Philo . . . St. John . . . St. Paul. . . .

Although Watts launched into an esoteric discussion of church history—a discussion of medieval man and his needs and religiosity—occasionally the bright shining penny that was Watts showed through, mostly in footnotes:

> *Renaissance art has little or no interest in nature as the soil. Nature is seen only in terms of man; landscape is a mere background for portraiture. The West has never produced an important school of nature-painters in the sense and mood of Chinese landscape-painting.*

The statement is arguable in *modern* Western times—more and more artists are becoming bemused by nature in different ways, having ignored her for so long. But the statement is thoroughly understandable to the layman, and it might start an argument at a cocktail party that would end up with black eyes. That's where Watts was really good. But as for this book—Eugene Exman must have turned off early and put it in the hands of a theosophical reader; it seems doubtful that he could have waded through much more without hip boots.

Certainly Alan Watts of 1947 was knowledgeable about what was then happening in the church, as well as the past that he had studied in Seminary. He gave credit to the Catholics of modern times over the Protestants, in making of the Roman Catholic religion something adaptable and understandable to the times. Jacques Maritain, Garrigou-Lagrange, Gilson, and von Hügel, he said, had it all over Bertrand Russell and Santayana and William James in making their faith palatable to a new generation.

Then—Watts predicted that the next great step in Christian theology would be the absorption of Hinduism, Buddhism, Taoism, and perhaps even Mohammedan Sufiism—all mystical religions.

To a man from outer space, or someone who had not grown up in the Christian tradition, it might make sense. After all, had not the Muslims adapted and adopted so much of the mysticism of the Jewish and Christian faith? Why not? Why not, indeed. To make such statements to practicing ecclesiastical Christians, was to wave a red flag before a bull. If the flag was small, and tucked away in the middle of a paragraph in the center of a book, it might go unnoticed by many of the religious book buyers and non-readers. (Bishops are notable for not seeing such things). But someone, somewhere, sometime was going to notice all this, and if that someone knew Alan Watts, he was going to draw certain conclusions.

The satyr-priest was now at work with his pipes, playing his songs of happiness.

Watts said that the mystical in religion—Christianity or other—must be superior to the ritual. Too many, said theologian Watts, held to the mechanistic or sacramental view of religion. Those people were suspicious of mystical experience; if a woman went to a priest as Eleanor had done in New York and said that she had seen a vision of Christ—which she had—the priest's immediate reaction would probably be—which it was—that here was a woman who needed a good psychiatrist.

That kind of thing can shake the religiosity of even the most faithful. For one of the truths of religion—at least so the priests always said—is that God is always with us (*Dominus vobiscum*). Well, if He is always with us, then why should it seem so unusual for somebody to catch a glimpse of Him once in a while?

That's what Watts was saying.

More, he was saying that a religion in which God did not appear to the faithful in one way or another was scarcely better than no religion at all. He called it the religion of infancy and adolescence. If it did not lead into mystical consciousness, then the whole world would become mechanical and as lifeless as last Sunday's mashed potatoes.

Alan Watts did this with such splendid circumlocution that it would take a serious theological philosopher to see that he was challenging the very root concepts of the established church. Five hundred years earlier he would have been tried, convicted out of his own books, and burned at the stake. There is hardly any doubt about that, on the record of the Established Church. In 1947 a troubled church was looking for answers, and so even serious departure from the norm was acceptable, if a churchman did not insist too much. And in clothing his arguments in the balloon words of theology, Father Watts was following accepted practice: it was all right to raise shibboleths and try revolutionary tactics as long as the people did not understand what you were up to. Don't stir up the animals!

The first half of the book was mellifluous intellectualizing, the sort of exercise a scholar gets into in order to flex his writing muscles and remind the world of the church that he is alive and vigorous, ready for any important tasks that might be awaiting.

Almost midway the book livened up: this was where the Reverend Watts reverted to Master Watts, the student of Asian philosophy. For when he spoke of Christian things, Father Watts used Greek and Roman quotations and leaned heavily on syllogism and the formal church-type of argumentative posture. But when he spoke of things Oriental, his argument reached down into his bag of joy—he told anecdotes, one after the other, some of which he had told before, but obviously not to this audience.

> *One day Master Pai-chang was asked by a follower what to do: the questioner had been seeking reality but did not know how to go on seeking. Pai-chang answered that it was very much like the man who went out looking for an ox when he was riding on one.*

That was an aside in a bit of discussion of East vs. West—and as always in Father Watts' pages, the East won by a knockout.

Watts argued *for* mysticism within the established church, using the materials at hand. He said that the individual must be able to free himself from the formal symbols of Christianity (confession and penance, 17 Hail Marys if you were a Roman). And the final realization of this would be the development of the religion of the Incarnation—and that meant God's union with the entire universe.

Reaching into his bag, he tried to lighten it with an example from the church itself, and the best he could come up with was the Breviary hymn:

> *From that Holy Body broken*
> *Blood and water forth proceed;*
> *Earth and stars and sky and ocean*
> *By that flood from stain are freed.*

That argument, going to the heart of his book's contention, just could not stand up against the arguments he could summon from the top of his head for Buddhism.

It ended Part One of the book, in fact. And Part Two plowed on through dust as dry as the middlewestern plain. The problem, as Watts posed it, was the finding of the true relation between God and the universe.

In a trice, Father Watts was back writing with a heavy pen.

> *Theology . . . can only say that whereas creatures cause things out of themselves or out of pre-existing material, the Creator causes things in the manner proper to a first cause—independently of pre-existing material. . . .*

And whereas to the Orientals the universe *is* God, to the Occidentals the universe cannot be God and to say it is God is to be pantheistic and thus subject to the stake when it might be reintroduced as a way of getting rid of wicked deviationists.

Desperately Alan Watts tried to leaven the book with some of the interest he could inject into all his writing. He tried a quotation from Dante in the Italian, but all it did was show his erudition. It did not help unstricture the dreadful prose of Western theology.

And no matter how Watts struggled, it always came back to the same invidious comparison between Eastern and Western views.

Even in his symbolism for the Holy Spirit, he turned to ideas that were basically Asian:

> *The symbols of the Holy Spirit are wind and fire—wind which is masculine in its strength and feminine in its softness, and fire which is masculine in its brilliance and feminine in its warmth and volatility. . . .*

After all, he said, there was the traditional symbolism of angels playing on harps in celebration of God—and no one could really believe that angels kept flying around up in heaven playing endlessly on harps. So there must be room for an extension of symbolism to include manifestations of the Holy Spirit, the least developed facet of the triumvirate God in Christian theology.

Watts was, in other words, offering the church an out that would make it appealing to thoughtful persons, and especially the questioning young.

The last pages of the book comprised a plea to accept contemplation, mysticism, and an outreach of religion away from the old forms. *The Life of Contemplation* was the title of the chapter and it went as far into professing the need for incorporation of the Eastern religions as anyone dared go in the West.

When the book was finished, and the agony of rejection by Harper's had been stomached and overcome, Watts did find a publisher in Pantheon Books, where Paula Van Doren took his affairs in charge. The editors at Pantheon read the book, without having been tainted by association with the old Watts, the spellbinding popular Watts—and they saw in it an interesting exercise in the modernization of the Christian religion. So they agreed to publish.

The book was a modest success with the public—but it was not really intended for the public at all, but was at one time Alan Watts' *apologia* for his faith and an exploration of the manner in which he might achieve real Christian belief for himself. By his own statement, at this point he had not done so.

The Episcopal world was in ferment that year, and the progressive leaders of the church were looking for just this kind of discussion. That is not to say that the church as a whole was ready to put an imprimatur on what Alan Watts proposed—not at all. But had he been interested in struggling through for a number of years, by his own statement he thought he had a good chance of becoming a bishop. And indeed this must be so, for he was an impressive speaker, an impressive person, and he was beginning to be heard.

The Reverend Bernard Iddings Bell, then Chaplain at the University of Chicago, shared some of Watts' problems and thus some of his outlook on life with students and the youth of America. He called the Watts book "one of the half dozen most significant books on religion published in the twentieth century."

F.S.C. Northrop said that he regarded the book as "the only first rate book" in recent years in the field of religion. It went to the heart of the problem of Protestantism, he said, and proposed the only cure possible, at the basic metaphysical level.

And there were other reactions. Soon the Reverend Mr. Alan Watts became a Master of Theology—a degree awarded him by the Seminary in honor of the success of his book. His work was lauded and his contributions welcomed fervidly to *Holy Cross Magazine*.

So in one of the senses that was important to Watts, the book had succeeded past his wildest dreams. It had brought him acceptance in the religious community.

But in another sense it had failed completely. It had not quieted his own concerns. In the debates that followed and in all that he could see about him, he recognized his own spirit as differing completely from the religion as it was practiced.

One of his contemporaries at Seabury-Western Seminary read the book, and announced to his friends that Watts was obviously a man on his way out of Christianity. It would be simply a matter of time—for the church was not going to do what Watts suggested, and he was certain of it. The church had been muddling along for 2,000 years. Not since Henry VIII had there been a major change in Anglo-Catholicism. It was more likely that the Episcopal church of America would rejoin the Roman Catholics—and that was not very likely—than it was that the church would absorb Buddhism and the rest.

So the year 1947 ended in a strange state of affairs for the budding priest of Episcopalia. He was an undoubted success in what he was doing. The way was clear for him to fight, along with James Pike and John Robinson, and Bell and others of modernistic ideas, if he wished to do so. But within himself Alan Watts was undergoing a new crisis of spirit.

CHAPTER THIRTEEN

THE GENUINE INFLUENCE

"You eschew all false, devious actions. Your emotional life is disrupted by an intense need of freedom and independence. Also by a very idealistic attitude that eventually sees the hidden flaw in all humans and immediately turns off. . . ." So wrote astrologist Christine Carter in her analysis of Alan Watts, written so long after his death (two years), and with no knowledge of her subject except his astrological information.

But how true it was. For even now Alan Watts was beginning to look back on his entrance into the church as an "experiment." It seems doubtful that he did become a priest as an experiment at all, but as Zen has it, the past is not just one part of the continuum, but an illusion, so one's illusion of what the past was today is not necessarily the same as the illusion of those same events will be tomorrow.

In 1947 Watts was asking himself why he had entered the church. A number of problems were bothering him.

It is a truism that dissatisfied women tend to fall in love with their obstetricians and their ministers. The whole of the Christian church is dedicated to either celibacy or monogamy, some think to prevent this situation from getting out of control, but literature is filled with tales, references, and allusions, from Boccaccio through the Canterbury Tales and into modern times, of the clerics who could not keep their cassocks down:

There was a young matron from Yew.
Who said to her husband: Go screw.
The vicar is quicker,
And slicker and thicker,
And six inches longer than you.

This grave truth now threatened the marriage of Eleanor and Alan Watts. For as the years had passed, nearly a decade, Eleanor had been content to have babies.

In the Evanston picture, she was what Margaret Jacobson and the other students called "the one jarring note" in the smooth introduction to religion that Alan Watts brought the youngsters. "They were as ill-sorted a couple as I have ever seen. She was fat, dumpy and stupid," said Margaret Jacobson. She and others wondered among themselves how Alan Watts could have married her. "It was only after reading his autobiography that I realized her money must have been for something in his marrying her," she said.

That cruel youthful opinion was not shared by all in Evanston certainly, but as time went on, Eleanor did draw around herself a circle of friends quite different from those of Alan's world. She grew stout and matronly, while Alan seemed to grow younger with the challenge of the ministry.

"He looked like a man completely sure of himself and happy as a saint," one student said of him. "And to me with his Jesus Christ-like whiskers, at a time when no one else wore them, he was as exotic as a Tibetan monk. . . ."

The young, male and female, clustered around, and made Alan's life bearable at Northwestern.

He hated Chicagoland—the food was bad in all but a handful of restaurants, and the company, particularly of suburbanites, was deadly in the extreme. His students and graduate students at the university were the bright spots. Somehow, many a party and many an encounter seemed for him to end up in a bedroom.

Eleanor knew, and it became a matter of increasing friction between them. In Alan's mid-thirties, he realized that his marriage was coming apart, and he knew precisely why:

> *My own sexual mores are largely principles of style and taste concerning how and with whom I should participate in the most intimate pleasure that people can give to each other. . . . I do not believe that I should be passionately in love with my partner—though it is the best of pleasures under such circumstances—and still less, married. For there is a special and humanizing delight in erotic friendships with no strings attached. . . . My life would be much, much poorer were it not for certain particular women with whom I have most happily and congenially committed adultery. . . .*

The Reverend Alan Watts performed marriages for many a young couple, but in his heart he was beginning to doubt that institution too. And it was all a part of his movement back into Zen, away from the proprieties of the Western world.

By 1947 Alan Watts had gone back to the practice of an interior life—taking a part of each day for some bit of contemplation. He still could not do Za-Zen—he never would—but he could go for a walk or lie down and achieve what he wished to do in that manner.

Everything, it seemed, was pushing him away from the organized Christian religion, even as he was becoming one of the "bright young men," and his chaplainate at Northwestern was gaining national prominence.

He was becoming less impressed with the authority of the Christian tradition, and he came to feel that the church's claims were arbitrary and not revealing.

Odd—just as Watts was achieving what every right-thinking young ambitious cleric wanted—national recognition and growth within the church—he was moving away from it.

The signs of success were sure and obvious. He was written up in *Time* as one of the new *enfants terribles* who would bring the church into line with life. He was invited to various colleges and universities to lecture. And being on the road brought him new temptations; to most of them he succumbed joyfully. And as he became more secure in the church, he was less afraid to state his libertarian views. They upset many churchmen. They upset Eleanor worst of all, for his actions were a betrayal of the Christian marriage, and his statements about it were little short of braggartry. All would have been easy enough, except that there were two children, Joan and Ann.

But as this domestic pot boiled and bubbled, Alan Watts was being dragged into the limelight and into a new study of theology.

In the summer of 1949, the domestic boil came to a head. Eleanor found she could not stomach more of his affairs, and she left home to go and visit her mother in New York, pleading overwork and illness. That left Alan and his children at the Canterbury House (they always had help, courtesy of Eleanor's money) and joy seemed to become even more unrestrained than it had been in the past. More and more the *real* Alan Watts was standing up.

From the social standpoint, the new Alan Watts was not a character the conservatives in his church would admire. At this point, Margaret Jacobson came back into his life and saw him in Evanston. She had graduated from Northwestern and gone to Washington where she took a job and saved money so she might go to Europe to live for a time.

In October 1949, Margaret came back to Evanston for a visit. She looked up her old guru, the Reverend Alan Watts.

Immediately he invited her to dinner. He also invited Bob Morse, her old flame. And here is her account of the evening:

> *The evening was drenched in sensuality. (Alan was first, last and always a man of the theater). He prepared a Lucullan feast for us, soused us with wine, and then a dozen or more candles in the living room and read to us a weird story called, I think,* The Green People, *in a magnificently haunting voice. At that point he had Bob and me where he wanted us—ready to fall into one another's arms. It was only years later that I realized he had deliberately set out that night to play God.*

There were more such incidents—Alan Watts had begun to spend a good deal of time in the kitchen, and was fast becoming a cook with some reason for pride in his work. He could put out a meal that would rival most of the first-rate restuarants of Chicago at least, and in Eleanor's absence, the pots clanged and the wine flowed in the Watts' establishment night after night.

And yet, how the past drags with us into the future! Even as he was becoming ever more the free spirit, and recognizing his own road as diverging sharply from that of the Christian church to which he adhered, Watts was writing a new *apologia* to set forth a strengthening of the views he had expressed in *Behold the Spirit*.

Partly this was the press of publishing—a successful book always begets its copy or sequel, and critics who have liked one product plead for repetition. Partly it was the sorting-out process still in motion—by now it must be apparent that Watts' deepest thoughts were in his writing; this particular kind of solitary contemplation "turned him on." He would sit down at his desk, or maybe not at his desk, and sit at his typewriter, and the ideas would begin to flow. He was in that summer of 1949 groping again for his personal truths.

First there would come a bit of meditation to clear his mind. He would take a walk, ostensibly to get fresh air or think through a sermon, but he was really "absorbed in mystical silence of the mind." He did not recognize it then as planned meditation, but rather thought of these solitary jaunts as "exploring a state of consciousness out of sheer interest."

The Supreme Identity was, in essence, an extension of the high point of *Behold the Spirit*, wherein Alan Watts attempted to synthesize the wisdom of the East within the mantle of the Holy Ghost. One basic difference in the new book and the old is that, having achieved so much within the Episcopal community with *Behold*, Watts no longer felt the need to put on a display of furious academic footwork, so the reader was spared much of the syllogism and quotation that sometimes seemed more designed to impress than to inform.

The essence of the book was stated in outline form:

That modern society is falling apart because it has no principle of unity to stick it together, and that men of the twentieth century (Western men, that is) have no workable knowledge of the meaning of life.

All else has failed, and so the answer must come from religion—but not the Christian religion as we know it today. What Christianity needs is a new interpretation, the absorption of the metaphysical knowledge of the East and that which can be found within the church itself, and the translation of this into terms and practices that fit the world as it is and not the world as it was at the time of the Reformation.

Having said this, Alan Watts suggested that among the Christian faiths, the Catholic "in some form" was the only likely vehicle to work. Watts had always stood strong for the Catholic church as opposed to the Protestant—he had chosen the high Episcopal because it was almost precisely Catholicism with the language changed—and after the Vatican put the mass into native tongues, it was even more similar. The Greek Orthodox fascinated Watts more, the more he learned about that faith.

The Supreme Identity must be placed in its time. These were the days of the formation of the Committee of Atomic Scientists and the World Federalists—days when troubled intellectuals of the Western world were concerned about our ability to survive in an atomic world which had suddenly emerged at Hiroshima, and which now threatened to spread as the Russians gained the same powers that the West had achieved. There was questioning of the whole of the Western past and present. Communism seemed to be on the march in Western Europe and the Balkans, not only as a political and military force but as an economic and social alternative.

So we see the new Watts book written in the language of its day. There are new ideas here, and new jargon—one must give Alan Watts tremendous credit for being in tune with the times. Perhaps it was his close association with the youth of the nation, through his particular priestly function—but he had all the words and phrases, and the iconoclastic ideas they represented.

That is not to negate Watts—it was an achievement that must not be overlooked, for it would become increasingly a part of his mode of life and his search. Watts may have aged in years as the time went by, but he did, as the astrologer predicted for him, also seem to grow younger in spirit.

There is new language in *The Supreme Identity*, a new ambience, of a man no longer looking for the approbation of his clerical peers—a man standing confidently on his own record.

Watts in this book was now talking to a more sophisticated world—a world in which the atomic bomb had brought into common use such terms as cosmology and macrocosm and microcosm. The universe, with the popularity given the considerations of Einstein and other thinkers at such places as Princeton's School of Advanced Studies—the old universe that had appeared mostly in Oriental considerations in recent times—had become something new to contemplate.

This time there was no pussyfooting about the comparison between cultures—East and West. Watts had already made the point that the West had much to learn from the East, and that point had been accepted by his peers in *Behold the Spirit.* So he launched into the comparisons in the introduction to the book which was, as can be seen, an extremely timely and fashionable book. The secret of Alan Watts, from this point on, is to be found in his gait—he was able to run alongside fashion in a manner unsurpassed by any other older American. I say older because Watts was then at the magic age of thirty-five. And although he aged along with the rest of us, it was not apparent; each year he appealed more, not less, to the younger generation.

The Supreme Identity begins to tell us why.

Immediately after the introduction to the book, Watts plunges into the subject of infinity—scarcely a Christian tradition. And he does not even deign to bring Christianity as it exists into this.

> *There is no point from which knowledge of the infinite can begin, other than the infinite itself. From the start we are in the disconcerting position of setting out to understand something which has no beginning, which cannot be approached from any ordinary finite point of reference.*

For 56 pages, Alan Watts performed the circumlocutions and difficult strategems of trying to explain infinity—the easiest thing in the pages was a circular chart. Then he broke it up with an old limerick about God and infinity and the existence or nonexistence of anything when there was no one to behold it:

There was a young man who said: "God,
I find it exceedingly odd
That a tree, as a tree,
Simply ceases to be,
When there is no one around in the quad."

"Young man, your astonishment's odd;
I am always about in the quad.
So the tree, as a tree,
Continues to be,
Since observed by yours faithfully, God."

But very little was easy, for the Tao te Ching is not easy, as we have already seen, nor is the Isha Upanishad, or Theologica Mystica. They were not meant to be simple, they were the serious attempts of men, and the compilations of the efforts of wise men, to achieve an understanding of the universe. And this, no less, was where Watts was heading in this book. Not the scientific universe—which might not exist as far as he was concerned. The universe of belief.

In this book, Watts took his reader much deeper into the thoughts and moves of the Asian mysteries. And not only those, but of St. Augustine and other Christian mystics of the past.

He also opened on a new vista—something that had not troubled previous generations, but was beginning to trouble a postwar generation. Watts saw it early, described it, and came to grips with it: the crisis in identity.

". . . nothing is so profound an enigma as the internal mystery of man's own identity. Certain as we may be of the reality of our own being, its nature and origin elude us to exasperation. . . ."

Watts then discussed the self, not as ego, but as the physical being, and told something of what the Asian faiths believed of man.

It was a complex book, in a way more complex than *Behold the Spirit,* because it was obviously conceived for a different purpose; not with any thought at all of establishing a cachet—which is so apparent in the other, but in Watts' own troubled wrestling with the materials at hand from which he was fashioning his philosophy.

He discussed good, he discussed evil. He discussed involution—the self identifying with a separate ego, and evolution, the self recollecting its own true nature.

It is no good trying to give a capsule view of this book—it is too complex, and too specific in its address to the metaphysics of belief. One section follows and depends upon another. Anyone who wishes to understand *The Supreme Identity* must read it and then make up his own mind.

But the last chapter of the book shows where Alan Watts was going. It was termed The Way of Realization, and it dealt with such factors as prayer and meditation, concentration (yoga type), detachment—the letting-go process of the East, living in the eternal now (another Eastern concept). Once again the book came to life when Alan Watts described Krishna and told his anecdotes through which understanding was achieved. O, that Christianity could be so told. And finally, Watts came to the very end. Fittingly it was a tale of Zen, and the Zen Master Hogen.

> *A scholar said to Hogen, "When I was studying under Seiho I got an idea as to the truth of Zen."*
>
> *"What is your understanding then?" asked Hogen.*
>
> *"When I asked the master who was the Buddha (that is what is Reality), he said 'Ping-ting comes for fire.'"*
>
> *"It's a fine answer," said Hogen, "but probably you misunderstand it. Let me see how you take the meaning of it."*
>
> *"Well," explained the scholar, "Ping-ting is the god of fire. When he himself comes for fire, it is like myself, who, being a Buddha from the very beginning, wants to know who the Buddha (or the Self) is. No questioning is then needed, as I am already the Buddha himself."*
>
> *"There!" exclaimed Hogen. "Just as I thought! You are completely off. Now you ask me."*
>
> *"Who is the Buddha?"*
>
> *"Ping-ting comes for fire."*

And there it was. The great imponderable. It was just exactly what Alan Watts had believed when he started out with this whole wretched Christian business. . . .

思 始

CHAPTER FOURTEEN

THINKING IN THE BEGINNING

By the time Alan Watts had finished the manuscript of *The Supreme Identity* his marriage was in shambles. Eleanor had uprooted and gone to New York to be with her mother, and try to achieve some understanding of what had happened to her and her family. As for Alan, he sensed that a climax was coming. In a way he had forced it with the new book, because it was certain to be more controversial than the last. Very little obeisance to the Christian orthodoxy was paid in this work—and while it was increasingly popular to throw stones at poor old Mother Church, Watts was going to have to continue to write, to define and clarify and fight for these principles.

But it was really his personal life that brought an end to the path he was walking. And a witness to the drastic change that had developed in him was again Margaret Jacobson.

She was still bound to go to Europe, but plans were delayed by events. In March, 1950, Margaret again found herself in Evanston, and once again she called Alan Watts, and he insisted that she come immediately to his home.

"I rushed to Canterbury House, and there met with a violent shock—Alan minus his beard. He looked hideous. He had a rather long upper lip, and a set of frightfully bad English teeth which I had never noticed before."

Eleanor and the children were all gone now. Watts invited Bob Morse over to the house too, and he spent the evening openly suggesting that Bob and Margaret bed down with one another right there, "which at the time," she wrote later, "struck me as a scandalously naughty thing to do, in a *priest's house!* What was the world coming to? He seemed almost diabolical."

All that evening Alan besieged the pair, to bed and to marry. "He ticked off my past list of boyfriends—this one was a cipher, that one a pederast, another would never amount to anything, but with Bob I would have a fascinating life. . . ."

It was no go. The way to Margaret Jacobson's heart lay through Paris, and Bob Morse was just getting ready to be ordained and go to California.

So the importunations of the odd priest at Canterbury House did not bear fruit that evening. But the three of them went here and there during Margaret's stay. Not a word was said about Eleanor's absence, and Margaret suspected nothing, because so many times in the past Alan had left his wife at home while he went out "on the town" with the young people.

On Margaret's last evening in Chicago the trio went to the Red Star Inn, one of the city's best restaurants, and dined on Oysters Rockefeller.

How Alan Watts had changed from the priest she had known as a young college student. After dinner they put her on the airport bus:

"I remember my last glimpse of them. They had already forgotten me and were absorbed in an animated conversation, their faces wreathed in smiles. I thought to myself: 'They are true to the philosophy of Zen—the Now is the only thing that counts, and since I am no longer a part of it, they have put me out of their minds.'"

So Margaret Jacobson went off then, not to see Watts again, she thought, and quite unsettled about her own reactions to the changes in him. They had come as quite a shock, to see how he had moved in his ideas.

Then came another shock that settled the whole affair of marriage and church with remarkable speed. It changed Watts' life.

After consideration, and consultation, and her own kind of meditation, Eleanor left New York, and went off to Nevada to see how she might dissolve a marriage that had become a mockery because of her husband's constant violation of the seventh commandment.

She dissolved the marriage in a fashion that could be considered purely devilish—if one were of that turn of mind. For instead of getting a divorce, which would have created enough *furore* in the church, Eleanor produced evidence and caused her marriage to be *annulled*, on the grounds that it was no marriage at all, but a union of maidenly honesty with false principles. In their quarrels before the end, Alan Watts had been driven more and more to state his innermost ideas—and the belief that free love was the only kind of love really meaningful was one of them. By that Alan meant real love.

In his autobiography he cautioned youngsters about the rules of love: let there be no pretense if love is not felt, do not demand love as a duty and—important to Watts—there should be no strangulation. The partners must be free to be themselves.

That last was his main point. Alan Watts must be a free spirit. If he was to be married, he must still have the right to conduct himself as he pleased, and being a highly sexual creature that meant his friendships must be allowed to pursue their course, to bed if it meant that.

No step taken by Eleanor could more swiftly have wrecked Alan Watts' ministerial career. For if there is one thing society will not tolerate, it is violation of the code of conduct by those who have special positions of trust. The physician who persuades young women to undress and then seduces them is the object of many crude jokes in Americana; but also that spectre represents a real fear. The priest who raises his robes and seduces the spiritually ailing is equally the subject of verbal joust—but also of a lingering social fear. And so, when he knew what his wife had done, Alan Watts was under no illusions. He gave up the property rights she had turned over to him. He was now back in the world again, to make his living by his wits.

He was broadening his scope. For some months he had been making lecture tours here and there, presenting his new amalgamation of the wisdoms of East and West as the salvation of the Christian church. Spring became summer—1950—and then the blow fell.

Watts had been away in New York on lectures. When he returned to the Evanston house in June, he found a letter there from Bishop Conkling. The prelate had learned of the decision of the Nevada court to dissolve the Watts marriage. Did the Reverend Mr. Watts indeed believe in Free Love, as opposed to the sanctity of the Holy Sacrament of marriage?

There was absolutely nothing to be said. Or, rather, there was ever so much to be said—none of which would do the slightest bit of good.

Alan Watts sat down in the privacy of his study in Canterbury House, and composed a long letter to the Bishop. It was defensive, and thus not one of his more notable efforts at prose. He was at needs to explain that he had entered the church under a misapprehension. That was not strictly true—he had entered the church because he saw the need for a vocation, and he believed he could tailor his personal views so that they would find a place beneath the broad roof of the church. He had very nearly succeeded—*Behold the Spirit* was the proof. Had he been able to maintain the position, he would have become at least as celebrated as Bishop James Pike. In the end, Pike would go the same way. But now it was Alan Watts who was going.

Watts' letter must be a resignation from the ministry. He knew that. The tone of the Bishop's inquiry was official. The offense was clear. The proof was there. Only by resigning could Watts avoid a long inquiry and trial which could come out only one way—at what cost to the spirit? It might have been that he would have served his own cause best by dragging what he said out into the open and forcing a canonical trial that would most certainly attract worldwide attention. Yet Alan Watts was not certain enough of the position he took, not strong enough to put his future on the block in that fashion. He did what most of us would do. He took up his pen and wrote the letter of resignation.

He justified. He complained that the church's authority was abused by a group who had taken over the affairs of the institution and imposed their own morality on all.

He said that churchmen seemed unable to face love and marriage frankly; their attitude came from a need for security, and security could never replace love as the adhesive element in marriage. Watts said that the laws for an institution like marriage pandered to the political and social rather than the spiritual.

He wrote similar letters to many of his friends, telling them of his reason. The letters had to be read, of course, in context of what he had done and what had been done to him. The particular brutality of Eleanor's annulment was not against Alan, but against the children, who officially became bastards by the act. All the more indication that what he had to say against marriage and the church had its own wisdom. For no matter who might be guilty in the marriage between Eleanor and Alan—if anyone be guilty—it most certainly was not the children of that marriage. And it grieved Alan more than anything else that they might be the ones to suffer most.

Yet beneath the surface there was boiling on both sides. Eleanor left the two girls to Alan's custody, and almost immediately he sent them to England to be raised by his family. Their son stayed with Eleanor and Alan did not object to it.

He was apparently quite content with the resolution of the affair. There was no public mention of the quarrel, of course, nor at any time did his children's names become public property.

Before and forever after, it was always Alan Watts' way to protect those he loved. They played no role in his public performances. They were more a part of his private life than his friends, who might be exploited as they might exploit Watts. Perhaps it was for the sake of his children, and not only because of the bruises to his spirit, that Alan Watts chose not to make a public quarrel of his private problem.

Speaking from the standpoint of love and freedom there was much in what Alan Watts had to say. Love should be unfettered, and should need no bonds to tie two lovers together. At the outset it should be as Alan Watts told his young couples when he counselled them before marrying them: they were seeing each other at their best in the full bloom of youth and the starry gaze of love; as time went on, one, the other, or both of them might disintegrate while the other grew; and they must not cling to one another and use the bond of marriage as a leash.

But examine Alan Watts' truth for a moment. Is it possible to expect so much from mere humanity? A couple decide to marry. Probably they have already been sleeping together (that has been going on since long before the NOW generation; for proof see *Canterbury Tales*, written 600 years ago.) They are starry-eyed, completely saturated in one another. So they marry. Along come children. The husband grows and matures. The wife sinks back into the chocolate-cum-church cum-bridge-club of suburbia. The husband becomes involved with his secretary who is interested in his work. What to do?

Or vice versa. The wife becomes a serious citizen, a painter, a musician, a social worker; the husband spends his weekends on the golf course and his nights in the club bar. She is attracted to a serious person in her own milieu. Or to several of them, altogether or *seriatim*. What to do?

The church, of course, *had to* take the position that marriage was not something one put on and took off like a pair of gloves. Otherwise the church's interest in marriage had to be either cynical or be dissolved.

In some ways the argument is reminiscent of the arguments regarding the Free Love of the Soviet Union in the early days of the Communist Revolution in Russia. American and English pulpits thundered with bombast against the Godless Russians who permitted marriage by the simple matter of a couple appearing at a government registry office. Divorce was nearly as simple.

It is remarkable how the furor against that kind of marriage in Soviet Russia had died down in the thirty years between the Revolution and Watts' troubles. For instead of turning out to be "free love" as all the church world had suspected, Soviet practice made marriage as binding and as respectable as it ever had been. Human beings need stability, and they find their stability in one way or another.

Watts, the idealist, could not win against the established church. Had he been willing to sacrifice his personal honesty—and sneak around with his extramarital affairs as others do, he could have remained within the church, perhaps. He was not willing to cower, not willing to compromise. Thus he could be accepted by neither Eleanor nor the church fathers. It was a tragedy of major dimensions, the irresistible force had met the immovable object, and both were the worse for the encounter.

Watts' apologia was not strong. His position was not good. His friend, Canon Bernard Iddings Bell, was shocked and surprised and sorry. The Bishop was unhappy. But that important and thoughtful theologian, the Reverend E. Stanley Jones of New York, put the whole problem in context in his reply to the Watts apologia. He noted that one of Watts' reasons for leaving the church was his study of the wisdom of the Orient, and he wondered if Alan needed something of the Eastern philosophies to "piece out Christ."

"In Christ," he wrote, "we do not have a religion but a Gospel. There are many religions. There is but one Gospel."

And there Mr. Jones had hit the nail precisely on the head: All Alan Watts' works had been an attempt to correlate East and West. His last two books (one of which the Reverend Mr. Jones had not yet seen at the time of the letter) had indeed been attempts to "piece out Christ," for it was Watts' contention that the entire metaphysical base of the church must be revamped to take on a new and more liberal aspect if the church was to survive the stormy years ahead. The Reverend Mr. Jones drove the nail home when he stated the hardline church position: *there are many religions, only one Gospel.* Believe, do not question. Argue if you wish, but keep your argument around the periphery; God is not mocked by the amusements of tiny men if they do not challenge him.

No one could have summed up the basic quarrel between Watts and his church better than E. Stanley Jones had done. It was over, ended by one great conflagration over a matter that was not central to Alan Watts' problems of faith.

From Yale University came a letter from Professor Theodore M. Greene in which that theologian suggested that he too had worried long as to whether it was possible to remain within the established church and hold his own religious views. He had said yes, and had done so. He was not sure he had taken the proper road. Perhaps Watts' road was indeed the right one.

So with that much small comfort, Alan left the church forever, and headed into the cold world alone, bereft of wife, bearing the weight of a family still to support and succor for what had been done.

That summer there was refuge for the Wattses. A liberal wealthy friend owned an old farm at Millbrook, New York, close to the Connecticut border, in the midland along the Hudson that was dedicated to the dairy industry.

There was one little footnote to it all, the kind of ironical happening that would appeal more to a biographer than any other. For in the year that Alan Watts broke irrevocably with the church over matters of doctrine and behaviour, he published his last attempt at integrating his soul within the percepts of the church. Henry Schuman brought out a little book called *The Meaning of Easter*, highly decorated, some of it by Watts himself, much admired by librarians and reviewers, who pointed with pride at this filling of so great a need for young and old. It was a paean of religious love, somewhat mystical, but wholly acceptable within the religious community.

And in referring to it later, Watts would call it a pot boiler.

CHAPTER FIFTEEN

BEING DIFFERENT FROM ORDINARY MEN

Although Watts had just stepped out of one marriage, which was lost to him because of his feelings about the universality of love and the impossibility of one person giving himself entirely to another, he stepped immediately into another marriage, with an attractive girl, one of the students at the university and one of his friends—Dorothy DeWitt. She was a mathematician, and an intensely practical person. He hoped, in one way, that her practicality would rub off on him. He did not seem to give serious thought to the anomaly of moving from one marriage to another with the views he held. Neither, it seemed, did Dorothy DeWitt.

The next six months were spent sorting things out. Watts took walks through the pleasant hilly New York countryside, the ground covered with leaves from maples and beeches and ash, the lush fields blooming with their high grass fed by the innumerable springs and creeks. It was a haven of birds and rabbits and small game. Deer coursed the hillsides in the summer and fall. The vague, bifurcated town-city of Poughkeepsie was not far away, offering the needs of the writer and very little of the wickedness of the booming city. During these six months, Watts meditated in his fashion, walking and thinking or not thinking, observing or not seeing, and turning about the topsy-turvy world in which he lived.

Out of it came a new serious book, the logical sequel to *The Supreme Identity,* a book that would be titled *The Wisdom of Insecurity.*

Watts' psychological problems ended with his flight from the Christian religion. All the tensions that had made his last two books works of circumlocution were gone. He had tried to come to terms with reality within the Christian religion. He had given more than his share; he had set up arguments with the church that were accepted as sound by thoroughgoing and eminently respectable followers of Christ. And all of this had failed. He had put it down, part of it, in his letter of resignation.

He was convinced, he wrote, after studying both Oriental teachings and Catholic theology, that the church's claim to be "the best of all ways to God" was both a mistake and a "symptom of anxiety." The church was strangling itself, he said, and he could not countenance its proselytizing thus.

All very well, but if Alan Watts was to live at Thornecrest Farm in Millbrook and support his family, something must replace the twin losses of Eleanor's fortune and the small but real stipend he had received each month from the Episcopal church for his efforts as chaplain at the university. The answer lay in a foundation grant, and he managed to secure one from the Franklin Matchette Foundation, which gave moneys for study in science and metaphysics. Watts could promise that he was itching to write something so new and so different that it would burst like a starshell across the heavens.

So he set to work.

He knew now (for according to the Way there are no life facts and all is illusion) that he had been living under the specific

Christian illusion for nine long years. It was as obvious to him in 1950 as it was to a reader of his earlier works that his books written from 1940 to 1950 had been *apologia pro vita sua* in a way—theologian Watts' attempts to bring his own thoughts around to Christianity, and to adjust to Christianity the Tao and the other Eastern beliefs on which he had based so much study, thus making of Christianity a synthesis that could appeal to all the world.

What a noble attempt.

On retrospect there is only one conceivable way that it could have succeeded. That is if no less authority than the Pope of the Roman Catholic world had, without consultation with the College of Cardinals made the declarations of faith that Watts had made. In other words, one Super-Encyclical. Then all the Christian world would have noted. For except in the obvious traps into which Romanism had fallen (the right to life being the most deadly of all for the church) the Roman church is the leader of the Christian world. The Church of England, the Lutherans, and all the rest, even down to the hardshell Baptists and Holy Rollers, always look up when the Pope speaks. Any action of the Romans is subjected to the most minute scrutiny, and if there is anything in it for the Protestant sects, they come along sooner and later and follow suit.

But Watts, one lone cleric, might have devoted his entire life to the pursuit he had abandoned—and if he was very lucky, two centuries after his death he might have been seen to be right.

Now, of course, what he had built was already falling into disrepair. His place had been taken at Northwestern by a new and more "stable" priest. His book *Behold the Spirit,* which had earned him a degree and much respect, was thrust into the back shelves of the Christian libraries. The truths that were true were no longer true—that was a Zen way of looking at what had happened; with the disgrace of Watts the truths became monstrous falsehood.

After several weeks of contemplation, it came to Alan Watts in one of those Zen flashes that by losing all he had gained all. It was apparent to him that all he had tried was totally impossible. His whole nine years of Christianity had been one giant koan—a spiritual and religious problem that he had battered again and again until his mind reeled. And only when he had been disgraced, humiliated, and run down to nothing had it come to him, that he was on the Way.

It was not possible to manipulate Zen into Christianity. It was possible to use Christianity as an opening for Zen. And this was another part of the great truth that came to him in that lonely farmhouse near the bogland. He now postulated the "backwards law"—that is, in true Zen fashion that when you struggle to swim, you sink, but when you relax to sink, you float. When you hold your breath, it escapes you in a painful whoosh. But if you relax, you need breathe hardly at all. Putting it into terms that conformed to his own immediate situation and were reminiscent of the past 10 years, he could say *Whosoever Would Save His Own Soul Must First Lose It.* For in the searing experience of the months just past, he came through such a fire.

In the preface to his new book, there was much to be done and a great deal also to be undone. For the reader was going to discover the New Alan Watts, with his new truths, and they were going to be contradictory to the old Alan Watts with his old truths. Watts tried to convince the reader that these contradictions were only apparent. They were contradictions.

The Wisdom of Insecurity was a different *kind* of book than anything Alan Watts had done before. Previous works had been stuffed with literary and religious allusions and studded with footnotes, most of them learned citations of other works. *Wisdom* had only seven footnotes and no bibiliography at all. Of the footnotes, by far the most were expositions of the text, or parenthetical observations that he had not wanted to put on the page and interrupt his flow. This was Alan Watts being Alan Watts, an important thinker in his own right. He had indeed sacrificed everything to win his own position as an independent—but an independent what? Aye, there would be the rub. Was he philosopher? Was he teacher? Was he entertainer? Was he charlatan? He has been called all of them, and he has admitted to all but the last, and even there, he has hinted that there was considerable degree of this in him.

Others said these things much more strongly. One time during the Northwestern period, Margaret Jacobson brought a friend to one of the Watts lectures. This particular man was a newspaper reporter from the Chicago *Daily News* and "cynical as they come."

"After we had spent an evening at Canterubury House, listening to Alan lecture as he did in his usual fascinating manner, I asked what he thought. He snorted and spat out 'That man's a *charlatan*'."

And later, when Margaret brought her mother to a session, she went away declaring gloomily that Alan was interested not in religon but in religiosity.

But whatever he was, in 1950 he was *what* he was—for the first time. At the age of thirty-six he had found himself. From now on anything that Watts was, was Watts.

The more he studied the world around him, said philosopher Watts, the more impossible he found it to put up his world in neat little packages. And with the feeling of troubled times belief was going begging—organized religion had lost the adherence of millions. Science and religions were as far apart as ever in their approaches to life. Science, which once denied God, had by 1950 found God to be irrelevant.

Watts addressed himself first of all to the age in which he was living—the age of anxiety. And, with one of those clear insights of which he was so capable, he limned American society of the 1950s, the society about which a musical philosopher was writing a song called "Ticky Tacky," and Watts did his job in three swift paragraphs:

> *. . . consequently our age is one of frustration, anxiety, agitation, and addiction to "dope". Somehow we must grab what we can while we can, and drown out the realization that the whole thing is futile and meaningless. This "dope" we call our high standard of living, a violent and complex stimulation of the senses, which makes them progressively less sensitive and thus in need of yet more violent stimulation. We crave distraction—a panorama of sights, sounds, thrills and titillations into which as much as possible must be crowded in the shortest possible time.*
>
> *To keep up this "standard" most of us are willing to put up with lives that consist largely in doing jobs that are a bore,*

earning the means to seek relief from the tedium by intervals of hectic and expensive pleasure. These intervals are supposed to be the real living, *the real purpose served by the necessary evil of work. Or we imagine that the justification of such work is the rearing of a family to go on doing the same kind of thing, in order to rear another family . . . and so on* ad infinitum.

This is no caricature. It is the simple reality of millions of lives. . . .

And so it was. Americans could recognize themselves in those paragraphs—if they wished to do so. More than the people who so recognized, the young adult children and even the teenaged middle children of these parents saw the futility of it. They saw it in their schools, in the press, and in the fight for ever more education and the growing competition for what?

There were, said Watts, but two alternatives to face such a life philosophically. One was to discover a new God myth. The second was to dissociate one's self from the God myth altogether, to assume a mechanistic stance toward the universe. We all came out of squirmy things in the mud and that's where we're going to end up—that sort of thing.

But no, there was an alternative. And here Watts turned about all that he had argued in the past. The Christian concept was useful in talking about God—he said now—if one considered that God was a part of the Godness of the universe.

Does the reader see where Alan Watts was heading, even by page 25 of his new book? Right back to Zen.

Let there be hope, said Watts. There is a God, just as there is water and there is sky. But what the people of the Western world must do is learn to look in a different way at the world about them if they were to find God.

He was not going to be found in the Thomas à Becket chapel in Canterbury House in Evanston, Illinois. Not any longer.

The real God was not to be found on the cross, nor in the blinding lights of heaven, or even—sadly—in the Holy Ghost. The real God could be found only in abandonment of all the old pictures and idols. Indeed, the early Christian tradition, in which the fish played an important role, had it that there could be no graven images, no idols, no icons, no symbols. This was much closer a resemblance to the God that Alan Watts could find than the God of the Christians in the twentieth century. Watts went back into his Oriental mysticism to find his God this time, a most satisfactory, helpful God.

The second step in this new book was to explore the problems of consciousness; his finding was that the more conscious we are, the more we pay. The more sensitive we are, the more we hurt, the more love we feel, the more pain we feel when the loved one goes away. And he summed it up: "Consciousness seems to be nature's ingenious mode of self-torture."

And now without using the Oriental terms, the pipe-playing Pan who was Alan Watts was leading us in the stream of Buddhist thought. For the answer, he said, was to eliminate the "I" of our consciousness, and to see that I is simply a part of All. We must remember that everything we say and do and even think is a matter of the way in which we were taught to do so. He raised the point that even a thought is an illusion—it is a thought because we have been taught to call it so and for no other reason. Most things are not what they seem. Gold is wealth. So is paper money. But gold is permanent, and so to a degree is paper money. Wealth is food, which is impermanent. So there is the question. Is real wealth food or is real wealth gold? Which could you live with if you had to choose one?

Gold then becomes a shorthand way of representing wealth. This was not Adam Smith but Alan Watts, and he did not pursue that theme too far. His purpose was simply to show that we think in symbols—that if we are going to understand nature and the world about us we have to change those symbols.

One can see, right here, why Alan Watts would appeal to youth and would turn off the old. For how can you ask a woman who has been going to St. Mark's every Sunday for 40 years to suddenly avow that the figure on the cross is not Jesus, that God does not sit on a golden throne in heaven with angels flying around. But a youngster—ah, what a different matter that becomes.

The younster knows, intuitively, that his elders have not found the Way. He sees in the world about him every evidence of corruption and crookedness and convolution and pain. And he believes there must be a better way. How best to find it? What could be more sensible than the need to knock out all the old clichés of thought—for it is certain they have not solved the problem. After all, Jesus has had 2,000 years to return and put to right the world. He has not shown up. So is he relevant? That is the kind of questioning that Alan Watts provoked with his ideas on the I.

What one must accept, said Watts, was that neither religion nor science has a way of plumbing the depths of life. Both deal in shorthands and symbolism; neither makes life a bit happier.

But—said Master Watts—playing softly on his pipes, there was a way, and it had been found and lost and found again, and many traditions in the world other than the Christian have it.

Watts was on the way to becoming a great translator and transmitter of the wisdom of the East. Undoubtedly his 10 years of Christian training had done this for him. For in 1940, when at twenty-five he was fumbling for a vocation, he could not deal in the terms of Oriental mysticism without leaning on the crutches of Suzuki or some other. Now, having gone through the wringer, Watts saw with a new clarity that he had been more nearly right in his fifteenth year, when he eschewed Christianity and avowed Buddhism, than he had been ever since. The years from fifteen to twenty-five had been spent exploring his own mind and learning. The learning process is useful, but it had not very much to do with the Godhead, the processes of achieving revelation and satori. He was closer to satori at fifteen than at thirty. Now at thirty-six he was back again, but oh, so far forward. For thousands, literally thousands, of books—the compendium of millions of ideas on the subject of religion—had been passed through that brain, and whatever tiny grain of truth there remained was distilled in the unconscious mind and retained all through the painful koan years of Christianity.

In this new book, Watts was Lao Tzu, he was Chuang Tzu, he was his old mentor Sokei-an Sasaki—he was every Zen master who ever existed. He had suddenly emerged, there in the modern wilderness of Millbrook, New York, as one of the enlightened ones. There was a sureness in his presentation that said that He-I-You-Thou-Me Alan Watts *knew*. He *knew*, and knowing he could transmit a sense of that to those who were willing to apply themselves with open mind to what he had to offer them.

In later times Watts' detractors would sneer that he never did a thing for philosophy. Well, he was a great showman and translator of Zen to the American people, they would say, but really what did he ever do for philsophy?

They have missed the point, as Lao Tzu would have put it. They have missed the point entirely, as Master Watts would have put it.

The End

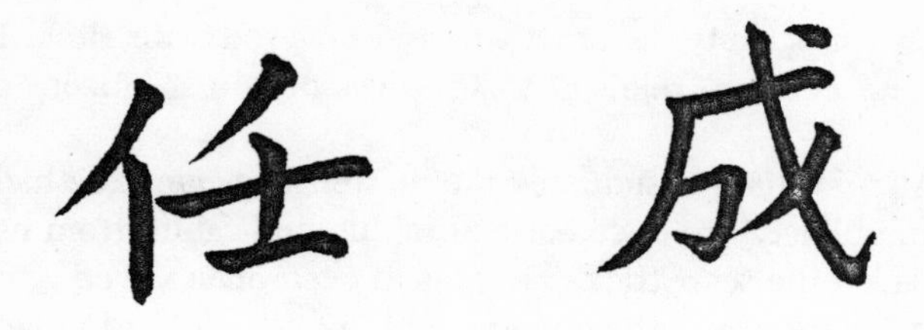

CHAPTER SIXTEEN

THE TASK OF ACHIEVEMENT

The Wisdom of Insecurity is an exciting book, for in it one can see that Alan Watts for the first time is exercising his maturity, and that here is his first creative effort as a follower of the Way. Everything before this has been preparation. There was juvenile fumbling in *The Spirit of Zen.* Mock it not, for it was the best thing of its kind in England in 1935. There was an equal fumbling in *The Legacy of Asia,* plus the cockiness of a youngster who is full of himself because at twenty he is an author and is accepted by grownup men. Everything written during the Christian period is truly irrelevant, except to the student of Christian mysticism, and to the history of Alan Watts. It is rather more valuable to the latter than the former—for Watts succeeded more than did any other in making Christianity, as practiced and covered with ritual in the twentieth century, relevant to the lives of young citizens of the century.

Alan Watts was suddenly the master magician. You had seen him, fumblingly, produce hat and rabbit, and rabbit from hat. He had played the scarf trick, and he had even once sawed a woman in half. There was nothing *wrong* with the way he had done these tricks—his mastery was enough to maintain the illusion, whether he was writing about the Christian marriage ceremony or the Buddhist koan—but in the past you had not really *believed.*

Now, suddenly, in *The Wisdom of Insecurity* the words leaped out at you from the page and the Watts approach seemed to be magic because it called for no conscious effort on the part of the student of his way.

> *. . . it was not through statements that we learned how to breathe, swallow, see, circulate the blood, digest food, or resist disease. Yet these things are performed by the most complex and marvelous processes which no amount of book-learning and technical skill can reproduce. This is real wisdom—but our brains have little to do with it.*

That, Watts said, was the kind of wisdom we needed to approach the real practical problems of life.

He was talking of the unconscious mind, of course. And of phenomena in nature that are beyond explanation, the power of homing pigeons and migrating birds to find their way. And then he moved to another sphere—the war within the body. The mind of people—Westerners particularly—is conditioned to want things that the body neither wants nor needs. Left to itself the body will eat until satiated and then stop. But because of anxiety, the human often eats and eats and eats and grows fat.

Most people, of course, do not think of things in this manner, and thus the suggestions of Alan Watts strike like a torpedo suddenly exploding against the side of a ship. How easy the dieter's lot would be if he could manage to conquer the anxiety that he knows drives him to nibble in the kitchen when he should be busy at the typewriter or in the garden or out for a long walk. Could Watts help?

He could, but only for those who were willing to read his whole book. No excerpting, as done here, can do justice to the Watts language, the Watts theme or the new emerging character that was Watts, full of the strengths of inner certainty that despite the tribulations of the past, he was now on the proper road.

The trouble, said Watts, is that we live in the future, at the expense of the present.

The future—since it is not known—is abstract and is like a phantom. The faster we race after it, the faster it eludes us. That is why so few enjoy what they have and keep seeking more and more.

Western society, said Watts, consists of a stream of artificial stimulants designed to produce cravings for more and more of the products of the Western society. And, he said, this system conspired to persuade people that happiness was just around the corner. But when they came to the corner—whoosh—happiness had run ahead to the next corner, beckoned once, and disappeared, so they ran ahead again, buying, wishing, wanting all the way.

In this first excursion into independent thinking, Watts pointed out that Western houses were so built—with tiny kitchens and huge showy living rooms. Western sex was so organized; Western man is so sexually stimulated so much of the time that impotence of men is a common failing. Their brains are trammeled by sex during most of their waking hours, so that when it is offered them, they cannot perform physically, because, as Watts put it, it was a case of "his brain pursuing what his genes do not at the moment desire."

He had many examples: sex was one, man's slavery to time was another. He went on, and on.

What Watts was doing, in this exploration, was to see if he could present the foundations of Eastern thought in a manner to attract the West. This was a primer; it was necessary for Western man to divest himself of his loose veneer of civilization before he could begin to accept and assimilate the learning of the East.

And here, of course is the reason that Alan Watts had to turn to the "counterculture"—although that name had not yet been invented in 1950, nor was the dissatisfaction with the Western style of life so apparent then as it would become in the middle of that decade.

Alan Watts set himself to several tasks. First, he pointed up in new ways the oddments of Western society. Second, he redefined terms, materialism and spirituality in particular. And by Chapter Five he was getting into Zen.

He contended that most people are almost totally unaware of the world around them, and that they can change this situation if they will.

For several pages he dwelt on pain, showing his readers how this was a part of the process of being aware. And he told tales in the manner of Zen masters, the purpose to persuade readers that they must get away from the I concept of Western man, and accept the You concept—which he said was also to include the I.

Complex. Of course, it was complex. Otherwise it would have been done a hundred times before. No one had until this time succeeded in taking the processes of Eastern thought, refined over so many hundreds of years, and starting from a different sense than Western—no one had yet translated these processes so that Westerners and particularly the Americans would be able to understand and work with the materials. This is the problem to which Watts now addressed himself.

One might ask why did Watts do this from the farmhouse at Millbrook. The answer is at once simple, direct, and cynical at the same time. All that Watts had directed himself to do, he was doing. He had recognized his inability to function in the business society when he was twenty years old. He had no training for government. He had failed in his religious profession because of his innate character as a "loner." He had none of the patience or humility it would take to be a journalist. He did not take himself so seriously as to become a philosopher. So it was natural that he should do what he did best—write about the spirit and the East. He understood these things. He had begun to understand his own power to attract people, and the lure of mysteries of the East to the "advanced thinkers" of the society, to the intellectuals who felt out of it, and to the youth who were already seeking something.

Of course youth had always sought the better way. Not the generation of the late 1930s. That came to maturity just in time to go to war—for they had no chance to protest that the world was a "helluva place"—the proof was right there before them and they were sent out to fight and stop it from getting any worse. But by 1950, the uneasy peace had fallen apart already. The Russians and the Americans were standing on two sides of an Iron Curtain. The Chinese Communists had conquered China and lowered the Bamboo Curtain. The war in Korea had begun. Americans were being sent to fight for things that were supposed to be all over and done with, only five years after the end of World War II, when so many glorious promises had been made.

So naturally there was dissatisfaction, and it was growing very rapidly in this summer of 1950 as Alan Watts worked on his book.

Looking backward on the phenomenon, it was easy to see a convergence of market and material. If publishers could work from hindsight, every book would sell better, for they could judge what the market would be. This year, as Watts labored over his desk and walked in the woods to think over his concepts, the world was becoming more troubled, and the old philosophies more burdened to explain why all was so unhappy in the West.

The Wisdom of Insecurity is hard going for one accustomed to the thoughtless progression of the West. Having entered on the Zen concept, Watts pursued it relentlessly, however, and by Chapter Five was deep into the matter of awareness and sensation. It would be no service to him or the reader to try to recapitulate the complex arguments.

He retells stories from other books—including the one of the monk who wants his mind pacified and is finally told that it *is* pacified. But there is reason for the retelling: the story is to the point of what he is discussing at that moment. And it is most unlikely that the readers of *The Wisdom of Insecurity* would hark back to the older books.

The mysticism begins in Chapter Six; Watts tells the tale of a Chinese sage who was asked how to escape the heat, and who suggested that the answer was to step into the middle of the fire. This was symbolic: he in this case meant pain. But it was also indicative. We have all wondered (if we have seen the phenomenon) how Indian fakirs can walk across fire without burning themselves. Watts suggests without ever using that analogy that the conquest of pain is far simpler than most of us believe. Pain is a kind of experience. As such it must be accepted, and once it is accepted, it vanishes.

The Wisdom of Insecurity is filled with revelations for the Westerner—things the thoughtful people of the East have known for a long time. On the question of religious thought, for example, he said that the best ideas of man come when thinking has stopped. A problem may seem impossible, but when man stops thinking about it—all at once the solution appears.

To Watts, this was the normal method of problem-solving, the proof that the mind is superior to the computer.

Having established the preliminaries, Watts then turned to what he called the Transformation of Life, which is a further exploration of the reality of Zen. To *know* reality, he said, "you must enter into it, be it, and feel it."

That argument is one of Watts' central themes in all his religious studies, and he repeats it and varies it and plays it in his books as a composer works with a theme in a long piece of music.

Watts knew that man *had* his problems. And he tried to set up answers—or the Way to answers. In the final analysis, he said, it comes down to love. But that is not the kind of love that most of us think about. It is Zen love.

知難

CHAPTER SEVENTEEN

THE DIFFICULTY OF BEING KNOWN

The end of *The Wisdom of Insecurity* deals with organized religion. It simply had to do so, for the bitterness of his recent experience was still in Alan Watts' nostrils and would take some getting out. Bishop Conkling had warned Alan in their last exchange of communications that he must guard himself against falling off the Way. Of course the Bishop's Way and Alan's seemed quite different—more so than they must have been—but the Bishop suggested that when a man moved so far from society as Watts had done, there was really nothing left to say. He hoped that Watts would be a leader and have a "genius for truth," but he did not really believe it.

Alan Watts' problem was to find a society into which he

could fit, given his failure in the middlewestern society of Ecclesiastica. But before he moved on, he must break with the past totally, and then find his way.

The whole of *The Wisdom of Insecurity* represented this breach, but the specifics of it came in the final chapter of the book, when Watts settled down to review religion and put it into place in his scheme of things.

His quarrel was that you could not get theologians to talk in terms of things that are. They speak about a God in the past, and a God in the future. They say that the supernatural world is unlike the universe as studied by science, and that it exists on a different plane. To Watts, that all sounded pretty psychic.

Now one of his basic points: ". . . metaphysical language is negative because it is trying to say that words and ideas do not explain reality . . ."

In one way or another, quoting Lao Tzu, and Sasaki and all the rest, Watts had been saying this—toned down in his Christian period—for many years. It is a key to understanding what he was driving at all the time.

Thinking, worrying, considering, acting—all his life western man goes round in a circle, and Watts was trying here to get men to stop, and relax, and consider, let their minds work for them, and become free.

So concluded *The Wisdom of Insecurity.*

In this period of his own insecurity, Alan Watts went back to his Asian philosophers. He spent much time with the writings of Krishnamurti, which he had begun to appreciate back in England. He also read and reread the works of Ananda Coomaraswamy, and got to know that author's widow. He became acquainted with interesting people—like Joseph Campbell, the historian of magic and mysticism, and John Cage, the composer. He liked free spirits. He liked parties and the descriptions he gave of his cooking at the farm show how well he could play the gourmet role.

These were hard times in many ways, these months of 1950 and 1951. Watts was trying to establish a new marriage with a woman of strong character herself. He had two children to look after from the first marriage. He had no visible means of support. His friends rallied round. His publisher was now Pantheon, and he was allied with Kurt and Helen Wolff, while they were connected with that house. He gave Joseph Campbell credit for helping secure a grant from the Bollingen Foundation to keep bodies and souls together. No, it was not an easy time. It was the most difficult period of his existence, because until then he had not experienced financial troubles.

The new world came to Watts courtesy of Frederic Spiegelberg, his old acquaintance from the days of the Buddhist Lodge in London. In recent years, Dr. Spiegelberg had held a chair as Professor of Indian Thought at Stanford University. But in the winter of 1951 he was undertaking a new intellectual voyage, and there was a place in the boat for Alan Watts.

For years the Asian aspect of American culture had been neglected; almost always the eyes of the United States looked across the Atlantic, not the Pacific. There were a few exceptions—the Perry expedition to the Far East in 1851, and the involvement in Asia during the Boxer troubles, and then the whole Philippines adventure. But by and large Americans paid little attention to the Far East. That fact became painfully obvious during World War II when it was essential to send men overseas. The governors of the nation found that practically no Americans except Japanese-born knew any Japanese. It was the same with Chinese, with Tagalog, with the Indian languages. Americans simply knew virtually nothing about the Far East. And the situation was only somewhat remedied by the war. Once students had been trained by the military in Asian languages and cultures they came home to find almost no use for the training. So most of them went into other fields and promptly forgot all they had learned about Asia.

But with the growing ferment there—the coming of age of Indonesia, the conquest of China by the armies of Mao Tse-tung, the schism in Korea, the development of the war in Indochina, the split in India—it became essential to learn something about an Asia that was beginning to be a world force in its own right.

Louis P. Gainsborough, President of the Login Corporation of San Francisco, became concerned about the need and enthusiastic about a way in which it could be filled. So he got Dr. Spiegelberg, with his fine reputation in the field, to put together a faculty and begin a new institution for the study of Asian affairs.

It was an advanced institution. The students had to be college graduates. The purpose, as noted in an editorial in the San Francisco *Chronicle* was "to provide practical training for leaders in government, education, politics, industry, foreign trade and social service and to serve as a testing ground in Asian subjects for all U.S. education."

It was a considerable honor for anyone to be chosen to teach here. The advisory board included Carlos P. Romulo of the Philippines; Madame Pandit, the Indian ambassador; Robert Gordon Sproul, President of the University of California; and Stanford President Wallace J. Sterling.

The faculty was also distinguished. It included Spiegelberg and Dr. Haridas Chaudhuri, Professor of Philosophy from Krishnagar College in Benares, India; a Tibetan monk, Lama Tokwan Tada; Dr. Judith Tyberg, a student of Sanskrit from Benares; and "Alam (sic) W. Watts, Orientologist and advisor to the Bollingen foundation."

Watts was so described in an article in the San Francisco *Chronicle* in February, 1951. The newspaper would not long be misprinting his name, for Watts was to become one of the Bay region's most famous citizens in a short time.

But now he was on his way to California, travelling across the southwestern U.S., for in winter one cannot approach San Francisco by way of Salt Lake City and the Sierra—the roads through the Sierra Nevada are closed by snow.

Watts and his family crossed the desert on U.S. 60. They went to Los Angeles, where Watts looked up a few people, such as Floyd Ross, Professor of the History of Religions at the University of Southern California. Ross was valuable: he put Watts in touch with Zen masters and Taoists and followers of Krishnamurti and others. He gave a few lectures in Los Angeles, and got into the midst of a great religious argument with Gerald Heard and Aldous Huxley and a whole mélange of people all concerned with Eastern religion and Eastern thought, some of them in saris, some in more pretentious robes. He stayed just long enough to become deeply enmeshed in the big religious squabble among the practitioners. And then he was off, up toward Santa Barbara, and Big Sur country, where other groups of free spirits (or kooks, depending on point of view) were known to live.

There was Henry Miller, who later became a friend. There was Maud Oakes, another. He stopped by, and then went on, past the scores of houses and huts and yurts and revetments of the faithful and the faithless, the whole and the maimed, the true believers and the unbelievers that were the colony loosely called Big Sur. California, and particularly southern and south-central California, would beckon him back time and again, because of the freedom from cant, the willingness to allow all points of view, and to mix them up, that this society offered almost alone in America.

Then it was on to San Francisco, to begin.

The *Chronicle's* slightly erroneous announcement of Alan Watts' coming was on the nose in one sense—for he came as Orientalist, which was not a very meaningful term. Dr. Spiegelberg knew that Watts had a gift of gab, that he always had something to say and a very interesting way of saying it, and further than that, Watts was searching for his own way.

From the beginning, the school was in trouble. For the teachers and the businessmen had different approaches to the whole idea. Founder Gainsborough approached the problems as the practical matter of training people in the ways of Asia. He had been in the business of foreign trade for 25 years, and he knew what was needed. But by setting up so pretentious an organization (the school promised to give Masters and Ph.D. degrees in Orientalia) as Watts so sagely noted, the school put itself up against Harvard's Yen Ching Institute, or London's School of Oriental and African Studies—and there just was not the substance available to sustain that status.

They began with high hopes. At first the offices were in a building in the business district—Gainsborough's building on Sansome Street. Later they moved to an old mansion on Broadway, in Pacific Heights, overlooking the Golden Gate and the harbor.

The spring of that year was a busy time. The school was trying to expand and announced scholarships and the broadening of the program, to include Middle Eastern studies as well as Far Eastern.

Watts was busy, organizing and teaching, and travelling. His family settled down in Palo Alto, to live the life of suburbanites. He travelled each day to San Francisco to teach and to lecture. He became involved in a series of radio programs with the Pacific

Broadcasting group, and later with educational television. For as these showmen soon learned, there was no showman-teacher like Watts. No one could expound the mysteries of the East and make them more mysterious, yet let the people believe they had almost reached the brink of understanding—no one in the world could do it as well as Watts.

From the outset, his California life was charmed. Soon he was moving freely around the artist and "thinker" colonies of the state, engaging in seminars, speaking to university groups, lecturing in various temples, talking with encounter groups, and the money was coming in very satisfactorily. He was deeply involved in every way with the American Academy of Asian Studies. This provided his base of operations, and gave him the mantle of respectability that one needed even in California. But aside from that, he was doing very well. Within a matter of months from his salad days in cold and dreary Millbrook, he was a grand success.

His older children were growing, and his second wife Dorothy was planning a family of her own. Watts divided his time between being the "family man" in suburbia (he was never very good at this) and the showman-philosopher of Sansome street.

He ranged in his lecturing as far north as Portland and south to Los Angeles. His fame spread, and with it came more offers to write. He wrote. He kept a steady stream of writing going, for radio, for television, for little magazines and big magazines, for serious magazines and flippant magazines. Starting in 1951, almost as soon as he arrived, he found that he had managed to fly in like the robins with the "counterculture," and he became a moving force in this revolutionary little volcano.

Harper's, realizing his popularity, decided to bring out a new edition of *The Meaning of Happiness*, and Watts wrote a new preface for it. His philosophy, he said, had matured. Still, he felt the essential theme he had explored here was as valuable and as much a part of his philosophy as ever, even though he had since written in very different terms to express the idea. (There, of course, was an oblique reference to any contradictions that the reader might pick up between this pre-Christian work and his Christian books, and now his latest non-Christian book.) He brought forth some of his new popular symbolisms. He was talking more about the Brahman, now, having been in close association recently with several students of Indian affairs, where before most of his association had been with those of the Japanese and Chinese cultures.

He was beginning to repeat himself a bit now—the preface to the second edition of *Happiness* had many of the catch words and ideas of *The Wisdom of Insecurity*. But why not? He made no pretenses. It was his hope to make people understand the mysteries of the East.

There were difficulties at the Academy. In the fall of 1952 there was still no complete sense of direction. Founder Gainsborough's dreams were hard to realize. On the other hand, there was no hope of this academy matching the University of California's Orientalia program, or Oregon's or Washington's. It was not in the cards for a popular, private school to do so. There was expansion, most of it in directions that did not entirely concern Watts. Sir Chetpat Ramasqwami Ayar joined the staff, to teach social and legal courses about India. The school added an extension division—so that some far away could study by correspondence.

By the fall of 1952, hopes were still high and rising. The school moved to Pacific Heights that fall. It began to receive various little attentions: a collection of Buddhist scriptures was presented by Princess Poon Pismai Diskul on behalf of the reigning family of Thailand. Dr. Gunapala P. Malalasekera, President of the World Fellowship of Buddhists, came to join the staff and teach Sanskrit and Hinayana Buddhism, plus courses in the civilization of Ceylon and other southern lands. These were, of course, anything but the Zen views of Watts, but the coming of Malalasekera made for interesting discussions in the school and for nice arguments outside.

That year there were only 65 students registered. The school would hardly become self-sufficient at that rate. At the moment there was plenty of money about, the school was getting good publicity, and foundations were open-handed. But how long would it continue? To Watts it did not seem too important. He was so busy, fulfilling lecture dates, talking before college audiences, and doing what he wanted to do, that he soon had little time even for writing. He studied calligraphy, and Chinese, and he walked and talked and meditated in his own way, to the disgust of the traditional Zen Buddhists, and more to that of the Hinayana believers. But Watts was doing just fine as his second year passed by. That year, 1953, he moved his family to Mill Valley, in Marin County, north of the Golden Gate bridge. The community was receptive to the kind of people the Wattses were. His good friend Elsa Gidlow lived there, and a half dozen others.

The longer the school stayed in operation, the greater its problems became. The Ford Foundation was approached, and refused to grant any money to an organization many looked upon with deep suspicion. California abounded with odd religious cults, many of them claiming a background or adherences to some Asian group. And Louis Gainsborough was glad to foot the bills as long as he could stand it, but how long would that be? They hired a pair of fund raisers, and discovered what many other organizations have, that fund raising takes up most of the funds raised. So they staggered along through the year 1953. To broaden the base, they brought in Watts' old friend Rom Landau, to teach courses in the History of Morocco. They added Charles Malik, the Lebanese U.N. delegate, to the board of the Academy. The idea was to broaden the base, attract more students, solve the financial problems. Spiegelberg and Watts were not particularly interested in these problems, but they saw that their school was in trouble and did their best to promote support. One way Watts could help—and did—was to lead seminars in Zen, which was then becoming popular on the west coast. Down on Bush Street a Zen temple was created in an abandoned synagogue, several Japanese priests came there, and Watts began to renew his studies of the Orient for the first time with outside help since he had left New York and his mother-in-law's Zen master.

CHAPTER EIGHTEEN

ALLOWING MEN TO TAKE THEIR COURSE

The year 1953 found the Asian Academy in serious trouble. From his record and his own accounts of his life, one would scarcely believe that Alan Watts would be of the spirit to expend huge amounts of his energy to save *any* institution. He had carefully nurtured the concept of a complete libertarian, concerned with his own pleasures, and of showman-shaman, so that any thoughtful loyalty had been concealed.

But the fact was that Watts was a loyal professor, an adherent of and believer in such an organization as the one to which he belonged. Cynics could say that he needed the base—that might have been true in 1952, it probably was not true in 1953, for by that time the lecture offers were coming in, those nice fat college campus invitations with their big fees and small responsibilities.

Louis Gainsborough did everything possible to make the American Academy of Asian Studies self-sufficient and successful. The number of students was not large. Too many needed financial aid. As costs rose steadily in America, so did the demands and real needs of the faculty. If the Academy was to work it had to be further broadened in scope and that cost money.

They tried bringing the Academy to the community. In the spring of 1953 they secured a full-length documentary on the life of Mahatma Gandhi, perhaps the best-known of modern Asians in the Western world. The premiere of the film was held at the Academy and it brought out the community. The hope was that more people would become interested in the overall program.

Next month, July, the faculty wracked their brains and came up with a series of community lectures. Haridas Chaudhuri would discuss Vedanta and Western Thought—one of his specialities. He was a follower of Sri Aurobindo Ghose, the religious leader of Pondicherry in India, who had written widely on Hindu philosophy. One could see, in Watts' writing and speaking at this time, how much affected he was by his burgeoning knowledge of the Indian varieties of faith, for he quoted them more as he learned more about them. This knowledge was transferred because the Academy was quite unlike the average academic institution. As Watts put it in his autobiography, they were concerned with *living* the ways of life they espoused, and not only with talking about them. It was simple enough to go to Berkeley or other fine universities and have Taoism, Zen, and other beliefs described to one. But at the Academy you were supposed to immerse yourself in the studies. And to help, the faculty held weekly colloquia, at which they aired their own views of life and affairs under the genial glance of Dr. Spiegelberg. Outsiders were welcome. This way the school began to attract the progressive intelligentsia of San Francisco—the way-out group. Artists, writers, students, and bums came to the Academy to see what was going on.

Sir Chetpat Ayar and Chaudhuri and Watts argued endlessly about the various karma and the various illusions of mankind. In one way one could say that Watts had a real nerve in putting himself up against these gentlemen, who were native-born religionists of Asia and highly trained scholars to boot. But this was not the same Watts who we have seen come from England. It is true that he had still never visited Asia, but he had read nearly everything of note translated into English on his subject of Buddhism, and much that was translated into French. He did have formal education, those years in the Seminary. He held degrees of Doctor of Divinity and Master of Theology. So, although there were many in San Francisco who regarded Watts as a genial fake, he had done one thing to protect himself—he had covered himself with the mantle of *academe* that was almost sure protection in American life.

Watts came in for a good deal of ragging because he would follow no regimen. A Zen Buddhist *was supposed to* sit on his ass—and other followers of Zen who did so were shocked at a Watts who professed the faith but refused to follow the cardinal principle. It was as if the Archbishop of Canterbury had refused to conduct morning prayer. But of course, since most Americans were unaware of the requirements of Zen form they did not worry about what Watts did himself, but only about how he translated the thought of the East for them—and this is where he had his magic.

He traded argument for discipline, and for his own welfare he made it work. He was the mystic with the golden tongue, and as his reputation spread around California, he began to draw ever larger crowds. His good humor and his handsome form did not hurt anything either. He was a real charmer, this man with the red beard who grinned at them and posed them wonderful questions and drew such fine analogies, words that made one sure at the moment that one understood precisely what Watts was saying—although 10 minutes later, just as with St. Augustine—no one could quite remember what it was that Watts had said that was so clear. Donovan Bess, one of San Francisco's most literary reporters, reviewed one of Watts' books and said precisely this:

> *Give Alan Watts a batch of ineffable Oriental philosophy and he turns it into words that make you believe you understand. You don't understand, but you believe you do. You believe in the splendid package of words that Watts makes for you.*

Entertainer, that's what he was.

Charlatan, that's what his enemies said.

But Watts would argue. He was perfectly *capable* of seeking the Way in the the "right" way. Of course, that would have obviated the way he lived his life; Zen Buddhists were no showmen but contemplaters. Watts was not a contemplater but a showman.

Meditation, he argued constantly, was only reasonable insofar as it showed the meditator that his whole approach was wrong—that he could not learn anything by meditating. So Watts did not meditate, he drank and ate and fornicated and made speeches and wrote books and walked on the beach and climbed Mt. Tamalpais, and laughed with his friends and played with his children, and winked at pretty girls instead. That was Zen, Watts style.

His friends among the faculty at the Academy ragged him unmercifully as a lazy bastard who would not get down to work and utilize his obvious ability in the right directions. Most of his fellows liked him, although they did not admire him. Most of the youth he encountered admired him, for he was making life work the way he wanted it to work—and he had a prescription for the rest of us, if we would only follow it. Of course, not all who heard him were either capable or in position to live the happy life, but for those who were—and a million dollars, debt free, would be a nice way to start—it was the ideal existence.

And yet, whenever anyone who knew Watts was ready to bat him down—to disregard him as a fake—one had to contend with what he was doing at the Academy.

Gainsborough was encountering difficulty in the summer of 1953 in holding the American Academy together. It was not turning out precisely as he had hoped, for he was a practical businessman, and he was watching his dream child fall into trouble.

Of course it was easy enough to shout that the community did not appreciate the goodness of what was offered, or the excellence of it either. But that was the way of the dreadful world. Gainsborough was the major angel. And as he watched, the child was turning more philosophical, and less practical. One result of this was to teach businessman Gainsborough that culture is a very iffy thing. He had financed the making of the Ghandhi movie—and it was not very successful at the box office. He had brought all these teachers, foreign and domestic, together to give San Francisco insight into India, Pakistan, Thailand, Tibet, and Burma—as well as into Zen and other exotic exercises. And he was right, right, right, right. But right is right is right is right—and San Francisco bubbled around the building at 2030 Broadway up on sunny Pacific Heights, and paid very little attention. So, when tentative feelers for the movement of the whole academy from San Francisco to Los Angeles or perhaps to Houston came along, angel Gainsborough was beginning to give them attention. He was running out of free capital.

The faculty of the Academy sensed the danger. Watts, in particular, had found his home on the shoulder of Mt. Tamalpais and he never wanted to leave the place for more than a few days to pick up some money.

He felt a vigor and a happiness in northern California that he had not known before. He was close enough to Big Sur to visit those who would recharge his batteries. He was close enough to Los Angeles to go on a far-out trip if that was needed—or to make money by participating in the adventures of one of the kook institutions down there that had its own, sometimes rich, following. And the old Bourn mansion on Broadway was a pleasant place to use as center of his activities.

The summer of 1953 was a critical time for the Academy, and all concerned knew it. Two years had been test enough to try the resources of the community without response.

Watts and Dr. Spiegelberg and Haridas Chaudhuri tried hard that summer to bring a new look and a new life to the Academy. They organized four new conferences to bring out interested prospects for the Academy. Dr. Spiegelberg would discuss his psychological researches and the work of C. G. Jung on four different lecture occasions in the next few weeks that summer. Chaudhuri would lead a conference lasting over a month on Vedanta and Western Thought. And Alan would take two conferences upon himself, one on the foundations of Oriental philosophy, and the other on Zen Buddhism.

So the summer was a busy place at the Academy, with strangers and reporters buzzing around listening in on the thinkers as they expounded on their philosophies. But was this what San Francisco wanted? Was it what Gainsborough needed to let his wonderful experiment survive?

It did not seem so. The lectures were successful from the standpoint of the lectors. Out into the ether of the world flowed all this marvelous philosophy—all this distillation of human knowledge. Not a person who attended was but the better for what he or she learned.

But the school?

Next month, September, Alan was addressing a meeting at the school. It was a desperate effort—an organization was to be formed called the Friends of the American Academy of Asian Studies. Anyone who has had any experience with organizations knows that when a "Friends of . . ." is formed there is usually only one purpose—and that is to put the bite on the Friends and the friends of the Friends. Alan was the keynoter. He was the best speaker, the liveliest mind, the finest promoter.

But "Friends of . . ." did not do the job either, as no one really expected they would.

In another month Dr. Spiegelberg quit. He was getting along, he did not need the position, and the "hassle" was growing too great.

Alan began to take over, for there was no other capable of managing. Gainsborough could not continue the sole financing of the school. It was going to have to learn to fly on its own wings if it flew at all.

The school began to do what it might have done earlier; it presented programs a little less "far out" for the public. That fall of 1953 the school announced the addition of three new courses. First, and most practical: students could learn almost any of the Far Eastern languages here: Tibetan, Chinese, Japanese, or what you would. There would also be courses in Chinese painting and in the arts of the Far East.

And of course, there was also to be an addition in Alan's special sphere. There would be seminars in Chinese philosophy and Zen. And besides that there would be seminars in Tantra, the psychology of non-violence (Indian) and Hindu psychology, and a special training course for teachers in Buddhism.

This was material that could scarcely be studied elsewhere in America and it offered hope for the future of the Academy.

By January there seemed to be a chance. The Academy was attracting a good deal of attention in the community. The winter term they opened language classes to all who wanted to study, regardless of academic background. They taught Arabic, Bengali, Burmese, Mandarin Chinese and Cantonese, Hindi, Indonesian, Japanese, Malay, Persian and Siamese Sinhalese, Tagalog, Urdu, and Vietnamese. The language classes were given in the evenings—the tuition was reasonable, $15 admission fee plus $20 to $40 per course.

In spring, Alan was the Dean of the Academy, and he called for public support to replace the failing financial aid given by Gainsborough. Alan began giving more seminars, and devoting more of his time to the school. He was doing his best to save this vehicle. On Mondays and Wednesdays he gave evening lectures on the Philosophy of Lao Tzu.

Still it was not enough. But Watts and Gainsborough were men of action. They scouted around and found that the college of the Pacific up in Stockton could be interested in the prestige to be attained by having the college's own graduate school in Asian studies. The faculty was adequate—more than adequate for the task, for there were people here of attainment and of letters. So by mid-spring, 1954, it was arranged, and plans were made for the Asian Academy to award its graduate degrees through the College at Stockton in the spring commencement exercises. This move helped strengthen the grip of the Academy on *academe*—for the College of the Pacific was California's oldest institution of higher learning. Gainsborough now hoped that the school would become self-sustaining within the next three years. He had stepped up from President to Chairman of the Board. The faculty consisted of Alan and six other teachers, and the student body of 30 graduate students and 150 special students in the adult education division.

Alan Watts was content in his work. Long since, his personal financial problems had ceased to trouble him much. He was not one for Rolls Royces or castles in Spain. Three children had been born of the new marriage by 1958, and Watts was not only apparently settled in with his family in Mill Valley, but he seemed to be established. He was getting to be very well known in the community. He was studying Chinese more seriously than at any time previously. He was learning the fine points of calligraphy from Hodo Tobase, the Zen master who taught at the school.

One way in which Alan Watts made something of a local name for himself was to get embroiled in a clash between the liberal KPFA radio station in Berkeley, the Pacific Foundation station, and its "advisory board." The cause celebre involved the management of the station by the managers—the advisory board quit in a huff in protest over station policies. Watts had been broadcasting for the station for some months when this furor began in 1954, and he brought in 34 signers of a petition to back the management—and signed himself Dr. Alan Watts (remember the Doctor of Divinity degree) when he did so.

It was a battle. Gainsborough quickly disaffiliated the Academy from the whole business. Watts and his group claimed the management had been harried by the advisors. The advisors claimed the management was unresponsive. It was not the last controversy that Watts was to involve himself in.

And as for self—by 1956 he had undergone a really remarkable change for a man who six years earlier had left the Episcopal ministry under conditions that must be described as desperate.

CHAPTER NINETEEN

LOVING ONE'S SELF

One of the most cutting statements made to Alan Watts when he circulated his letter of resignation from the Episcopal church had come from Canon Bernard Iddings Bell.

Bell did not doubt Watts' honesty, he wrote, but he felt the letter, apologizing Watts' position, was both rationalization and incomplete. He hoped that Watts might find different and clearer views in the future.

It is hard enough to take insults from your enemies when you are in a negative position; it is much worse to see your friends registering pity and disbelief.

In resigning his post and abandoning the Episcopal priesthood, Watts had said that the church had become victim of its own forms, and had not changed with the times as it must. That was no more or less than the argument he had used within the church in his earlier works. But with the stinging of Canon Bell's words in his mind, once Watts had put aside the past, with his little renunciation *The Wisdom of Insecurity,* he felt impelled to answer his critics and put into words the major complaint he felt against the church he had left because of the quarrel over his first marriage.

The result was a book written in 1953 called *Myth and Ritual in Christianity,* which was published by Vanguard Press.

He began by anticipating attack from his old friends and mentors:

> *A book on Christian Mythology has not, I believe, been written before. There are some sound reasons for this omission for the subject is one of extreme delicacy and complexity, not because of the actual material, but because the whole problem is in a very special way, "touchy."*

What Watts meant here is that even he, the iconoclast, would have hesitated long before he would have written such a work while he remained under the roof of the church. Nor could such a book be written by one who was not once a Christian minister or priest, or at least that learned in Christian theology. So now, out of the church, he could write this critical essay. Not before. He continued,

> *There are extreme differences of violently held opinion about Christianity itself—both as to what it is, and as to whether or not it is a "good thing." Similarly there are rather wide differences as to the nature and value of Mythology, which has only quite recently become a subject of serious study. [Watts' friend Joseph Campbell was the principal serious student.] But when one takes the two together, one is doing something best expressed by the colloquialism "sticking one's neck out"—and sticking it out very far.*

True words, or they certainly would have been had he been writing as a Christian. But having eschewed Christianity for the second time during his life, Watts must be regarded here as the vengeful outsider, proving the point he wished to make for so long.

Considering the Christian church, Watts went to fundamentals (which he believed anyhow and always had), taking the Catholic church as the Christian church. It must be remembered that Watts would certainly have spent his second Christian period as a Roman Catholic, had there been any place for him in that church. Married, he could not conceivably have become a priest; in his day the Roman church had no practicing deacons of the hand-laying variety, which they were to develop in the 1970s in the enlightenment of the Holy See.

So Watts' first vengeance on his old associates of the Episcopal church was to disregard that church as "irrelevant" when considering the rite and rote of Christianity.

As for mythology, what he was going to discuss, Watts defined it as "a complex of stories—some no doubt fact—and some fantasy—which, for various reasons, human beings regard as demonstrations of the inner meaning of the universe and human life."

Oh, how the traditional churchmen would squirm under this lash. For the church to be discussed as a Mythological Beast was sheer torture to a fundamentalist churchman, who believed in the body and blood of Christ, in the actuality of the sacraments, in the letter of the history of the church.

Now examine if you will, the language:

> *. . . Jesus himself actually claimed some type of divine origin or affinity. . . . Why, for instance, was the mind of Western man captured by the Christ-myth rather than the story of Mithras?*

He brought forth C. G. Jung (remember those lectures back in London in the 1930s?). Jung he cited to show that the myth of Christianity originated in dreams and daydreams. Jung ascribed the Christ myth to the collective unconscious of the Western world, and Watts speculated why the Christ myth might have survived, while the Osiris myth subsided, why Isis, the goddess of Ancient Egypt died, and the Virgin Mary lived on.

Anyone who wonders what kind of impact this discussion of Watts' would have in Christian circles is welcome to try that last paragraph or two on the parish priest or the minister when he next comes to tea. It should provide some interesting pyrotechnics.

Watts' next authority on the Christian myth was Ananda Coomaswaramy—and here he leaped off into a dissertation on Hinduism, Buddhism, and Taoism which had something to do with myth, but little to do with Christianity.

The words were different. The words were always the key to Watts; he could no more avoid the pejorative when he was angry than words of praise when he was glad. Hügel, Gilson, and Maritain, whom the reader of this book will recall having encountered as Watts' "authorities" in his discussions of Christian mysticism in the past, now became "modern Catholic apologists" in *Myth and Ritual.*

It might be possible, said Watts, to give the solutions to the problems of Christian myth through the terms of the official doctrine. But really no, it could not be done because the "church's doctrine confuses its own position by trying to include within the myth, the dogma" and to claim that the church's way is the only true way.

Watts' implication was already clear (this was page 20 of his prologue): that the Christian myth was far from the only "way."

Watts was going to look at Christianity from the outside. "It would seem," he said, "that in the present state of our knowledge of other spiritual traditions than the Christian, there is no further excuse for religious provincialism. This knowledge is now so extensive that it is becoming hard to see how anyone can be considered theologically competent, in the academic sense, unless thoroughly well versed in traditions outside the Christian alone. . . ."

Does it sound familiar?

The book has the ring of that first Watts discussion of Christianity, so far back in his life, back in 1937, when he published *The Legacy of Asia.* A restrained, confident, and tolerant Church of England looked upon this youngster then as an interesting phenomenon, and his book as a clever little put-on. This was the same Watts grown up. He was saying about the same things in his grown-up way that he had said before in his childish way—with one great exception. Back in the 1930s Watts had been convinced that he could reform Christianity by bringing into it the truths of Buddhism. Now, having spent 10 years in the bosom of the church, having made his impact as an individual churchman of high visibility and strong personality, but not through any effect on the doctrines—Watts was wise enough to give up the reform of Christianity and abandon it since he could not stay within it—and look upon Christianity from the outside.

Watts then delved into the fears of churchmen about the discussion of the myths of Christianity. First, he said, they were afraid of the emergence of a new religion which would adapt their ways as they had adapted others'—the Roman Sun God feast as the feast of Easter is an example of that adaptation. Some say it was done at a critical period to propitiate the Roman Legions.

And the dreadful thing, from the doctrinaire Christian point of view, was that Watts proposed to discuss the whole of Christian belief in terms of a *myth*. Shades of Billy Graham, indeed.

And so, in the best scholarly fashion, telling all the reasons why he was going to do as he pleased in this discussion of Christianity, and not do as the usual run of writers would do, Watts then turned to the Christian religion.

He began with the beginning: John 1: 1-2:

> *In the beginning was the Word,*
> *And the Word was with God,*
> *And God was the Word.*
> *He was in the beginning with God.*

Well, who was God? Here we go—on the chariot ride of Christian mysticism and myth.

God was the secret, the Hebrews' Unutterable Name—. YHVH, the Tetragrammaton of four Hebrew letters, meaning *I Am*. God was the great *I Am* then?

That's the myth. The great *I Am* was always, there was never a time that He was not, and He was not created by anyone, and He existed for a long time before He got around to creating anything else. In appearance He was pure light, except that afterwards He was believed to look like man because He had created man in His own form.

And He was also Three, because we had God the Father, God the Son, and God the Holy Ghost. But the three were hard for Christians to consider at this time, because Jesus Christ had not yet been born on Earth. So it was confusing, so confusing that the icon painters of the Eastern Orthodox church painted icons in a number of ways, including the use of Sophia as Jesus—which is another facet of the myth.

How Alan Watts has matured in this book. How erudite he now is in 1953. Consider his footnote (page 31) explaining the apparent confusion caused by the use of Sophia, the Godhead of the Orthodox, instead of Jesus, as one of the three manifestations of God.

He noted that one of the *arcana,* or obscure mysteries, of mythology is the fact that the Son as Wisdom, Sophia, is *feminine* and the Church also applies the above passage (Proverbs 8: 22-31) to the Virgin Mary, since it is used as the Epistle on the Feast of the Immaculate Conception. The great cathedral of Constantinople, Hagia Sophia, is dedicated to God the Son in this aspect.

Such words, *cult, myth, obscure*—they would make those churchmen shudder, those people who had cast Watts out—or forced him out.

And can one truly believe that this Wattsian effort was done from spite?

Of course not. Spite may have had its part—(it must have pleased Watts each time he got to a phrase like "the cult of the Virgin Mother.") But he was doing more, he was staying in character. He had to write this book; it was as much a part of his apologia as anything he would ever write, and Canon Bernard Iddings Bell would most certainly read it and understand that here was his friend's answer.

This was another of Watts' intellectual manifestos, and sometimes the footnotes ate up a third of a page. The first 50 pages were devoted to the discussion of theology and to Creation. The next 30 pages treated God and Satan. The next portion of the book was devoted to the Advent, or coming of Christ. Chapter IV dealt with Christmas and Epiphany. Thence the book moves on through the Christian year, with a useful glossary of terms at the end. The book was illustrated by a combination of woodcuts and old pictures and line drawings by the author. Alan Watts had ever shown some aptitude for drawing, and he was fairly well skilled.

Had Watts not left the church, he could very easily have produced almost this exact book—without the opening denial that the Christian mysteries were the real truth of the world. He had everything but faith. He knew the material, and in a way it could be a very useful book to Christians and those interested in the history and procedures of the church. Written slightly differently the book could have been quite acceptable to the church, and perhaps titled *The Christian Year.* It was certainly a throwback in the sense of Watts' enlightenment; it was as though he had stopped in his peregrinations, stopped completely, and created this out of the fabric of the past. In good part that must have been what happened, for the book has virtually no "Watts" in it after the opening materials.

In another sense it is all Watts. He had, since the earliest days in the church and before that, felt that his place in Christendom was to reform, to recreate his personal Christianity with reference to the Eastern mysteries and the Eastern view of life. So we see it again in the closing pages of *Myth and Ritual:* the call to Western man to live in the present and not either past or future.

> *So understood, the marvelous symbols of Christianity might well—one is tempted to say, might begin to—have a message for Western man, that anxious and restless eccentric who has "no time" because he has reduced his present to an abstract dividing line between past and future, and who confuses his very self with a past which is no more and a future which is not yet. He, too, needs to be turned outside-in, to live in the real world which he thinks is abstract, instead of the abstract world which he takes for reality. And for this he must know that the true place of Bethlehem, Calvary, and Olivet is no more in history, and that Death, the Second Advent, and Heaven are not in time to come. His "sin," his missing of the point, can only be forgiven if he repents—turns back—from his past, as from the future which it implies, and returns again to his Creator, the present reality from which he "ex-ists." Whereupon the life which had seemed momentary would be found momentous, and that present which had seemed to be no time at all would be found to be eternity.*

The book was generally well-received. There were not that many people in America concerning themselves with the future of the church, and it was mentioned in *The New York Times,* the

Herald Tribune, and even the *Times Literary Supplement* in London.

Most reviewers did not quite know what to make of the book. Most of them did not know who Watts was, nor did they get into that aspect of the matter at all. The *Herald Tribune* was not quite sure what to do with it, so its reviewer did what was proper in the circumstances, he detailed the contents of the book and let it go at that.

The Virginia Kirkus service, usually more waspish in its approach to all but its handful of favorites, noted that the book was "irritating in its complacent assumption that from the very beginning the true meaning of the Christian mythos had been missed by everyone else." And the reviewer spoke of Professor Watts—which must have done Watts' heart good, for it upgraded the Academy.

Library Journal's reviewer was more to the Christian point: "it will be rejected by most Orthodox Christians," he said.

The *New York Times* had the most balanced review. "Few readers will go all the way with Mr. Watts in his interpretations but his learning is considerable and he has much to say that will interest anyone interested in cultural and religious history. . . ."

It was Watts the showman who had triumphed again. He had a fine way of spreading out his knowledge, as a peacock spreads his tail, and in so doing bringing a great deal of color if not light to a subject. In that sense, *Myth and Ritual in Christianity* was a success. It also marked the end of the whole Christian experiment for Alan Watts and was its valedictory for him. He had placed Christianity in his scheme of things for once and for all.

CHAPTER TWENTY

THE WAY OF HEAVEN

In a way, one might say that it took *Myth and Ritual in Christianity* to clarify Alan Watts' mind after 10 years as a practicing Christian minister. That is an oversimplification, and yet there is truth in it, because the smell of the altar candles lingered on. In his resignation from the church Watts had known himself well enough to understand that he must continue the road he had chosen, that of priest, even though he was changing not just denomination—that had been done before many times—but his entire structure of religious organization. Not his faith. That had remained basically the same through the Christian years, and his books indicate it all. All the Christian books except the last show his desperate attempt to fit his own beliefs within the historic and ritualistic mold of the church—without success.

In 1954 and 1955, Alan Watts was totally immersed in the Academy in San Francisco. Within the walls of the old mansion he could find anything he desired. He went out only to play and to live with his family, and to make speeches and broadcasts and write articles for a dozen publications.

Most of these articles are rather hard to find, for they were written for publications not usually saved by the mass of libraries. Watts was a creature of the new liberation, the counterculture that was spreading across the United States in the 1950s as the "Beat Generation" heralded it.

From 1953 until 1956 there were not too many of the articles—for Watts was filling the unaccustomed role of administrator, in addition to practicing his calligraphy, studying his Chinese, still learning Zen from Oriental experts, making love, drinking and dining, and getting into discussions whenever possible on the differences between East and West.

Despite all this fulfilling activity, it would be easier to take Watts more seriously if he had done so himself.

Watts left many with the definite impression that he was a rogue, a lovable rogue, perhaps, but nonetheless a rogue, skating through life, enjoying himself immensely, and ripping off everyone in a giant con game of his own.

Only Watts' temperament and his adherence to the Way could save him from endless worry. The Academy was failing and there was virtually nothing that could be done about it, it seemed. The *Chronicle* might note editorially that of the hundreds of American diplomats abroad in Asia, only some 30 had any formal training in Asian affairs, languages, or ideas. But that did not bring the State Department running, as probably it ought to have done. A handful of initiates and curiousity seekers continued to haunt the halls of the Academy, but by 1953 it was a failure as an American enterprise and everyone knew it.

Watts and the others must receive very high marks for trying their best. They brought in new teachers and new subjects. They added to the library—a new collection of Arabic works was announced in the spring of 1954 and Rom Landau came back again to teach Islamic civilization. Such studies were useful and necessary; if the Americans knew virtually nothing about the Far East, they knew even less about the Middle East. But the Academy did not "take" with the general public, and even the association with the College of the Pacific did not solve the problem. Certainly Gainsborough tried. He became a trustee of COP, and worked from within for his old Academy. Watts brought in more and more people from the East. He hired Saburo Hasegawa, a well-known Japanese artist, to teach part-time at the Academy.

Watts became involved with the Soto Zen temple, and spent more and more time studying his language and his Eastern mysteries. Yet he was indefatigable in bringing the finest of available lecturers to teach his students. D. T. Suzuki came. So did S. I. Hayakawa, the San Francisco State College man who later came to fame in another way, and even Ruth Sasaki, Watts' former mother-in-law, who was now a Zen master in her own right in a way that Watts would never be.

He took students to Stockton and to Big Sur, and to Chinatown. They had the best of everything the Oriental communities could offer—including argument, for the Orientals by and large were integrating themselves into American society and had been for a hundred years, while Watts wanted them to retreat to the same kind of appreciation of their ancient cultures that he had.

But as an administrator Watts was no more successful than one might expect. If anyone at all could pull together the financial strings of the Academy he was not the one. And when the Academy affiliated itself with the College of the Pacific, it accepted a whole new set of strictures that made his life totally miserable. Academe is as ritualistic a world as that of the church, and by 1956 Watts knew that he had no further place in it. Nor did he need it. The small salary he drew from the Academy was nothing compared to his income from publishing and writing for magazines and speaking. He was being lured farther and farther afield by interest shown toward him from universities and colleges in the East and by his own interest in Zen in particular. And each month he was growing more expert at the forms of the spirit he espoused.

The Beat Generation was beginning. Alan Watts was playing the drums, and in the summer of 1956 he was finishing up the book that would make his reputation international as a leader of what was coming to be known even then as the "counterculture," as that negation of "the American way" took shape.

The book was *The Way of Zen.* The idea behind it was the most ambitious that Watts had yet entertained. For in the past he had been occupied with learning, and he had accepted the complaints cheerfully that he would not espouse a formal system of meditation. But now, Watts was doing something new, he was stepping forth as the apostle of the new Way, and it must be a new way, for he sensed that Americans could not simply meld into the Buddhist system.

He did not favor importing Zen from the East, for the Oriental cultural tradition made an adoption of Zen in a very different America implausible. But there was much that we could learn from it, and adapt to our way. Zen offers much to us, Watts said.

Zen "has a way of being able to turn one's mind inside out, and dissolving what seemed to be the most oppressive human problems into questions like 'Why is a mouse when it spins?' At its heart is a strong but completely unsentimental compassion for human beings suffering and perishing from their very attempts to save themselves . . ."

There was in 1956 no fundamental text on Zen. Watts (with considerable charm) discounted his own earlier writings on the subject. He revealed for the first time publicly, a fundamental difference with Christmas Humphreys over his old mentor's addition of doses of Theosophism to his appreciation of Zen.

No, there was nothing printed in America to lead the young people who were turning to Zen in increasing numbers. Zen masters lived here, in some number in the hills and byways of California, but none of them had sufficient command of English to do the job. Therefore, Watts would write his own book, bringing to the subject the appreciation that he had of the difference of basic cultural premises between East and West.

From the standpoint of the institution—Zen included—Alan Watts was his usual outrageous self. He suggested, by way of putting up a straw man, that one really should be a student who had studied for years under a Zen master. But no, not really.

He was saying that neither the person closely associated with a religion—such as a priest—nor an outside observer of completely objective view, could possibly write about a religion. Monsignor Fulton J. Sheen certainly would have challenged him on that contention, as would indeed, St. Augustine, and Lao Tzu. But we are dealing with Alan Watts, not Fulton Sheen or Lao Tzu. That was Watts. This was how he was. And he believed what he said.

Watts was honest enough with his reader:

> *. . . I cannot represent myself as a Zenist or even as a Buddhist. . . . I claim no rights to speak of Zen. I claim only the pleasure of having studied its literature and observed its art forms since I was hardly more than a boy. . . .*

Was it artless? Or was it artful?

This question would be one to come up time and again in the appraisal of Alan Watts. Was he a modest, unassuming man in his early forties, an unfrocked priest who was troubled by the world, and sought to have and give the world he knew an insight into the road to happiness? Or was he the charlatan, artfully dodging his critics by pretending to know nothing, when actually he knew a good deal, by disclaiming responsibility as an "official" interpreter of Zen, so that his critics would not bring up the fact that he had never studied under a Zen master (which was not quite true although he had never followed a regimen), and, perhaps most telling in a way—*he had never been to the Far East.*

If one took the position that a true Zen student must have gone to the Orient, labored in a monastery for months and years, and acquired the Way thus—then Watts was indeed a charlatan. The argument there can be buttressed by an allusion to Japan. For years, before World War II, English was a second language in Japan, taught in every prefecture, taught in most of the schools. But it was taught by Japanese who had been taught by Japanese who had been taught by Japanese. And the end result was an English that no Englishman or American could understand. Was this not the danger that Watts ran, by learning his Zen at second hand?

Fortunately for Watts, he had not entirely learned second hand. He had studied *with* Suzuki, as well as of Suzuki. Not for long, but the influence was there. He had studied with Sasaki. Not in the way he should have, perhaps, but he had. More recently, and this was to show like sun over a cornfield in the new book, he had been studying with the masters here in San Francisco Bay country.

Indeed how it showed.

First of all, as he pointed out in the preface, the book contained 16 pages of appended material *in Chinese*, written by someone who not only knew the written language but was an expert in calligraphy as well. Perhaps this was Watts (although it seems doubtful that he had achieved so much in so short a time). Whatever, the calligraphy is expert. Second, Watts had been led into study of Oriental sources for the first time. Until now his Zen was almost entirely the result of works written in English. Even now he claimed that his base was the works in European languages.

The new Watts had a whole new list of teachers: Sabro Hasegawa, Gi-ming Shien, Dr. Paul Fung, Dr. George Fung, Dr. Frederick Hong, Charles Yick, and Kazumitsu Kato, of the Soto-Zen school in San Francisco.

And as an additional attribute to his own scholarship, he attached to the book a table showing the Wade-Giles system of Romanization of Chinese characters into words.

Then the book itself—it was a remarkable work. His friend Joseph Campbell, reviewing it for *The New York Times* called it the finest work of its kind extant. "No one has given us such a concise, freshly written introduction to the whole history of Far Eastern development of Buddhist thought . . ." he wrote.

Nearly all the reviews were good. "The most comprehensive work on Zen yet," said London's *Listener*. "The most explicit and orderly account that has yet appeared", said Maurice Richardson in *The New Statesman*. It was for either scholar or student, and the fact that Mr. Watts was detached from any organization made it better—said Jean Burden, the poet, who was Watts' good friend.

The more Watts knew on a subject, the more simply he could write about it—that much was certain in this book. Contrast this book with his very first work, *The Spirit of Zen*, and there is *no* comparison. Here in *The Way of Zen* Watts wrote with the authority of the old pro, a man who knew what he was talking about and need not lean on others in footnote and allusion. There are references to the work of others, but for good reason, and not for the purpose of citation, which seemed to be part of the writing of the young Mr. Watts. But why not—there was nearly a quarter of a century between books—Watts had learned his lessons well, and he could now truly teach others who did not have the linguistic and cultural familiarity to undertake Zen study in Japan, the center of the culture and the religion.

This book is more than a book on Zen—it is a primer in Asian culture and understanding of the Asian outlook as well. It ranges across a broad field, discussing the processes of communication, the history of Taoism, the I Ching (the very early Chinese book of history and philosophy and divination, which became very popular in America at about this time).

Watts rings the changes again: the history of Buddhism, the rise of Mahayana Buddhism, the development of Zen. In this last he is not much more specific and detailed, for in the previous three years, aided by a Bollingen Foundation grant, he had the leisure to study the field for this work. Bollingen spent its money well—Watts had absorbed and could now tell the American people more about Zen in a more concise way than anyone had done.

There are, of course, the same charming stories that always seem to "get at" the Westerners who contemplate Zen for the first time.

These little tales are always dropped into the middle of long dissertations. They did not enlighten perhaps, but they brought amusement and relief.

Usually they were tales of how some monk sought or achieved enlightenment. They described it but they did not tell it. They indicated but they did not show. They played but they did not sound. They created what Donovan Bess called those magnificent words of Watts—and if they were nothing else, they were tremendously immersing and amusing. When one had finished a chapter of Watts, this new Watts, one had the feeling that one had been to an Oriental bathhouse. You might not be much cleaner, but you were certainly wetter and warmer, and had enjoyed yourself, relaxed yourself and been happy. And what is the real purpose of the bathhouse?

Poems, sayings, statements, quotations from the sages, all were brought together to try to give the Westerner a feeling for the Zen. In this the book was certainly successfull. If it failed in making the Westerner *understand* Zen—then the reader must remember that Watts had spent 25 years at the task and had accomplished more in his field in the past three years than in the first 20 by far.

In the history of Zen, Watts went into much detail that probably was mental exercise more than anything else. But out there in the wilderness were some few who really must appreciate what he was saying. As for the rest, it gave the youth of the counterculture something to fling into the faces of their elders, and the few something serious to contemplate.

One tale obviously gave Watts great pleasure as he told it: It was the story of Huai-jang, the Zen master.

When Huai-jang was initiating the monk Ma-tsu into Zen Mastery, that latter monk was sitting in meditation at the monastery of Ch'uan-fa. Ma-tsu had been spending many weeks in hard meditation.

"Your reverence," said Huai-jang, as he spoke to the other, "what is the objective of sitting in meditation?"

"The objective," answered Ma-tsu, "is to become a Buddha."

At this point Huai-jang picked up a piece of tile from the floor and began to rub it on a rock.

"What are you doing master?" asked Ma-tsu.

"I am polishing it for a mirror," said Huai-jang.

"How could polishing a tile make it into a mirror?"

"How could sitting in meditation make a Buddha?"

Oh, how that story was right down Watts' alley.

And this one, too.

He told how in the ninth century the teaching of Zen became peculiarly "disturbing." The master Nan-ch'uan came upon his monks one day and found them arguing most disreputably over some minor matter. It was, in fact, the ownership of a cat.

Furious, Nan-ch'uan picked up a spade and said he would cut the animal in two to solve that problem, if none of the monks could immediately show his own Zen.

There was dead silence.

The master cut the cat in two, and left it on the floor.

Later in the day, Nan-chu'an related the disgraceful incident to the monk Chao-chou, who looked at him, put his shoes on top of his head, and left the room.

Nan-ch'uan followed him, and said if Chao-chou had been there the cat would have been saved.

And Chao-chou became the successor to Nan-chu'an.

The reader, of course, is always left by these tales with the feeling that Watts had just said something tremendously important that should be understood. And sometimes, if one has been reading much of Watts at a sitting, and is half somnolent, one has the feeling of great understanding of the universe seeping through the page. Then one wakes up and it passes.

The tales delighted the Watts audience and delighted the Watts readers. One gets the feeling that with a little more brain power, a little more effort, one *will* understand. Or maybe it is to come back to these truths with a fresh mind, or with a tired mind, or with a drunken mind. Somehow, since there is a question, there must be an answer.

But the real point is that as he grew older and more assured, and more immersed in his subject, Watts' revelations of the Tao grew more specific, and better adapted for his audience. His major argument was for living life fully as it is, without worry. A wonderful philosophy, particularly for the young turned-off generation.

All this questioning, all this doubt, all this discussing of revelation was presented to the reader in the first half of the book. The second half was more specific.

Principles and Practice.

It was to show *how to.*

This discussion takes Zen into the realm of the practical insofar as it tells what the Zen practitioners are trying to do in achieving their end.

Where there is good there must be evil.

Man finds it hard to think in any terms but good or bad or an unclear meld of the two. Yet Zen, Watts said, releases one from this stricture, for according to Zen, it is absurd to choose—because there is no choice.

Well, it is simple—almost. There was something in the way Watts put it that seemed to have a handle on it. And he could dot your eye out with footnotes, once again.

But he always gave you something to think about.

Going back, he picked up his old friend Sokei-an Sasaki, who had earlier done as good a job in presenting something of the reality of Zen as any Oriental ever did in America.

Here is Sasaki's description of a religious experience of his own:

> *One day I wiped out all the notions from my mind. I gave up all desire. I discarded all the words which I had thought and stayed in quietude. I felt a little queer—as if I were being carried into something, or as if I were touching some power unknown to me. . . . and Ztt! I entered. I lost the boundary of my physical body. I had my skin of course, but I felt I was standing in the center of the cosmos. I spoke, but my words had lost their meaning. I saw people coming toward me. But they were all the same man. All were myself. I had never known this world. I had believed that I was created, but now I must change my opinion. I was never created; I was the cosmos; no individual Mr. Sasaki existed.*

The question is natural, to wonder why Alan Watts does not describe experiences of his own. *The Way of Zen* is devoid of these. Watts is our guide, our preacher, but he is never our experimenter, never our witness. He tells us how to, but never how he did. He describes Za-Zen, and the koans, and satori, and the places and ways of these things. But it is all descriptive—it is the *National Geographic* taking us on tour of the monastery we have never seen, and bringing us sidelights of history as we walk.

When that chapter is over, we want to jump up and ask, Yes Mr. Watts and what have you done with koan? How has it worked for you?

And when we do that, the air is silent.

CHAPTER TWENTY-ONE

STANDING ALONE

There is no doubt about it, the reader of *The Way of Zen* wants a witness and wants Alan Watts to remove his mask of Professor and *be* that witness. But he does not get his wish. For the last chapter of the book is again descriptive—Zen in the Arts. It does well by us, it tells us how to appreciate a Chinese scroll painting, and how to see a Sung dynasty landscape for what it is—an essence of what was viewed. It tells us a good deal about Japanese painters, and serves in every way as an admirable introduction.

We also learn something of haiku, the 17-syllable Japanese poems that have long been the delight of the monks and other intelligentsia. Watts shows us haiku and tells us how we should enjoy it. He gives us enough haiku to whet our appetite, and perhaps to set us to work ourselves. Good! He tells us of the art of tea—the tea ceremony. He tells us of calligraphy, of Zen breathing exercises, he rushes us along on this travelogue of Japan now, for that is where we have suddenly emerged with Zen, having come through China with Tao. And there Guide Watts leaves us, typical guide Watts, with a paragraph and a thought:

> *"Yet when it comes to it, this moment can be called "present" only in relation to past and future, or to someone to whom it is present. But when there is neither past nor future, and no one to whom this moment is present, what is it? When Fa-ch'an was dying, a squirrel screeched on the roof. "It's just this," he said, "and nothing else."*

So we come to the end of the Watts travelogue, somehow enriched, and liking it, and yet somehow dissatisfied and undernourished.

Is that to complain?

Readers did not. Watts' *The Way of Zen* sold in the tens of thousands. It was called a "Best Seller." It lined the pockets of the publisher and did not hurt the author's either. It was published by Pantheon. Watts had wandered from Pantheon here and there but after *The Way of Zen* he was not to wander. It was a most satisfying publishing experience.

Alan Watts, who had been in training all these years, suddenly emerged into a world where Zen had a magic sound. This book caught the fancy of the young. And Watts became America's principal interpreter of Zen.

The Zen leaders did not like it at all.

The traditional Zen priest Sohaku Ogata, observing the furor and examining the work, complained that Watts' book reminded him of "a portrait made of a cat by someone who had intended to paint a tiger."

Watts learned of that remark and laughed, a marvelous belly laugh—because he was a man with a fine sense of humor even when the joke was on him. Then he turned the joke.

The old Zen master Sengai, said Watts, once painted a tiger being scared by a cat.

And so?

And so, the deep suspicion of the legitimate Zen community continued. But this was a small community, highly specialized, demanding tremendous sacrifice and concentration and time. This was not the Zen that the American people wanted. They wanted ready-made Zen. They were used to department stores and they wanted to go in and buy their Zen and take it home with them. Homogenized Zen.

This Zen is what Alan Watts supplied, and because he knew it, he began styling himself a religious entertainer. He was more than that, he was the guru of the new disaffected society, just as Allen Ginsberg became the poet. The youth of the 50s, rejecting the profit motive, rejecting education, baths, and haircuts, began flocking to the cities, and particularly to the west coast, and here they learned of Zen and Alan Watts. Between 1953 and 1957 Watts became a celebrity of the counterculture.

In reviewing Watts' autobiography in later life, Thomas Lask of *The New York Times* found it very difficult to understand a Watts who was totally unconcerned with the real world about him. Lask was perturbed because nowhere in the Watts book did he find any mention of causes. There were no protest marches against Vietnam or Korea or for marijuana or just about anything else. Lask was disappointed, disgusted, and leaped to the conclusion that Watts did not care a fig for anything but making money and leading the good life.

But this was not true. It is true that Alan Watts was preoccupied with leading the good life. But in the matter of not concerning himself with the issues of the day that burned so hotly with some of his friends, the judgment is harsh and not altogether truthful. Did he not side up with the management of Pacifica against the handful of people outside who wanted to run the station? Did he not take responsibility and devote countless time to trying desperately to shore up the American Academy of Asiatic Studies when Dr. Spiegelberg and others had given it up as a lost cause?

Anything he did, in fact, would be a reversal of the Buddhist position—for the Buddhist, by his very nature, has given up the outside world as hardly worth the trouble. If this was more true of the Hinayana Buddhist than of the Mahayana, still in China and Japan Buddhist monks were not the ones a person turned to for a capsule view of world affairs. At least not until the war in Indochina.

The Watts approach to Asiatic studies failed, and the governors of the Academy decided they wanted someone with better Asian credentials than Alan Watts to lead their affairs. He still had not been to Asia, nor in the traditional sense was he ever a student of Asian affairs. He never gave a fig for politics or the high wigwag of economics. The College of the Pacific was in charge of its graduate school, and things had changed. So Watts' leadership ended in 1956 and next year the Academy was taken over by Ernest Egerton Wood, author of some 20 books on Asian affairs, who had lived for 38 years in India. That "experience" was more like what was wanted on the American scene.

So Watts was on his own.

But if anyone was ever ready for it, Alan Watts was.

He had a radio program. He had his lectures. He had a television program on KQED called Eastern Wisdom and Modern Life, and the program was distributed to educational TV stations all across the country. Terrence O'Flaherty, the TV columnist for the San Francisco *Chronicle* gave him several good writeups, which did not hurt. Once a viewer tuned in, he was on his own, but Watts need not worry. Clean-faced now, with a crew haircut that made him look something like a Buddhist monk, and also far younger than his forty-three years, Watts was wowing the TV audience.

Alan Watts in 1958 was the guru of the Beat Generation, and he had come into his own. He and friends were already included in Jack Kerouac's novel, *The Dharma Bums.* Beatness was wriggling its grimy way across America, and where it went so did Wattsian contemplation.

In the summer of 1958, in the *Chicago Review,* Watts the guru wrote an important essay titled *Beat Zen, Square Zen and Zen.*

The purpose was to warn the young, who were embracing Zen as "their thing." He spoke of the uneasiness that assailed Westerners, and told the young that they must learn a certain balance before Zen would work for them.

Watts did not want Zen turned into some kind of mystery of incantations and beads that would justify all sorts of young people not working or thinking or doing anything but sitting about and contemplating their navels with the self-satisfaction of those the world has wronged.

Those who scoff at Watts as pure showman would do well to read *Beat Zen* . . . for a good empirical look at what was wrong with American society from the period of the 1950s to the depression of the 1970s (which began to bring Americans out of themselves—a time when the struggle for survival began to put an end to bellybutton picking). Watts spoke of the disquiet of the world and said that it "arises from the suspicion that our attempt to master the world from outside is a vicious circle in which we shall be condemned to the perpetual insomnia of controlling controls and supervising supervision *ad infinitum.*"

He spoke now confidently of the "post-Christian west." He believed that Zen appealed to the youth because it did not preach or scold as did Hebrew-Christian beliefs.

There is no guilt in Zen.

The difficulty was that the Beats—those hipsters who wore their dirty lowslung jeans along the streets of North Beach and Greenwich Village, were dropping Zen words and phrases, and pretending Zen—while missing the whole point. Watts charged them with exploitation as intense as that of J.P. Morgan.

This was not the admirable Zen that Watts advocated. Indeed, after the publication of this article, Jack Kerouac's *The Dharma Bums* was published, and Watts was more than a little anguished to see that he had been used in the book, and that particularly a real Zen follower, Gary Snyder, had been brought into this thinly fictionalized account of Kerouac's experiences in California in 1956. Japhy Ryder, the hero, *is* Gary Snyder, the poet who had spent a year of study in Kyoto. But any resemblance between Snyder and Ryder was all in Kerouac's mind. For Snyder was not a part of the bohemian underworld. He could not disagree more, said Watts, with the Kerouac philosophy: "I don't know, I don't care. And it doesn't make any difference." That is simulated Zen, not Zen at all.

> *". . . just because Zen truly surpasses convention and its values, it has no need to say 'To Hell with it', nor to underline with violence the fact that anything goes."*

Watts was seriously disturbed by those he saw around him who were using the name of Zen to encompass an "anything goes" theory.

There is in this essay on Zen a key to Watts—to what he admired and loved and desired for himself. One can feel it in the passage where he describes his friend Snyder.

He first speaks of Gary Snyder's intellectual attainments in Orientalia. He had studied Zen for a year in Kyoto; he studied Chinese with Shih-hsiang Chen at the University of California. He translated some of the poems of Han Shan, the Zen poet. And he himself was, Watts claimed, one of the best poets of the San Francisco renaissance.

But, Watts went on, Snyder was "in the best sense, a bum."

> *His temporary home is a little shack without utilities on a hillside in Mill Valley at the top of a steep trail. When he needs money he goes to sea, or works as fire watcher or logger. Otherwise he stays at home or goes mountain climbing, most of the time writing, studying, or practicing Zen meditation. . . . the whole place is in the best Zen tradition of clean and uncluttered simplicity. But this is not a Christian or a Hinayana Buddhist style of asceticism. As* The Dharma Bums *made plain, it combines a voluntary and rather joyous poverty with a rich love life, and for Western, and much Eastern religiosity, this is the touchstone of deviltry. This is not the place to argue the complex problem of spirituality and sensuality, but one can only say, "So much the worse for such religiosity."*
>
> *This attitude has seldom been a part of Zen, new or old, beat or square.*

Where Watts faulted Kerouac and that writer's growing following, was in the confusion of "anything goes" at the existential level with "anything goes" on the artistic level. The trouble with Kerouac with all his warmth and winning ways, was that he was a caricaturist, and as such he was hurting the serious Zen movement.

He gave Kerouac some points. There were others he liked less: "the cool, fake-intellectual hipster searching for kicks, name dropping bits of Zen and jazz jargon to justify a disaffiliation from society which is in fact just ordinary callous exploitation of other people. . . ."

At this time, the drug fight had begun between the rebels and the members of the counterculture. And for the first time at least publicly, Watts addressed himself to the drug culture.

One of the problems of Beat Zen, he said, was the affinity for marijuana and peyote and the belief that there was any similiarity of the state produced by those substances with that engendered by satori. They were, Watts said, less habit-forming and harmful than tobacco and whiskey, but the "states of great aesthetic insight" they produced were totally different from the satori experience.

In the end Watts refused to be overly upset by the drug culture or by Beat Zen or Square Zen. Beat Zen was a deviation but "the fool who persists in his folly will become wise"—so he expected those who persisted to find the right way. As for Square Zen, the original Zen, the squares had a tendency to be uppity with the non-squares. That was all right, too. Watts' Zen could carry water on both shoulders and a bucket on the head as well. It was a great deal of fuss—even his essay was a great deal of fuss—ill-suiting Zen. So endeth the lesson.

守 微

CHAPTER TWENTY-TWO

GUARDING THE MINUTE

The Alan Watts who could take so statesmanlike a view of the misuse of Zen—and indeed, the abuse of his own position as a thinker in the field of religion and philosophy—was not the Alan Watts of eight years earlier. The Watts of 1959 was a serene man in a way, although his secret longings were to be found in his admiration for his friend Gary Snyder. That young man, going off to sit in a Zen monastery without a care in the world represented the Watts that might have been.

Watts had one problem that kept him from being as free as the bird that was Gary Snyder. He had a large family of children and a wife as anchor, a house in Mill Valley, and a sort of home life to which he must somewhat adhere.

This was his discipline, and one he felt so strongly that in later life he would write that it had been a mistake for him to become a family man. But that was the kind of mistake that had no undoing, save outright desertion. Watts was not the type for that.

Alan Watts was doing very well in 1958—very much better than the poor American Academy of Asian Studies. Ernest Wood was an old man, and he could not cope either with the exigencies of American economics or the demands of the College of the Pacific. Soon the college severed its connection with the school—and that was virtually the end of it. Haridas Chaudhuri went off to found his own Asian study institute. The rest of the faculty drifted away, and a hope disappeared into the fog above the bay.

As for Watts, he had offer after offer, and each more tempting than the last. He was asked to the Ivy League colleges—Yale, Harvard, Princeton—and waypoints between, and he commanded fees in four figures. His most impressive triumph came with an appointment to lecture at the C.G. Jung Institute in Zurich. This would give him a chance to return to Europe for the first time since the late 1930s.

On the way, Watts stopped off in New York to hold a seminar for a number of people who were interested in hearing his views. He charged $25 a person admission, which certainly was not cheap by 1958 standards.

Stephen Mahoney, a retired Beatnik, went to the seminar on behalf of *The Nation*, and reported on it, and on the Watts he saw there as well as the Watts described in *The Dharma Bums* by Kerouac.

The Watts he saw was our Watts—clean-cut, clear-eyed, crew-cut hair, youthful, and smiling and *alive*. Mahoney was much impressed by the U-accent (U meaning upper middleclass, and non-U meaning negative or lower middleclass) that was the intellectual rage then. Watts had everything going for him that day—his charm, his aura, his language. He was relaxed and his "gift of gab" shone forth like a bright star. He sat in an armchair in the big high-ceilinged room above 57th Street, the sounds of the city drifting through the open windows. And he spoke at three sessions, on a Friday, Saturday, and Sunday, saying what was in his books.

And Mahoney, who knew the people and the types, and the Kerouac book, presented another picture: of Alan Watts sitting on a log in coat and tie and trousers at "the biggest party of all time" held by the Beatniks in San Francisco, a party where some wandered about naked, others in their beads, and Watts in his "formal" clothes. In *Dharma Bums* he was the character Arthur Whane. He had conversations with the character Alvah Goldberg, who was in reality Allen Ginsberg. Whane-Watts also had conversations with Ray Smith, a heroic figure, and with Japhy Ryder, the hero-hero. They all climb Mt. Tamalpais and make appropriate remarks and do appropriate things about the beauty of it all. And in the end of Mahoney's presentation we have a picture of Two Zens—the Beat Zen, a dreadfully grimy way, and the Watts Zen, which is clean and clear and crewcut. And fashionable. My how it was fashionable in 1958. Watts had no trouble at all making a living. He was a hero.

The hero was glad to get away from home. Dorothy, his wife, was pressing him to settle down and live like other suburbanites. His wanderlust was pulling at him to live like a Zen priest. He did not regard himself as priest so much as philosopher-teacher (his term) who was concerned with his philosophy, with writing and teaching, and making the world into a little better place than it was that day. He was interested in ecology and the management of populations. He was interested in prison reform and the reform of mental institutions. He did some work in these fields, but he did not pick up cudgels in the way that Thomas Lask would have wanted him to. He was, above all, a propagator of Zen, and Zen does not hold with outrageous emotion to be attached to any cause. There are few Zen fanatics in the world—perhaps a lot of libertines—but few fanatics.

That year 1958 brought a new Watts book, which he finished before making the trip to the Jung Institute in Switzerland. *Nature, Man and Woman* was the title, and it was as different from anything he had written earlier as was *Myth and Ritual in Christianity.* But in its own way. It is not a Zen book as such. It is not a sex book, although it was called that. It is a love book, and the subject of the love is really *life.*

Watts argued for nature as opposed to science and technology—not the science of study, but the science of change, which seemed dedicated to the endless complication of human life. Here he brought forth the concepts and principles of the Tao, but in so gentle a fashion—unlike some of his past writings—that the reader had to go very carefully to understand that what he was getting here was the essence of Tao, as strained through the bright mind of guru Watts.

He had but recently been delving into Joseph Needham's monumental *Science and Civilization in China,* a work that was years and years in the making, in which Needham and any number of other scholars had gone back to trace the scientific aspects of Chinese life—or what the West called the scientific aspects.

Needham was then working on volume 3, and volume 2 was in print but just barely. One thing that was always obvious about Watts (as clear as his own expositions seemed to be) was his current reading. It was always reflected in the book he was writing. Needham and his findings on Chinese civilization were new, interesting, and "in." They found their way again and again into Watts' new book, although they were not strictly Tao, not strictly in line with the subject to which Watts had addressed himself.

To this reader *Nature, Man and Woman* is like one of Watts' addresses—I do not use the word speeches—in which he starts out in a low, mellifluous voice, with those broad A's that are so charming and disarming to the American ear, and then turns from one topic to another, like a handsome raccoon turning over the rocks of a stream. He is infinitely patient, infinitely slow-moving and careful, but he just keeps on turning over rocks, and delighting in what he finds beneath them.

Here we have a discussion of Japanese *yugen,* amplified by the words of the Chinese philosopher Chuang Tzu, and Chia Tao's poem about searching in the mountains, then a discussion of Alfred North Whitehead's scientific theories with a few Chinese words thrown in (by Watts, not Whitehead).

Then we race to a bit of J.P. Eckermann's *Conversations with Goethe* and the hodgepodge we have just traversed over (pages 82-83) leaves this reader breathless, confused, and impressed all at once, but mostly impressed by Alan Watts the word user, not Alan Watts the linear thinker.

By this time Watts had accustomed himself to the needs of the American society and had found the road to meet his own needs best by providing what was wanted and what would be paid for.

Little by little, Watts explained himself as he found himself. And as with every author, the process of writing was self-educating. He knew more when he had finished a book, and said what he wanted to say better by far than when he sat down at the desk to write.

The most formidable, indicative, and representative chapter in the book is the one entitled The World As Non-Sense. It is full of Non-Sense. This is the Tao as seen by Watts, and as known by him and interpreted by him. In a little poem, for example, he talks about the silver being white, and red being gold, and robes lying in fold. "The bailey beareth the bell away; The lily, the rose, the rose I lay."

Watts assures us that the words themselves are the meaning. The meaning of what? and to whom? And that is Watts' Zen, for they mean what you want them to mean. If that is not very satisfactory to the reader—then neither was Watts.

The key it seems, was here:

> *For as the nonsense of the madman is a babble of words for its own fascination, the nonsense of nature and of the sage is the perception that the ultimate meaninglessness of the world contains the same hidden joy as its transcience and emptiness. If we seek the meaning in the past, the chain of cause and effect vanishes like the wake of a ship. If we seek it in the future, it fades out like the beam of a searchlight in the night sky. If we seek it in the present, it is as elusive as flying spray, and there is nothing to grasp. But when only the seeking remains and we seek to know what this is, it suddenly turns into the mountains and waters, the sky and the stars, sufficient to themselves with no one left to seek anything from them.*

Watts again was chafing in his marriage, and the chapters on sex and love so indicated. But they were not so much an argument for freedom to love whom you would love, as a specific in how to do it, with attention paid to the teachings of yoga and other Asian forms. There is something about the way Watts tells of these things that indicates he is trying to tell us more—but is not yet ready to do so. He speaks of the partners, and the need for spontaneity and once again of *eros* and *agape.* He talks in terms of passion and death wishes—and it is all scientific, with many references to Asian and European mystics and psychologists, to say nothing of Kinsey, who is also cited. Somehow Watts is saying something to someone and no one quite knows what.

修 觀

CHAPTER TWENTY-THREE

THE CULTIVATION OF THE TAO AND THE OBSERVATION OF ITS EFFECTS

Perhaps Dorothy Watts knew. They were growing away from one another even though for a long time he tried to maintain the trappings of the suburban husband. His temptations were many—he was constantly having the same kind of sexual opportunities that he had enjoyed as chaplain at Northwestern, and that a psychiatrist receives from his upset, confused, neurotic and grateful female patients. How could he resist? He told the world in *Nature, Man and Woman* that he could *not* resist—and Dorothy began to get the message.

Under the auspices of the American Academy of Asian Studies small tour groups began to go to Japan, and soon Watts found that this was a good way to increase his income, and at the same time improve his expertise as an Orientalist. After all, in these days of easy travel, an Orientalist who had never been to the Orient was a ridiculous figure. He simply could not go on being a Zen teacher while he had never seen Zen in its native habitat. The remarkable thing is not that he went to Asia, but that anyone had taken him seriously *before* he went to Asia.

How much difference the Asian trips made is debatable. He visited his former mother-in-law, Abbess Ruth Sasaki, at her abbey, and he visited other Zen temples. He may have acquired some information or some insight that he had not held previously. It seems doubtful. He was primarily a tourist among tourists in Japan. He never made any particular pretensions about his trips, he played them down, for with his faulty command of the language there was no hope of being an expert. He was, really, on much sounder ground back in San Francisco climbing a trail along Mt. Tamalpais and meditating, or thinking about his next book or lecture.

In Japan, he was at the mercy of the real experts on the language and religion. But his insouciance carried him through. Mrs. Bergen Evans, wife of the teacher and TV personality, went on one of Watts' escorted journeys to Zen-land, and came home bubbling to her husband. Watts had done his job of charming and informing well. He *was* a tremendous entertainer, for the intellectual who wishes to believe his-her thought processes are being challenged and enriched.

One might say that *The Dharma Bums* made-Zen-made-Beat-made-Alan Watts. There would be a certain truth to that; the publication of the book brought new fame to Jack Kerouac and focused attention on San Francisco as the volcano from which was arising the cloud of counterculture. As the San Francisco *Chronicle's* Abe Mellinkoff put it, "Alan Watts was very big here." He was undoubtedly one of the handful of leaders of the San Francisco and northern California scene, along with Allen Ginsberg and Gary Snyder. Down south, especially around Los Angeles, it was a different scene, with Gerald Heard and Aldous Huxley playing approximately the Watts role, and literally hundreds of individuals doing their own thing—down south was always kookland,

and the people who lived at Big Sur and above were generally suspicious of anything below Santa Barbara.

Watts made many trips south to visit friends, temples of various kinds, to talk with other Zen enthusiasts and to hold seminars. He attempted to interest Dr. Robert Hutchins in various schemes. Hutchins had left the University of Chicago and gone to the Fund for the Republic, and then established the Center for Democratic Institutions at Santa Barbara—a shrewd move which set up Hutchins for life in pleasant surroundings, to do interesting studies, and effectively removed him from the center of American action. He has scarcely been heard of since, perhaps due to a certain mellowing process that caused him to reject the Watts schemes for spending Ford Foundation money.

So like most of the others of the Beat, and then Flower Child and Hippy and Peacenik generations and their leaders, Watts more or less went it alone. There were some foundation grants such as from Paul and Mima Mellon's Bollingen Foundation. They took an interest in the American Academy and tried to help save it. They made grants to Watts from time to time. By 1960 he hardly needed any more help; his books were bringing in healthy royalties twice a year, and his lectures were quite profitable. All the time he was learning the techniques of showmanship. Now he dressed in a black kimono not unlike a cassock in appearance, with a fan stuck in the belt, *a la Japonais*. He brought forth an easel and a big round Chinese brush, and drew Chinese characters to impress his listeners as he lectured. His calligraphy was getting better all the time. And he was busy as he could be.

One day, for example, he spent at Foothill College in San Francisco. At ten o'clock in the morning he gave a formal lecture with his trappings. Then he remained on campus all day long, meeting in the coffee shop with student groups for seminars and just plain bull sessions on the subjects of Zen and Oriental philosophy. At dusk there was a cocktail party and then a dinner for Watts, and at 8:15 he gave another lecture.

It was the way his days went—he was surrounded by young and admiring students and graduate students and faculty members of both sexes—and Dorothy was out in Mill Valley taking care of their brood of children.

On weekends Watts might be home, being nagged by his wife to mow the lawn, like a thousand other Mill Valley husbands. Alan Watts mow the lawn? The thought would send Buddha-chuckles coursing along the rich ripe bellies of Watts' Buddha friends.

There was the rub. The second Mrs. Watts wanted an American life. Mill Valley is an unutterably lovely area, sunny and bright and clean, just north of San Francisco in Marin County. It is full of intellectuals, college people, writers, artists, philosophers, and the retired who knew where to go for happiness. For most of them it is happiness American style, which includes the power lawnmower, the dishwasher, the Volkswagen bus for a flock of kids, a husband who putters with repairs, friends for cocktails and dinner, television, and maybe even the movies.

Watts, by his own admission, was not cut out to be a family man, not just because of his affairs outside the master bedroom, but because what he called "a colossal family enterprise" dulled his style, threw him into depression, and kept him upset much of the time. He was a free spirit—he said—and he simply had to be free. By 1960 Watts was growing very restless under the strictures of family life.

He was writing well, he always wrote well, and better as time went on. That year he published *This is It,* not truly a book but a collection of his more important magazine articles on Zen. He was established with Pantheon, a division of Random House, and this book was brought out by that firm. The *Beat Zen, Square Zen and Zen* essay was there. So was another well-known piece, *Zen and the Problem of Control,* which had first appeared in *Contact* and then as a booklet put out by the enterprising City Lights Books of San Francisco.

For the first time, Watts now began to speak of some of his own religious experiences.

Around 1933 after he had first begun to study Indian and Chinese philosophy he was sitting by the fire preparing to meditate one day. He pondered what attitude he should adopt to meditate in a manner of the Hindus and Buddhists. Several possibilities occurred to him and he tried to combine them—to no avail. In disgust he gave up, and as he discarded the planned attitudes, suddenly he felt light.

> *I felt that I owned nothing, not even a self, and that nothing owned me. The whole world became as transparent and unobstructed as my own mind; the "problem of life" simply ceased to exist. . . .*

Another of these experiences came years later when he had been involved in an unusually intensive "discipline"—for Alan Watts. He had been attempting to practice smriti, which to the Buddhists is constant awareness of the immediate present.

One evening someone asked him why he wanted to live in the present. Was he not completely in the present, even when he was thinking about the past or the future?

The remark gave Watts the same sensation that he had enjoyed that other time as a student. He had no weight. He floated. The present became a "kind of moving stillness, an eternal stream from which neither I nor anything could deviate. I saw that everything just as it is now is IT—is the whole point of there being life and a universe."

It was satori.

And *This Is It* became the title of the new book.

Watts revealed that he had since had the sensations of satori a number of times.

The second essay in the new book dealt with the matters of instinct, intelligence, and anxiety, the third with Zen and control of human emotions. In this latter, Watts gave his best definition yet of Zen:

> *. . . the adept in Zen is one who manages to be human with the same artless grace and absence of inner conflict with which a tree is a tree. Such a man is likened to a ball in a mountain stream, which is to say that he cannot be blocked, stopped, or embarrassed in any situation. He never wobbles or dithers in his mind for though he may pause in overt action to think a problem out, the stream of his consciousness always moves straight ahead without being caught in the vicious circles of indecisive doubt, wherein thought whirls wildly around*

> *without issue. He is not precipitate or hurried in action, but simply continuous. That is what Zen means by being detached—not being without emotion or feeling, but being one in whom feeling is not stuck or blocked, and through whom the experiences of the world pass like the reflections of birds flying over water. Although possessed of complete inner freedom, he is not, like the self-righteous, trying to justify himself. He is all of a piece with himself and with the natural world, and in his presence you feel that without strain or artifice he is completely "all here"—sure of himself without the slightest trace of aggression. He is thus the* grand seigneur, *the spiritual aristocrat comparable to the type of worldly aristocrat who is so sure of the position given to him by birth that he has no need to condescend or put on airs . . .*

Here is the man who has attained satori. For the first time in his writings we gather that Alan Watts is that man himself.

It shows in his writing and in the man. He was completely confident, easy and friendly, and living the life he liked. He was moving about the country, the principal apostle of Zen in America, and Zen was becoming very big on the college campuses and in the dens of the intellectuals.

The year 1961 was notable for his new book *Psychotherapy East and West,* for his breach with his family, his adoption of a whole new set of friends, his third important love affair, and his emergence as a "celebrity," attested to by *Life,* which devoted a spread that year to this elusive teacher of Orientalia.

The *Life* article showed him, youngish as ever, slender, short-haired and handsome, pondering a discovered spider web at the home of a friend at Big Sur. He was down there more and more, as he and Mary Jane, his new lady-love, sought companionship and interest in others outside the old Watts framework. He was shown grading entries in a haiku poetry contest, wearing white shirt, neat tie and suit jacket. He was Zen, but what a civilized Zen; he came on strong even with the conservative community; no sandals and ragged jeans or dirty robes for this teacher. He was shown at his desk, at work on a scroll, in a lecture at Brandeis University in Boston, in a New York studio with friends, and even at home with his four children.

He had made the big time.

One must admire Alan Watts for many things, accomplishments, feats, and points of character. One of the points of character was his ability to make use of virtually every experience that ever passed beneath that sensitive aquiline nose. In his new book he delved back to the Spiegelberg lectures and the Jung lectures of his London days, to the psychotherapists he had known there, and in New York, and since. And his new book was devoted to the whole concept of psychotherapy, neurosis, and the ways of the West and of the East in dealing with these troubles.

Those who have claimed that Alan Watts was a faker and entertainer only must not have read *Psychotherapy East and West.* It would have been easy enough for Watts to stick to the "Zen kick" and to make his living from that field, for there was opportunity enough. His 100 lectures a year around the country told him that. Those audiences were not very demanding. Zen was In, they wanted to be told about Zen, Watts was its American guru, so they tried to get Watts to explain.

But here was Watts doing something quite different, something of which pure Zenists would not approve at all. Nor could a true disciple have this to say:

> *I do not believe that the Eastern disciplines are the last word in sacrosanct and immemorial wisdom such that the world must come and sit humbly at the feet of their masters. Nor do I feel that there is a Gospel according to Freud, or to Jung, in which the great psychological truths are forever fixed. The aim of this book is not to say the last word on the subject, but to provoke thought and experiment. . .*

His discussion was slick and fast-moving and had the ring of tremendous erudition, as always. And indeed, in this field of psychology, Watts was tremendously learned; he had been educating himself with all that nervous energy for these nearly 30 years. In his credits in the book he went back to Eric Graham Howe, his old friend, the Harley Street consultant, and to Professor Spiegelberg. And there were others, from his Jung Institute period when he went to Zurich to lecture on Zen, and Joseph Campbell, the mythology expert, and many another. He could not resist the opportunity (he must have felt the need) to drop a few more names.

He had been, he said, associated in the past with many a fine institution, including the Yale Medical School, the Langley-Porter Clinic of the University of California, the C.G. Jung Institute in Zurich, the Washington School of Psychiatry, the Palo Alto Veterans Hospital, the Stanford Medical School . . .

Now there is nothing inherently wrong in this listing. Yet it is vague, and simply mixed up a lot of unmixables: e.g., to compare the C.G. Jung Institute in Zurich with the Palo Alto Veterans Hospital, in any connection, any language, any way, is simply absurd, and makes the reader flinch a little and scratch his head about Watts' bonafides. This was the showman overdoing his act.

Or to put it another way: Alan Watts was a self-styled "showman" of philosophy. By so saying about himself, he removed his image from serious consideration by the academic world. He, Watts, insisted as loudly as anyone that he was part charlatan. In this, of course, he recognized that Jung and Freud were showmen too. But they would not admit to this demeaning posture; by their assumption of superhuman dignity they attained it in the eyes of others.

Let us suppose for a moment that Alan Watts had as great a contribution to make to Western humanity in *Psychotherapy East and West* as many another student of psychology who wrote for the textbook field. Does anyone think the academic world would take Watts so seriously—particularly after he was known to admit that his basic purpose on earth was to enjoy himself? It would do no good in this sense to say that Watts was right and his detractors wrong.

He was just too slick an operator for the people in the trade.

So psychotherapy was another excursion into the Wattsian world of the conscious and unconscious minds, and it was apparently lucid and persuasive as was Watts always. Many pages of appended bibliographical notes lent verisimilitude to the facts. There was considerable repetition of some of the old Watts phrases such as "*Omne animal triste post coitum est,*" (Every animal is sad after coitus) which seemed to fascinate him. And as always, the outsider leaves the book ready to applaud a virtuoso number, but not quite sure that he has been convinced of anything, and wondering if it is all a giant put-on.

The reviewer for the London *Times* felt that way about Watts' work. It made him uneasy, he said. Speaking of his work, the Indian Ranjee Shahani wrote in *Saturday Review* that year that Watts was very quick to put down Hinduism and Hinayana Buddhism, and very quick to up the banner of Zen. "Words-words and mouthy," is how this savant characterized Watts.

Thus the reader can see that Watts was not an inconsiderable character. In the days of Kipling, a Westerner writing about the East was bound to be held by Eastern thinkers as beneath contempt—and probably he would have been. Now here was Watts writing about the East, even though he had spent virtually no time there. At least one thing could be said of all this: through the printed word, through translation, what Alan Watts read and digested and spewed forth was the intertwining of two worlds. It could no longer be said that East was East and West was West, for the twain were meeting all the time and the Easterners felt no compunction about criticizing Watts on the grounds he took. They even took him seriously, which probably was a surprise to Watts in the beginning, and then taken gratefully and finally casually. Thus were the pleasures and pains of public worship met.

Privately, Watts' life was again in crisis. All this moving around had led him to abandon his last ties with the family life that Dorothy Watts wanted, and to take up with the young lady he now called Jano. (He dedicated his *Psychotherapy East and West* to her in 1960 when he wrote the last pages.) So it was inevitable in the Watts karma that the second marriage would end in divorce. It did in February, 1962, when Dorothy DeWitt Watts filed for divorce in San Rafael, charging that he had deserted her and the five children, aged one to ten. So he had now given up two wives and a total of seven children for his art. In due course the divorce was granted, Watts went off to live the life he loved, accompanied by Jano, who became the third Mrs. Watts, and Dorothy Dewitt settled back into the house on LaVerne Avenue in Mill Valley, to collect $700 a month in support payments for herself and the children. Watts was free, but the price of freedom came high.

CHAPTER TWENTY-FOUR

INCREASE OF EVIDENCE

Alan Watts was no longer dismayed by anything. He had his philosophy and he was happy with the new, young Mrs. Watts. And he had a whole big group of freethinkers and artists and unbound intellectuals to whom he could turn for companionship and solace. Some lived in Mill Valley. Some, like Elsa Gidlow, lived down in Big Sur country near Henry Miller. Watts never got to know Miller well, but he knew many of the others, and he moved south to visit with Aldous Huxley and other students of the strange ways of men and spirits.

Intellectualy, he was free as a bird, and when the question of Zen came up, so did the name of Alan Watts. When Bobbs-Merrill brought out a book by Actor Sessue Hayakawa about Zen, the

Saturday Review chose Alan Watts to review the book, and although Hayakawa was a Japanese with six years of formal training in Zen, Alan found it not at all hard to take the Japanese lightly and denigrate his views on Zen. Watts remarked airily that Hayakawa really did not know what he was talking about, or at least did not say enough to indicate that he knew.

> *I do not wish to suggest that Mr. Hayakawa's reticence about the more interesting aspects of Zen is due to ignorance. It is more probably attributable to the Japanese feeling that nothing can be said about them which I find fainthearted because great literature and poetry are always attempts to express the inexpressible. When it comes to writing about Zen one must either put up or shut up. For if it is really true that its meaning cannot be put into words then one should not write about it at all. [Precisely the feeling of many Zen masters.] My own feeling is that Zen is no less expressible in words than any other form of life, and that if one refuses to describe it, then one should also refuse to describe the natural landscape or the subtleties of human character.*

How Watts had blossomed forth in every way.

His horoscope foretold it all. Here are Ms. Carter's raw notes:

> *. . .Periodic psychic abilities. A rich imagination and inner life. Were it not for strong Capricorn planets, you really wouldn't* do *anything, you can get such pleasure from your own mind, day dreams . . . fantasies . . . enough air, fresh air necessary.*
>
> *You are a natural politician, having a great respect for tradition, and yet being far sighted and innovative enough to see what is needed in the future. . . .*

In that connection Watts was exploring all the time the methods in which Zen could be adjusted to American life, or ways in which the two might be brought together. And as for the modern intellectuals he *was* the voice of Zen, and one of the leading "authorities" on Asian thought. When his friend Joseph Campbell brought out his *The Masks of God: Oriental Mythology*, the *Saturday Review* chose Watts above all others to report. Watts did not think the work as presented was particularly adequate and so reported, although he faulted the publisher for cutting the book more than he faulted Campbell's presentation.

The fact was that Alan Watts was involved himself in working with myth at the moment, and there may have been a jot of personal displeasure in the Campbell book for him. George Braziller, the esoteric New York publisher, had asked Alan Watts about a series of books on myth—*The Pattern of Myth*—of which Watts' contribution would be the book *The Two Hands of God.*

When the San Francisco *Chronicle* learned of the series, its editors asked Watts to explain what he was up to and he obliged in an article, suggesting something that Joseph Campbell seemed to have already rejected—that there was a collective unconscious mind at work in the universe, because the same general myths kept popping up at disparate places in the world.

Because Watts was interested, Ed Seaver, the editor at Braziller, chose him to edit this series. Then the adventure began. Watts wrote,

> *This wasn't easy, for the simple reason that there are very few competent mythologists, and that two of the best of them, Mircea Eliade and Joseph Campbell—were tied up with other writing projects. However, after brainstorming with a number of scholars, we selected six predominant themes and six author-editors to present them with appropriate introduction.*
>
> *The themes were the myths of Creation, of Death and Resurrection, of Polarity (the interdependence of opposites, such as light and darkness, male and female), of the Hero, of the Goddess, and of the Royal Father (or the God-King). Each volume was planned primarily as an anthology of texts and images (carrying from 23 to 32 illustrations) with running comments by its author-editor. . .*

It was interesting to see how Watts worked with this task and the names that came to him:

> *In default of Mircea Eliade, we got the next best thing, his number one student, Charles Long, now teaching at the University of Chicago, to write on the Myths of Creation out of his special knowledge of African and Polynesian sources. For the Myths of Death and Resurrection I picked two collaborators with a Jungian background, Dr. Joseph Henderson—dean of the Jungian analysts of San Francisco—and Maud Oakes of Big Sur, well known as an amateur anthropologist with special interests in the Navajo and Guatemalan Indians. And for the*

Myths of Polarity I picked myself, because the subject of the hidden unity of opposites has gone along with Zen Buddhism and Taoism as one of my main interests for many years . . .

The series offered Watts a new recognition—he was a popular figure in popular philosophy. Thus opened Watts' happiest years as a person. He had shucked off his family and was living just the way he wanted to live.

Yet there were tinges of a new bitterness:

"To hear her (Dorothy) speak of me, you would think I was the worst person that ever lived" he later told Margaret Jacobson when they met.

When the break with Dorothy had come, Watts had fled to Mt. Tamalpais, cursing the "suburban dormitory culture" he was leaving, and running to the "pad" of his friend Roger Somers, a free spirit, carpenter, and jack of all trades.

"So there it was," Watts wrote in his autobiography, "that I found a new self, . . . where we could strip to the waist, bang on drums, dance and chant through most of the night, or accompanying Charlotte (Selver) to similar uproars in Charlie Brook's Greenwich Village loft on Saturday nights after we had worked all day on our joint seminars . . ."

Happiness is.

Watts had many friends in East and West. Elsa Gidlow, his conferee in the series on myth, was living then on the edge of Mt. Tamalpais, writing and keeping busy in her garden. He met Ella Young, a charming old lady who taught Watts that plants are *people* and must be treated as such. (He was later bemused by experiments showing that plants responded to music and human talk.) And here and at Big Sur, he got to know Jean Burden, the poet and cat lady, Kenneth Rexroth, James Broughton, and many others as friends. These were the people he talked with, the people he did haiku with, the people he showed his calligraphy and discoursed with on problems of Zen. Dorothy Watts would not have fit in with these people at all. Dr. Joseph Henderson was one of the crowd—that's how he got the writing asignment for the myth series, for as Watts got to know Henderson, he (Watts) decided that Henderson was the spiritual heir to Jung. (This statement, out of the Watts autobiography, is the kind of simple arrogation that made many people turn from Watts in derision). These were the counterculture people, and they lived lives that were marked apparently by never-ending gaiety. Watts devoted an entire section of his autobiography to them, and it is the liveliest part of the book.

At this same time Watts was still poking around in Los Angeles and at Big Sur for sensation and new experience. Eugene Exman, his old editor at Harper's, encountered him in southern California, where Exman was moving about among the various philosophical and religious types, looking for books. Exman was strongly impressed with the change in Watts.

"He had been fresh and young and very sincere when I knew him in New York," said Exman. "He seemed changed, somehow very cynical. He was not at all the same person."

Watts probably would not have quarreled with that statement, or he would have laughed his big laugh and quoted from the Tao or its followers to the effect that the present *is*, and that the past is always seen as memory from the present, and that Exman's Watts of 1940 would not be Dorothy's Watts or Eleanor's Watts, or Ruth Sasaki's Watts, or even Watts' Watts. There is no future, there is no past, there is only present. That is the universe—at least it was Alan Watts' idea of the Zen universe.

So it was. In California it was mostly the Big Sur crowd and the Mill Valley wild ones. In New York it was Charlotte Selver and Charles Brooks, son of Van Wyck Brooks, and other friendly souls.

But Watts managed to keep track of old friends too. And to belie the charge that he had gone cynical was the joy with which he greeted their successes, and the pleasantness with which he assessed the old days. He was writing to Margaret Jacobson off in Paris at about this time. He was seeing a good deal of his old student, now the Reverend Robert Morse of the Episcopal church in the Piedmont section of Oakland. He was cheering Morse on just then as the young minister was "locked in mortal theological combat", as Watts put it, with the authorities.

"He couldn't even make it with Bishop Pike!" Watts laughed.

And Watts was seeing Emerson Harris, who had gone on to become associated with various space science projects, and others of the old Evanston and New York days.

No cynicism there. Not even any bitterness really toward his second wife, Dorothy, whom he now chose to describe as "a girl who turned out to be a total and militant suburbanite."

Many of Watts' old students at Evanston believed that Dorothy had been married for the raising of the children—which was scarcely true since Watts soon sent them off. She *had been* the babysitter at the Canterbury House a good deal of the time. And she *had* looked a good deal like Eleanor and Watts' mother, hearty and matronly.

Whatever the Freudianism of it, Watts did not seem to be so very, very unhappy.

And he had managed to keep the love and respect of his children of two marriages. His elder daughters kept in touch and he enjoyed their husbands, who were creative in their own ways (one as a musician).

He was having a good time.

Even in writing about it in the 1970s Watts exudes the atmosphere of good times and friendship that were in evidence here.

Watts and Jano had been living aboard a disused ferryboat, the S.S. *Vallejo,* deeply involved with the new culture that included drugs and parties and praying sessions and a good deal of honest work, at least for Watts and Jean Varda, the artist who shared the ferryboat with them. Watts was principal guru of the area, and he would be one of the major figures in promotion of the flower children's haven in Haight-Ashbury—before it became a sticky mess of hashish and penny candy and dropped off into a mugging station. He recorded Japanese poetry (doing the English part), conducted his seminars, and traveled widely about the country to speak and be with young people at the colleges.

Artist Varda, who was called Yanko, owned a sailboat called the *Perfidia,* rigged up like an Arab *dhow,* and many a pleasant day was spent aboard this craft in the glistening blue water of the bay or passing through the strong tide and current outside the Golden Gate and its huge red bridge.

This was Alan Watts' bohemia, a rich compendium of sights and smells and women and ideas, and liquor and LSD and pot and irreverent people who were all doing their own thing.

"There are great people in your sign and planet stellums," wrote Alan Watts' astrologer. "They are Darwin and Lincoln, Edison, Bacon, Kepler and Pasteur, for example." But Watts was content with the people around him. The cover copy of Collier Books' *The Two Hands of God* would call him "one of the most influential philosophers and teachers of our time."

What more could a simple philosopher-teacher-showman want?

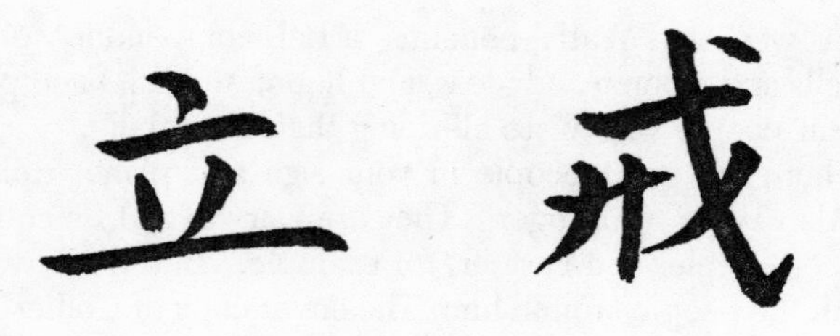

CHAPTER TWENTY-FIVE

CAUTIONS

In the middle of the 1960s Alan Watts had become the high priest of Zen in America. Back in the 1950s he had experimented with LSD under medically controlled conditions. He continued to experiment, under his own conditions. He knew there was a difference between the effects of satori and LSD hallucination—he had written about them, but he was interested in both and was working with both. These might be called The Drug Years, these middle years of the decade, for Alan Watts and other leaders of the counterculture in America. Drugs, however, were only a part of the Watts scene. It was, as he put it, a question of culture. "All culture," he said one day in response to a newspaper interviewer, "is a game of where do we draw the line?"

Watts made that statement when he was called as a character witness in the trial of a pair of gallery owners on charges of showing obscene statuary in a San Francisco gallery. Ron Boise, the sculptor, had made some lifelike and very active figures. The Vorpal Gallery in North Beach was showing them, and a pair of San Francisco traffic cops, stopping to write a few tickets on the block, looked in the window of the gallery, and promptly went inside and arrested Muldoon Elder and Michael Stafford, the proprietors.

The Puritanism of San Francisco copdom is to be taken for granted—what was unusual here was the awe that Alan Watts inspired in the community so that he would be called as a defense character witness.

Sculptor Ron Boise was to be congratulated, said Watts. Boise was pushing the cultural line back in his statues of copulation, just as Henry Miller and other writers had been doing in literature. In the 1920s and 1930s Henry Miller was an "obscene" writer, his books were published in Paris by Olympia Press, and most of his work was banned in the United States. He became a famous American author only because he stubbornly insisted on retaining his American identity in the face of ostracism for many years. In the 1960s Miller was a tame duck, an acquaintance of Watts, living quietly in Big Sur and minding his own business. Nobody considered him obscene or a menace any more, for literature had caught up with him.

In court and by the *Chronicle* Watts was identified as "a research fellow of the Harvard University Department of Social Relations and a resident of Sausalito."

Alan Watts was taken seriously indeed in San Francisco in 1964.

What he had to say was admirable in an American society looking quite the other way. American culture by and large seemed dedicated to violence; while love was seldom seen on network TV screens, murder was seen every day.

"They don't depict the consummation of love but they do depict the consummation of violence. Such work as Boise's could counteract the American obsession with violence and put love in its place."

As usual, Alan Watts was well ahead of his time. It would not be so long before they were not only *representing* the consummation of love on the screen but also showing it actually being performed, and *Deep Throat,* the controversial movie that could hardly be said to be about love, would show a different kind of sex.

The important matter in these middle years was that Watts had achieved tremendous respectability in America, and that he had done so in spite of the fact that he was a known LSD user. At Harvard Watts got to know Timothy Leary and he learned a good deal about the drug culture. One could scarcely say that Watts was primarily interested in drugs himself. They were a sideline issue—he could do without drugs what Timothy Leary did with LSD and it seemed much more satisfactory to Watts.

He was, however, enough into drugs that the *New Republic* called on Watts when it came time to review Dr. Sydney Cohen's book, *The Beyond Within: the LSD Story.*

The Watts review was as challenging as the book, perhaps more so, for while Psychiatrist Cohen predictably suggested that LSD and similar drugs be controlled by psychiatry, Watts offered another, broader view:

> *Yet when it comes to LSD and other methods of controlling or changing consciousness, who is wise? Few people are yet aware that one of the trickiest issues of the future—along with population control, atomic power, and the rest, is the problem of* neuropolitics. *By chemical, electrical, and other methods it will soon be possible to control the nervous system more effectively than ever, and this will put us in sight of being able to mold human character and emotion. And what types of character and emotions ought to be cultivated, and who will be allowed to remain uncultivated.*

In other words, who was to control drugs?

Alan Watts had some revolutionary ideas on the subject.

> *We will probably have to recognize that the transformation of consciousness and personality, whether by Yoga or LSD, is basically a religious problem, entitled to the same constitutional protection as freedom of worship. Our difficulty in accepting this is the inability to see that LSD enthusiasts stand*

> *today where Quakers and Presbyterians stood in the 17th Century, when they were regarded as perverts and lunatics and public menaces. . . .*
>
> *. . .In the end we shall doubtless have to regulate the psychedelics as we regulate such other dangers as alcohol, automobiles and firearms—with liberal licensing and strict rules of use. Too many people have become interested in these chemicals to keep them suppressed much longer, and by now we should have learned that prohibition simply passes their control to criminals and incompetent manufacturers, and their use is forced into clandestine circumstances where the psychiatrist and the minister cannot even be asked to advise.*

Alan Watts was stepping out of his role—he was taking a public position on a grave social matter and one well within his field of expertise. Had Watts been heeded this early in the game, poor floundering Timothy Leary might have gone on to become a respectable guru of the drug scene in fact, rather than a fugitive from justice and an exile in Africa, simply because of bad judgment and the flouting of a legal mechanism that has proved no more successful in controlling *any* drugs in America than the federal government proved in controlling alcohol in the 1920s. Watts knew that this kind of control would fail. He was right. It has failed. In the meantime the drug merchant would prosper and the addict would suffer, just as the bootlegger and rumrunner prospered and the drinkers suffered in the painful years of prohibition.

As the drug debate gathered steam in America, in the middle years of the 1960s, Alan Watts found himself in the middle of it, representing the sane side of the counterculture.

In the summer of 1965, Watts appeared for the first time in years in an Episcopal church. Drugs brought him there.

The scene was the Christ Episcopal Church in Sausalito. The characters were Watts, Bishop James A. Pike of the Protestant Episcopal church, and a number of concerned citizens who had set up a panel discussion of the marijuana problem in America.

The Bishop was the headlined character—he played the leading role. How it must have come back to Watts that night, as he later wrote, that had he remained within the fold of Mother Church, he might well have come to occupy a position as potent as that of Pike. That Bishop had not yet found that he had to go his own way, in the same manner that Watts had done so many years before. At this time, Pike was representing the "new look" in Episcopal churchmen, the look of concerned, liberal citizens, ready to break with tradition in order to satisfy the demands of a youthful society, yet to keep that society under the roof of organized religion.

The panel was called to discuss marijuana. Somehow all the troublesome subjects managed to come up at once, and in the same breath the participants were talking about Vietnam and the dreadful war there, nuclear war and the dreadful threat there, and marijuana.

All part of the same problem, said Watts. Teenagers were afraid of what was going to happen to the planet, so they smoked pot and worried.

And then they all agreed that pot was no more harmful than a laxative, not as harmful as cigarettes, that all the fuss should be toned down, that investigations should continue into the effects of drugs. Then they all went home.

Home to Watts was still the S.S. *Vallejo*—the old ferryboat. He and Jano had fixed it up, brought in his thousands of books, set up a fireplace, covered the floors with Japanese *tatami* and decorated with a small altar and a Buddha figure.

Sometimes Watts married his friends here. Even those who considered that the license was all that was necessary (and maybe not even that) were inclined to want the ministrations of some figure of authority—and Watts enjoyed being a priest.

"You are a priest forever," said Watts' friend Canon Bernard Iddings Bell, when Alan Watts left the ministry to travel along the uncharted path of his future. And of course it was true. He was a priest and he loved conducting religious ceremonies.

But his visitors and strangers could not understand just what kind of priest or what kind of creature the Alan Watts of the 1960s had become. San Francisco *Chronicle* feature writer Monique Benoit went out to Sausalito one day to visit Watts and discover just who he was. When she returned, and wrote her article, with a picture of a smiling Alan Watts, young and debonair as ever—the photo was captioned "half angel-half devil." Watts was fifty years old then. He did not look forty.

Miss Benoit was puzzled by the man she saw in sport shirt and slacks, lounging in this comfortable living room.

"I have always associated Buddhism with asceticism; you don't strike me as being an ascetic," she said.

Alan Watts laughed. "I am not a Buddhist or any other kind of IST. I am a bridge builder. My interest in Buddhism is an interpretation of Eastern thought to the West."

There was as clear and simple an explanation of the serious Alan Watts as had ever been given, by him or by anyone else. And there was a pattern to him, of course—ever since the days when he sat with Christmas Humphreys in London, he had been doing just that. All that Watts had done—if you examine it from that point of view—fitted into the mold. He had trained in England, he had seen in New York that the audience for the Orientalist was minor, he had hoped to find his place in the church, and he had failed. "I am much too Bohemian," he told Miss Benoit. He could laugh about it now, 15 years later. ". . . when you are a minister people stop treating you like an ordinary person; they put a halo around you. I couldn't take all that respectability," he said—and to show the lady that he was half devil and half angel, as he described mankind the angel gave her a recipe for paté and the devil a little lecture.

"Unfortunately people have the notion that if you speak of religion and at the same time enjoy the sensuous you are a hypocrite.

". . . But if you are a minister or a religious man and it is found out that you are sleeping with your secretary you are accused of being a hypocrite too. . . ."

Miss Benoit went away with plenty to think about. She liked the paté. What she thought of the deviltry she did not say.

For reasons of taxes and other financial problems arising from his marriages, in the 1960s as the money rolled in Alan Watts and his friends set up the Society for Comparative Philosophy which would sponsor his work, and when he died would carry it on insofar as possible. One of the early tasks was to handle the rights to *Beyond Theology: The Art of Godmanship,* which Watts delivered to Pantheon in 1964.

This book is an odd one in the Watts panoply. In a way it is a vicious little book, intended to strike back at organized Christianity in a way that would have been more understandable in 1950 than in 1964.

In the preface, Watts gave his reason for this new work:

> *My previous discussions did not take proper account of that whole aspect of Christianity which is uncompromising, ornery, militant, rigorous, imperious and invincibly self-righteous . . . developments are now swelling into a crisis on every level of human life—a crisis that cannot be handled unless we know among other things, the role that Christianity has played in bringing it about. . . .*

When Watts' ire was aroused by the Vietnam war and other developments in American life, he set out with this theme, and secured support from Laurance Rockefeller and the Bollingen Foundation again—to give him the leisure to write the book.

Beyond Theology is a wideranging gymnastic in search of God and a plea for the modernization of Christianity to eliminate the old hardshell beliefs and wipe away the sexual taboos—both facets of religion that were turning off the young of the Western world by the millions. No matter what Watts said about the church, his statements remind the reader that he is a reformer, not a revolutionary. He was not trying in this book to convert Young America to Zen Buddhism; in fact he was not even a professing Buddhist, as he told Ms. Benoit in that clear statement. Sure, he was labelled as the Prophet of Zen, but that was the American press speaking; having put the round peg in the round hole, the press pounded away at it.

Many of the ideas that Watts expounded in *Beyond Theology* were also presented by Christian theologists. Particularly in this book Watts hit the theme of *surrender*, and of course St. Augustine and others called on people to surrender themselves to God. It is in the trappings of God, the body of belief, that Watts could not bear witness with his Christian neighbors, and he insisted that the matters of belief and sexual custom were matters for the individual and not for the church to regulate.

Reading *Beyond Theology* the assessor comes to the strong conclusion that had Bishop Conkling been able to ignore the rumors about Alan Watts—or going further back, had Eleanor Everett Watts not so spitefully sought annulment instead of divorce—the Christian church would not have lost a priest. As Watts said himself, several times, his advocacies matched those of Bishop James Pike, who managed to remain in the church until he too was pulled away by the same basic reason. If the church could free itself from regulating the morality of its priests, it would have kept them both. Yes—would say the churchman—and if the church did that it would no longer be the church or have any right to be.

So there was Watts' eternal dilemma and if it still bothered him, which he denied, at least he was living the joyous life.

Unlike some of Watts' other works, there is relatively little of himself in this one. He tells some revealing tales that expose his essential Western outlook and strengthen his own statement that he could not possibly be a Zen Buddhist with his outlook.

Though the book rambles, it is what critics of the 1970s called in their lamentable jargon "a good read" and that is what always characterized Alan Watts' writing. There was something hypnotic about the man as he stood in his handsome splendor, casual, at ease, telling his tales before his Chinese calligraphy, or when he spun them out on the typewriter with all their artful artlessness. He *was* the showman he claimed to be, but more than that, Alan Watts was primarily a communicator. He *got to* people.

CHAPTER TWENTY-SIX

THE OPERATION OF THE TAO

Near the end of *Beyond Theology,* Alan Watts revealed his inner urges and deep beliefs of the 1960s, and the cosmology that had replaced theology in his personal view of the making of the universe.

> *My own feeling is that the most that should be claimed for any metaphysic, theology, or cosmology which is trying to say something about the way things are, about how the universe really works, is plausibility. For what one needs in this universe is not certainty but the courage and nerve of the gambler; not fixed convictions, but adaptability; not firm ground whereon to stand, but skill in swimming. Certainty might well be desirable in a universe where everlasting damnation is a real possibility.*

But, seriously, is it plausible to conceive our universe as something run on the lines of the Egyptian, Persian, and Byzantine monarchies with their thrones and judgments and their dungeons, torture chambers, and scaffolds?

No, Watts had perfected his cosmology, and it was simple; he called it "Negative Theology."

> *It is complete letting go. . . . Such letting go cannot be attained. It cannot be acquired or developed through perseverance and exercises, except insofar as such efforts prove the impossibility of acquiring it. Letting go comes only through desperation. When you know that it is beyond you—beyond your powers of action as beyond your powers of relaxation. When you give up every last trick and device for getting it, including this "giving up" as something that one might* do, *say, at ten o'clock tonight. That you cannot by any means do it—that IS it!* That *is the mighty self-abandonment which gives birth to the stars.*

So Watts in 1965 had gone beyond theology by his own statement and into cosmology. He was highly regarded in the upper reaches of the mystical intellectual community, as well as the flower-moving-to-hippy culture. He was also liked and respected by another group, not particularly organized, but very prominent in the California culture—the free spirits of Mill Valley and Big Sur. Of course many of these souls lived elsewhere—the freest of them sought places where the others did not congregate, and thus escaped being written about and gawked upon and considered "oddballs" if not "freaks." As Alan Watts noted about the good conservative middleclass: once the wild souls had found a place like Sausalito or Big Sur or Mill Valley, and had settled in there to do their thing, along came the good conservative souls and crowded them. It was the same with the wildest—they found the place and their own kind came in and pushed them higher into the hills. It is the Watts theory working there too.

In a way Watts had now come so far as to be a member of the "establishment"—a concept he would have resisted if you accused him. But it was true nonetheless. He wrote for *Saturday Review, The New Republic, Playboy,* and other commercial magazines. When a book review of psychoanalysis or Zen was called for, as like as not, Alan Watts would be the reviewer. When the people of Druid Heights—that is the section of Marin County that his kooky friends inhabited—wanted a moving spirit, why Alan Watts was always there. Like the old Zen masters, he denied disciples. He did not do this as a reverse psychological sales effort, as some thought, but because he did not need any disciples, and it was the tradition of the Tao to deny them. In many ways Watts was an old-fashioned thinker.

One of the books that established Watts in a way, with both the old and the new, was *The Joyous Cosmology*, a book about life itself, with a large sprinkling of notes about drug use. In this period those serious young Ph.D.s at Harvard named Richard Alpert and Timothy Leary were so impressed with what Watts was doing with the printed word that they wrote an impressive foreword to his book. For two years the eminently respectable university had been encouraging and financing Alpert and Leary in their Center for Research in Personality, and the pair had been carrying out a careful research in the use of mind-expanding drugs. Watts had taken drugs with them under controlled conditions. So had many others. The researchers were delighted with their results and with Alan Watts' description of them and said so in their preface.

This Watts book was indeed different from his previous works. In one way it was a handbook for the drug culture. It gave the history and dosages of drugs.

Alan Watts now contradicted himself. Earlier, having experimented with drugs, he said there was a difference between the experiences of mystical insight and drug expansion of the mind. Now he said there was essentially *no* difference. He had a caveat, he did not mention his own experiences here, but those of R. M. Bucke, William James, Evelyn Underhill, and Raynor Johnson. Why not himself? Was he copping out in the acid test? The question is not answered. Perhaps he was trying to make Leary and Alpert happy. Perhaps he had changed his mind in his further experiments with LSD.

The essence of the *Joyous Cosmology* is a 50-page, mind-expanding report on a "trip." Actually it represents several sessions with LSD, but for artistic purposes, Alan Watts has contracted them all into the one.

When he wrote the book in 1961, Watts was aware that LSD might become a public scandal. Already there were indications—too many youngsters were getting hold of it and being found naked in the streets or following their way up the roadway, declaring that they were birds on the wing.

But as he said in a prologue written nine years after the book was first published, he *had* considered scandal.

> *I ask myself whether I should have written this book, whether I was profaning the mysteries and casting pearls before swine. I reasoned, however, that . . . it was up to me to encourage a positive above board, fearless and intelligent approach to what are now known as psychedelic chemicals.*

But Watts was disappointed, by society and by authority. For what he hoped did not happen.

> *Thousands of young people, fed up with standard brand religions which provided nothing but talk, and (usually) bad ritual, rushed immediately to LSD and other pyschedelics in search of some key to genuine religious experience. As might be expected, there were accidents. A few potential psychotics were pushed over the brink. . . .*
>
> *. . .these incidents received full coverage in the press, to the relative exclusion of reports on the overwhelming majority of such splendid and memorable experiences as I describe further on. . . . There were even deliberately falsified stories in the newspapers, as that several young men taking LSD stared so long at the sun that they became blind. Psychiatrists raised alarms about "brain damage," for which no solid evidence was ever produced, and warnings were issued about its destructive effect on the genes, which was later shown to be insignificant and more or less the same as the effects of coffee and aspirin.*
>
> *In view of the public hysteria the Sandoz Company which held a patent on LSD, withdrew it from the market. At the same time the United States government, having learned absolutely nothing from the disaster of Prohibition, simply banned LSD (allowing its use only in some few research projects sponsored by the National Institute of Mental Health and by the Army in its investigations of chemical warfare) and turned over its control to the police. . . .*

The prologue of *The Joyous Cosmology* was as interesting as the book itself, and its criticism of the whole acid scene—as reflected after a number of years of hindsight—seems modest and moderate. A society which lets its alcoholics wander a hundred Skid Rows in our big cities, prey to every mugger, robber, and psychotic murderer in the land, has small business trying to regulate any other drug. But society will have its way, and the way is to suppress the new, ignore the old, and harry the proponents of change. It has been the same with birth control, where in 1975 a medical doctor performing a legal abortion in a recognized teaching hospital under controlled conditions *was convicted of manslaughter* by a Massachusetts court, for no other reason than that he did his job in an overwhelmingly Roman Catholic community.

In such a society, neither Alan Watts nor any other reformer stood a great chance of success.

Watts was a reformer, not a revolutionary, and that much should be apparent from this study of his life and career. His sense of reform led him to try to lead people toward a simpler, happier life, removing the bogeymen and artificial restrictions of the society in which he lived. He was not notably successful as the LSD story shows. Whatever effect he had was on the young, and cannot be felt for another 20 years when they assume the ruling power in the land. His personal success, his ability to live in comfort, was due to his pleasant personality, and his ability to write and also to perform as a public speaker—a group of attributes that are not usually found together.

貴生

CHAPTER TWENTY-SEVEN

THE VALUE SET ON LIFE

Who uses well his light,
Reverting to its source, so bright,
Will from his body ward all blight,
And hides the unchanging from men's sight.

from the Tao te Ching

Until Alan Watts achieved the ripe old age of fifty, he looked a much younger man. In his forties he appeared to be in his thirties, and even in 1965 photographs show him usually in open-necked sport shirt, clean shaven, and with the short haircut that could be described as either monk-like or crew-cut, depending on the state of mind of the viewer. But midway in the 1960s he began to age. Perhaps it was hardening of the arteries. Perhaps it was the regimen and busy social life he gave himself. But the turkey wrinkles began to sear his neck, the jaw became leaner and the pleasing layer of flesh dropped away from the face, leaving wrinkles and the signs of age.

Mentally he had never been more alert. His marriage was happy. It was totally out of character for him to be married of course, for in his previous two he had stomped and charged like a wild horse in confinement—but the years had slowed him down. Jano suited him, and apparently responded so beautifully to his every need that the friction was minor. But the years were wearing, and his literary output slowed down considerably. He wrote a good deal for magazines, but the books did not come so fast.

In 1966 Watts produced what he referred to as his nineteenth book. (That included booklets and other works.) It was *The Book: On the Taboo Against Knowing Who You Are,* and it was unashamedly aimed at the market that kept Watts going, the young people of America.

Watts was not always happy at being known as the Pied Piper of Sausalito; in 1958 he had gone to England to see his father and visit Chislehurst once more, and had been depressed to learn that in his own country (he was an American now, but still an Englishman at heart) he was a prophet without much honor. His books sold there infinitesimally, most of them were not published in British editions, and he was not at all well known.

But Watts the reformer was indeed well known in America and he was one of the principal gurus of the young.

In addition to his children Ti, Mark, Richard, Lila, and Diane by the second marriage, he had Joan and Ann by his first; now Joan had three children of her own and Ann had two. *The Book* was dedicated to the whole passel, children and grandchildren—Watts was hopefully moving into his second generational teaching. It was again a book about myth and the gods. This time, Alan Watts said, his studies had been based on the Vedanta. But he also went back to G.I. Gurdjieff, who was a friend and mentor to Dimitrije Mitrinović, that guru of Watts' own out of the dim distant past. But more than in that past, Watts' new work was a social commentary, a complaint against a society that created public parks and then so regulated them that most could not use them freely. Here is a typical comment:

> *Just try taking a stroll after dark in a nice American residential area. If you can penetrate the wire fences along the highways, and then wander along a pleasant lane, you may well be challenged from a police car: "Where are you going?" Aimless strolling is suspicious and irrational. You are probably a vagrant or burglar. You are not even walking the dog! "How much money are you carrying?" Surely you could have afforded to take the bus, and if you have little or no cash you are clearly a bum and a nuisance. Any competent housebreaker would approach his quarry in a Cadillac. . . .*

Now there is a new Watts. Secure in his position he has ventured forth into another field. Understanding the taboo against drugs, in 1966 he has had the good sense to get out of the general hullabaloo. He continued to use what drugs he wished—he took LSD as he chose—but he did it without fanfare and he did not crow about the glories of it any more. He had "settled down." His focus had changed.

And yet all the old Watts is there too:

> *The cat has already been let out of the bag. The inside information is that yourself as "just little me" who "came into this world" and lives temporarily in a bag of skin is a hoax and a fake. The fact is that because no one thing or feature of this universe is separable from the whole, the only real You, the Self, is the whole. . . .*

There is the Tao. There is the old Watts, back at his stand. The difference is in approach. For years Watts has been simplifying his approach to the Eastern mysteries, and in *The Book* he has reduced it to the point where a child might understand the fundamental concepts of the Tao. Not that the book was written for a child: "Nominalism, as we know, became the dominant attitude of western thought and especially of the philosophy of science. . . ." That is not childish talk. But the interesting aspect of Watts' philosophy is its reduction to simplicity: that is the way he wanted it, the old Zen masters were always pointing toward simplicity in those anecdotes and tales he told time and again. Now Watts was making up his own analogies and putting them in terms of a twentieth century American society.

It ends with IT, as his books were doing these days. And to sum up his philosophy, which was ever growing closer to that of the Tao—all the world is nonsense so have yourself a good laugh.

James Broughton, the poet (who was quoted in the book), reviewed it. That was a comforting thing to have happen—Watts was lucky that way—he reviewed his friend Joseph Campbell and Campbell reviewed him. Oddly enough, he managed somehow to escape the literary rule that the book review editor automatically puts the book into the hands of the author's natural enemy. The review was a good honest review, laudatory—but he could not be faulted for liking Watts, whom he called "a man of good cheer, good will, and good hope."

And indeed, Alan Watts was. In his middle years, living again in Mill Valley but keeping the "office" at the Sausalito ferry, Watts was asking not so very much of the world. He wanted to support himself and his wife and children (and his ex-wife, by fiat) and to enjoy himself. Much more than most Americans he and that tribe of wild Indians who lived in Druid Heights were managing to do all these things. Life could be beautiful. At least until the rest of America discovered it and somehow homogenized the process.

Lectures, radio broadcasts, television appearances, and even interviews were the way of life of the Alan Wattses of the 1960s. His wife was his principal aide. She read and corrected manuscript and typed. She was described by a friend as an enormously capable and winsome woman—she pleased Watts right down to the core, and she devoted herself to his affairs with a will that had not been apparent in either of his other wives.

Andrew Curry, the editor of *Dust,* a far-out publication, interviewed Watts at about this time. Curry had known him for several years—all in the California period, since the days when Curry had been a social worker at a state psychiatric hospital, where Watts was a consultant. The younger man always respected Watts: his first view had been of the man who had just written *The Wisdom of Insecurity*—and he found him then to be a "golden person." He saw Watts in 1960 and was taken with "rugged good looks," his casual dress, string tie, and the smile that brought back a Watts quotation from the East: "he that knows that he is a fool is not a big fool."

He liked Watts:

> *To my mind he is one of the most original and "unrutted" philosophers of the century; not because the book jackets say so, but because the expression of his life says so. After all, the essence of philosophizing is learning how to live and die. More precisely, in the vein of an old Zen saying, "When walking, walk; when sitting, sit—just don't wobble.*

So one night Andrew Curry and Leonard Fulton went down to the old ferry boat in Sausalito harbor, to visit Alan Watts and get an interview for their magazine. They found a relaxed Alan Watts, greeting them with an ample supply of Pinot Chardonnay which they drank as they talked. It was a stormy San Francisco night, with a thunderstorm brewing. And they sat, listening to thunder, talking, drinking, and smelling the incense that Watts burned for them in honor of the Buddha.

More and more Alan Watts dealt with what he saw as the major American problem—the need to make life somehow meaningful. And he told the young men from *Dust* his view, some of it repetitive of what he had said before, some of it more thoroughly expository:

> *There's a great lack of experimental adventure in not asking "Well, what sort of life could we live? What would be a new thing? What would be a new way of living?" I'm amazed by this because here is surely a fertile field for technology. We are the richest country on earth, powerful; but we have a very low capacity for pleasure, when you consider that we divide our lives rigidly into work and play. Almost all of us, except some few lucky ones, have jobs, a job means something you do to make money. It probably bores the hell out of you. But you have to do this thing because you need the money. So you work five hours or whatever, and you get that money, and you leave the job and you think, "All right, now comes play time." We make lots of money, enough to buy many things—what the hell do we do? You'd think that now with the great way of life, technology, all the powers that we have would enable us to go*

home, having done our duty to get that money, and have the swingingest time you ever thought of. But people just don't do that.

So Watts sailed through life, with a vigor and a sense of pleasure that is very well brought forth in his *In My Own Way.* The Watts of the late 1960s was in his prime, but the high point of his life was passing. He had reached the apex in those earliest years. His most beautiful piece of writing is undoubtedly *The Joyous Cosmology* in which he attempts to synthesize and recreate the psychedelic adventure. But all the while, all his life, he was changing. Only in the late 1960s do we see the repetition set in, meaning that he had achieved much of what he intended or could achieve, and was now practicing his trade.

Alan Watts was as busy as he had ever been. He spent a great deal of time on his calligraphy—and it was very good calligraphy, particularly for a Westerner. He studied his Chinese. He began a new book, *Tao: The Watercourse Way.* He started a novel.

The novel was one of Watts' most interesting literary ventures. For years, since the days of the Northwestern pastorate, Watts had been eager to write one particular book. He had been much impressed with some of the "divines" he had met; he wanted to create a work something along the line of Sinclair Lewis' mindstripping expose of evangelical doings. In a way, he wanted to limn his own life, and the title indicated it. *Charlatan* was to be the theme of his novel, for he always regarded himself as part charlatan. The story would be that of a man who makes a career of religion, then pretends to visions and supernatural doings—and finally becomes convinced in himself that it is all true.

Watts sat down to the work and planned it. He wrote some 90 pages, and he sent them to Tim Seldes. They were not ready—it was not enough—there was a good deal more thinking to be done before the novel was on the track. So he took them back and filed them away for future reference—and the future was not long enough.

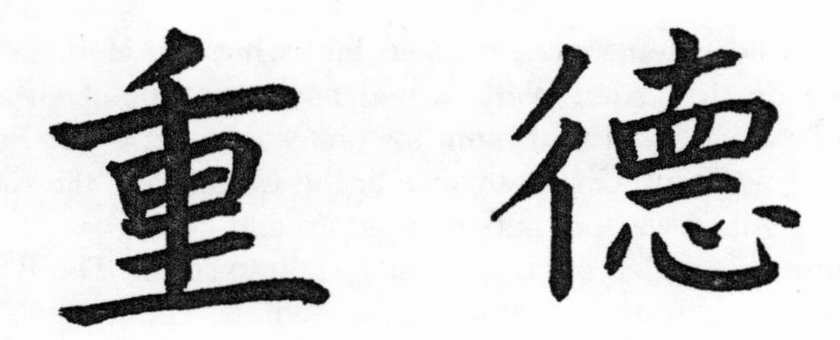

CHAPTER TWENTY-EIGHT

THE QUALITY OF GRAVITY

He always drew audiences. His was a specialized performance, and in these later years, he grew a new beard, red streaked with gray, and he donned the handsome black silk kimono, and used the fan as an Oriental would, for emphasis, to indicate impatience, or tranquility, or irritation. But he was the showman, and the principles were the same as in the past.

One night in San Francisco he appeared at the Avalon Ballroom, in behalf of a money-raising benefit for the Zen Mountain Center at Tassajara Hot Springs near Big Sur.

"Zen is inexplicable," he told them (quite forgetting that he had written in *The New Republic* that Zen masters must not start out that way). "I should just rap my fan on the microphone and leave," he said when someone asked him what was Zen. But he would not do that, Alan Watts would never disappoint an audience, so he stayed and told them his philosophy. In brief: Relax.

It was, as Frank Chesley wrote in the *Chronicle,* "the theme he has brought to western audiences again and again."

And he was called upon again and again to speak. The Bollingen Foundation supported some of his activities. The Esalen Institute of Big Sur sponsored a liturgy at the First Unitarian Church, all created by Alan Watts, including the part for the bongo drums. He did not stop his level of activity; he did turn from writing books to more personal forms.

The Unitarian affair was a fine party. Timothy Leary was there, and Watts led the singing and the chanting of the cosmic OM—the prayer in the heart of the lotus.

In spite of the complaints that he did not offer himself to causes, he fought for what he believed in. In Chicago he spoke out against making criminals of LSD users. It was not so easy to speak out on such issues in 1968.

That summer he went back to England again, to see relatives and old friends and there he was interviewed by columnist John Crosby, who sought him out as a guru of the young to ask what had happened to Haight-Ashbury, which was just then disintegrating. Watts had his usual answer—it applied to Sausalito and to Mill Valley too: where the hippies or the interesting people of bohemia come, the middleclass always follows. Once again, Watts was repeating. But a truth is a truth is a truth. He could not help it if an undiscerning journalistic world continued to ask him the same questions over and over again.

Watts now achieved something of a reputation in the San Francisco Bay area as an expert witness on drugs and religion. He was called from time to time by defense attorneys in their attempts to prove that drug-taking was a philosophical and sometimes religious adventure rather than a criminal act.

He was reviewing books for the newspapers and magazines, for he reviewed thoughtfully and well. His San Francisco *Chronicle* review of Theodore Roszak's *The Making of a Counterculture* was restrained and provocative, and unlike many a reviewer Watts did not use the medium as a takeoff point for an essay of his own.

Time was treating him badly. Here is the beginning of a long interview and descriptive article by the *Chronicle's* Maitland Zane, written in the spring of 1969:

> *BIG SUR*
>
> *"Are you breathing? Or is it breathing you?"*
>
> *Alan Watts, a guru with a little brass bell around his neck, was teaching 30 men and women how to turn off the endless chatter inside their heads and really listen.*
>
> *The place was Esalen Institute at the hot springs near here, in a big room with nothing in it but a springy wall to wall carpet. The afternoon sun was streaming in the windows. It was very still.*
>
> *Watts, wearing an orange-red velvet shirt, said in his well-born English voice, "Shut your eyes."*
>
> *He rapped a Buddhist gong, and the room shimmered.*
>
> *"We are going to explore the art of listening," he said. "You don't need to strain. Just let your ears alone. Let your ears be played with by the vibrations in the air. Just let it happen."*
>
> *Watts, who wrote his first book on Zen Buddhism when he was only 20, is a Capricorn of 54 who lives in Sausalito with his third wife and has had seven children and has several grandchildren.*
>
> *He looks it. . . .*

Oh unkind cut. But there it was. He who rides on the tiger may never get off—the same newspaper whose reporters of a different decade had remarked on Watt's agelessness now employed newer reporters, more critical, more caustic perhaps in the new school, but essentially reporting what they saw and heard.

Alan Watts had aged.

> *Except for his voice, which is as persuasive as a cello, and his laugh, which is that of a turned on Zen master capable of laughing at anything, especially himself, he could be taken for a seedy, bleary-eyed, fang-toothed loser from Sixth and Howard [San Francisco's Skid Row].*

But the reporter was honest as they come: he had obviously arrived full of skepticism. Watts had put the group to chanting, the Om, and the Aum ne Um, and a Vedanta chant, but shortly afterward had stopped them. It was like LSD, he said, the effects could be disorienting. A little went a long way.

And sure enough, said the reporter, the effects *were* disorienting.

So the reporter went away believing—but the damning evidence was there. Alan Watts was mortal and his mortality was showing.

He slowed down. No doubt about it. His next book was *Does It Matter,* a collection of essays written for various reasons and some for publications. Most of them had been written for his own *Bulletin of the Society for Comparative Philosophy.* Thus, as can be seen, Alan's intellectual efforts showed what Harold Ross of *The New Yorker* once called "a delicate sense of double entry bookkeeping."

These essays dealt with specific problems of life and happiness. "Wealth vs. Money" was one. "Murder in the Kitchen" was a second. "Clothes—On and Off" was a third. "The Spirit of Violence and the Matter of Peace" was the fourth. Not until the fifth do we come to "Psychedelic and Religious Experience"—and it is a rehash of much that Watts had written before, and not nearly so indicative as his *Joyous Cosmology.*

And yet when reporter Maitland Zane reviewed the book for the *Chronicle,* it was this essay he reviewed.

The essay "Wealth vs. Money" harks back to the teachings and plaints of Ezra Pound about money. "Murder in the Kitchen" is funny in spots, discussing food, materials, and implements involved with eating—even down to chairs. "Clothes" is an argument against and for comfort. All of them have charm and merit—and of all the books the least informative of the essays is the drug piece. But unerringly, reporter Zane found his target—for the press of this time was bemused by drugs. So the baby's bath water is in danger of costing us the baby—here—for Watts the character was being reviewed and not the writer. Mr. Zane's review really should have been run in the news columns and someone else should have reviewed the book.

Yet it was not an attack. The newspapers had a certain fondness for Alan Watts—he was good copy and he was urbane and apparently unflappable. He stayed out of the eyes and clutches of the law. If he broke the law he did so in decent privacy.

Watts was now dividing his time between the ferryboat and a little cottage on the back of Mt. Tamalpais, where the mist hung in late in the morning, and where the quiet and the peace made it beautiful for writing. Here early in the decade, he set out to write two new books, one a philosophical study of what life was all about, as seen from the mountain. It took the form of a journal. These pieces would be used in *Playboy*, in *Earth*, and in his own *Journal*, and then, since nothing is wasted in a philosopher's house, would be collected and printed in a book *Cloud Hidden, Whereabouts Unknown*—the title taken from a famous Taoist poem.

There is a sense of tranquility in these essays that must have been lost on most readers, so immersed in the razzmatazz of American life.

The title of one essay is "And the Mountain." It begins:

> *There is the water, and now there is also the mountain. (In Chinese the two characters for mountain and water mean landscape.) I have the use of a small one-room cottage on the slopes of the mountain Tamalpais—which I can see from the ferryboat. It is hidden in a grove of high eucalyptus trees and overlooks a long valley whose far side is covered with a dense forest of bay, oak, and madrone so even in height that from a distance it looks like brush. No human dwelling is in the view, and the principal inhabitant of the forest is a wild she-goat who has been there for at least nine years. Every now and then she comes out and dances upon the crown of an immense rock which rises far out of the forest. No one goes to this forest. I have been down to its edge, where there is a meadow, good for practicing archery, and I think that one of these days I will explore the forest. But then again I may not for there are places which people should leave alone. . . .*

Watts was at peace. He had not always been so. But now, he had adjusted to all that had happened.

That Spring Elsa Gidlow called on Watts to write an article about him for *California Living*, the magazine of the combined San Francisco *Chronicle* and Sunday *Examiner*. Elsa Gidlow had known Watts for 20 years, and she explored very sensitively.

She found Alan Watts living as he wished, with his wife and a handful of fancy cats (Burmese, Siamese, and Abyssinian) in that cottage on the shoulder of Tamalpais. She described a day of his life: up before dawn, several hours of writing, while Jano worked on the manuscript—surrounded by family, one daughter edited his subscription magazine *Journal,* living quietly, but busily, going from telephone to contemplation, dropping his work to help a friend, holding a seminar for a dozen people aboard the *Vallejo.* The seminar might be on Ecstasy—Sexuality—Death—Insanity. . . . Then back to the mountain again.

> *It is the close of another day at the retreat in the eucalyptus wood. Alan has worked since daybreak on his book (the first phase of his autobiography is now in progress). In the afternoon he begins replying to some of the less neglectable letters culled by his secretary. He jots notes on some for her to take care of. Others he will answer himself, the shorter ones handwritten in a distinguished script that most likely will be cherished by the recipient.*
>
> *Since breakfast he has forgotten to eat. He drinks some apple juice, nibbles a few nuts and goes out onto the deck that extends like the prow of a ship toward the valley. The air is very still, color accumulating and deepening in the sky from the sun's afterglow. At this hour Alan enjoys what he calls "walking meditation." He changes sandals for sturdy boots, puts on an enveloping shaggy sweater, takes his staff as tall as himself . . . topped by a Buddhist pilgrim's rattle . . . and starts down the rough trail strewn with eucalyptus seeds toward the valley. . . .*

Yes, a happy man. No money worries. A loving wife. His children adjusted. Why should he not be a happy man? He is. In 1973 he was that man.

In the spring the autobiography was finished. It was published that fall by Pantheon, and received very good, very solid, friendly reviews for the most part. It sold well, too, as all Watts books seemed to do.

He went on then, with his tranquil, friendly life, writing and talking, walking and contemplating, and eating the foods that interested him. In his late fifties he was still the happy man.

And so he died. One morning, before dawn, his wife moved to awaken him for the day, and found him cold and quiet.

There was mourning in Druid Heights and down on the shore of Sausalito. There were memorial ceremonies and processions and a sadness in the lively young community and the community of the young of heart with whom he lived.

Death had not been entirely unexpected. He had gone on a long and wearisome lecture tour that took him east and to Europe, and coming home exhausted he had been warned by his doctor. But now he was gone. There was a void. But was there?

Or fame or life,
which do you hold more dear?
Or life or wealth,
to which would you adhere?
Keep life and lose those other things;
Keep them and lose your life;—which brings
Sorrow and pain more near?

Thus we may see,
Who cleaves to fame
Rejects what is more great;
Who loves large stores
Gives up richer state.

Who is content
Needs fear no shame.
Who knows to stop
Incurs no blame.
From danger free
Long live shall he.

That was the Tao. And Alan Watts had found the Tao.

POSTSCRIPT

It is a tribute to the human spirit that a man's best work is often done in the very last period of his life; that is certainly true of Alan Watts. For in autumn 1975, two years after his death, Pantheon published Watts' final book, *Tao: The Watercourse Way.* The book surely deserved to be a grand success, for it was in almost every way superior to any of his other works. It was, in essence, a distillation of all that he'd learned in his years of study of The Way.

The work itself is brief, cut off in the middle by the untimely hand of fate. But for any who seek the roots and bases of philosophical Taoism and Zen, this book serves nicely as a primer.

The approach is quite new, representing a change in Watts' life that came over him in his last years. He tended to revert then, to the study of the Taoist writings, which were the foundations of Zen so long ago. He was going back to the source to strengthen and identify his ideas. Advanced students of Oriental philosophy—Orientals in particular—might criticize the work as puffed up and overconcerned with origins and forms. But this book was obviously written for eager young Westerners who had no background in Oriental life or culture, and yet wished to leap into that philosophy in one bound.

If there was a way through the forest for such people, then it could be that Alan Watts, sitting among the eucalyptus trees of Muir woods, drinking tea, and playing the bamboo flute, could be their guide.

Alan's great new friend of this period of his life was Al Chung-liang Huang, whose name is so marvelously tangled up by Oriental standards as to epitomize the entire problem of East-West transitions. Huang Chung-liang was the youth's name when he grew up in a Confucian scholar's family in China, and Huang is the family name. But Westerners put the family name last instead of first, and when the young man acquired the American nickname Al, it's something of a marvel that the polyglot could be written down. In any case, Al Chung-liang Huang became Watts' friend, and collaborator and teacher in things Chinese, and they spent a great deal of time together exploring the world of Taoist philosophy. It was not a one-way street, for Alan Watts knew a great deal about Zen that he could impart, and the student of Tao had much to give him in return.

So Al Chung-liang Huang became the literary editor of the unfinished manuscript, and when Watts died, tried to complete the book for Alan. But it was impossible. The book had been the most spontaneous outpouring of Watts' East-meets-West theme; there was simply no way that anyone else could finish it.

Watts' plan had been to let the book be a happening. He would allow the chapters to come out any way they wanted. And they did, with all that verve and beauty of which he was capable, all of what Al Chung-liang Huang called "writing the unwritable" and what Watts' critics would call literary froth. Watts completed a preface which showed where his mind was going and what he was using as the basic source for the book. That was Joseph Needham's *Science and Civilization in China,* a huge multi-volume scholarly enterprise for Cambridge University that involved scores of people and many years of effort. With typical Watts' one-upmanship he completed a prolegomana in which he dealt with the irritating problems of bibliography and romanization of Chinese characters and speech, showing all his old intolerance of the folderol and pretensions of scholarship.

Watts had lately become a serious student of written Chinese, a process that takes years for Chinese who grow up with it, and twice as long for any Westerner. Few if any Westerners ever attain a real familiarity with the brush. Realizing that, Watts made arrangements for his character-illustrations, and translations to be done by Al's mother, Lee Chih-chang, who had a very nice touch.

There are twenty-four pages in Chinese, brief quotations that both illuminate the book, and should illuminate the minds of those who can read them, and give a sense of something worth striving for to those who cannot. That, likely, was Alan's prime reason for including the Chinese ideographs. Of course, one must never forget the recurring Wattsian motivation, the need to dazzle his audience with prestidigitation and the unusual.

Watts' purpose in exploring the Chinese language was to try to give his reader an indication of the Chinese approach to life, and he does so for those who are willing to stop and think as they read. The difference between that approach and that of Occidentals is so great that most readers will give up or simply leave the chapter, stunned.

The second chapter of the book deals with Ying and Yang, the Oriental polarity. Here Watts enters the philosophical realm for certain, with more sureness than he was able to bring to any book since *Myth and Ritual in Christianity*. That is why *Tao* is Watts' finest book—he is more certain of his subject than ever before, and he brings his teacher's loves and his shaman's showmanship together in a sparkling display.

The chapter, like the book, is filled with anecdotes that illustrate the weird and wondrous approaches of the Oriental philosophers to life and the world beyond understanding. And he sums it up in pure Watts:

> *Let your ears hear whatever they want to hear; let your eyes see whatever they want to see; let your mind think whatever it wants to think; let your lungs breathe in their own rhythm. Do not expect any special result, for in this wordless and idealess state where can there be past or future, and where any notion of purpose? Stop, look, and listen . . . and stay there awhile before you go on reading.*

Watts now adhered to the simple theory of the watercourse of nature. "Let your mind alone" was the basis of it; let your mind wander and dictate your ambience. In the third chapter, on Tao, he explored that philosophy, not talking of Zen, but back beyond to the roots of Zen, and telling by anecdote and example how the old ones worked out their lives.

The fourth chapter of the book, *Wu-wei*, refers to the principle of inaction or nonaction, which again emphasizes the philosophy of letting matters take their course without excitement. And again, as in the past, Watts is full of quotations and tales to illustrate and prove his points. It is a highly footnoted work, as perhaps it had to be, since he was exploring a subject he'd not treated before, and he knew he would be facing the rude gazes of Western scholars of things Chinese, and they would be much more harsh on him than Orientals. But there is more to the footnoting than that; the notes show a relish for the subject, a learning process in motion. As he was writing, it was apparent that Watts was studying, learning, absorbing the Chinese language as much as the philosophy that he and Al Chung-liang Huang were essaying.

There is not much reference to Zen in the book—except again to explain his own eschewing za-zen or "aching legs" and "sitting on your ass" Buddhism. He is more interested in what he had just learned and in passing that along.

The final completed chapter of the book, *Te*, which refers to virtue, is more or less a summation of the Tao or way of life, and adjuration to disciples to live without effort. Watts again here shows his marvelous capability of combining references to Chuang Tzu and Thor Heyerdahl in the same chapter without appearing absurd. It was natural for him to do so. And that, after all, is the essence of Watts: do what comes naturally.

It was here that Watts was cut off in the middle of November, 1973, and so the book ends with an appreciation by his friend Al Chung-liang Huang. And it is a gentle, precious flower of its own, giving the reader a lasting feeling for Watts, and for the joyous nature of his last period and the pleasure of his company.

There was also a touch of the sadness of it, of the heavy drinking and admission that liquor had become an essential of this happiness—an admission that would curl the hair of the puritan in the American at least. Al Chung-liang Huang identified even Watts as the victim of the world in which he lived—a world dominated by the *Yang* or power force.

"He revealed the crux of this tragedy shared by most men in this unbalanced time by admitting, 'But I don't like myself when I am sober,' as he surrendered to another shot of vodka at a time when he knew he need not and should not rely on it any more."

Where would the book have gone had Alan Watts lived to finish it? There was indication that it would have remained a work heavily dependent on the Tao, and that Alan Watts was transcending the Zen he had absorbed and transmitted for so long. (Zen Buddhists will not like that idea.) But perhaps not. Perhaps he would have returned to his old concept of Walking Zen, and certainly he would have returned to his old showmanship and love of the art forms of religion, the shamanism that he adored.

But that is all conjecture. The reality is that he died in midstream, and left this unfinished, yet poetical and positive book as his testament. He left a sense of peace behind him that seems to have been transmitted to those close to him, for when asked at a memorial celebration in 1974 what it had been like to live with Alan Watts, his widow Jano replied that it had never been dull, always full of fun and surprises, ". . . and the biggest surprise of all was on November 16 last year."

You could sense that she almost heard him laughing in the hills.

And then came another surprise. In the summer of 1975 a thief broke into Jano Watts' apartment in Marin County. He stole a color television set and a little Tibetan urn. There was a Watts-ian touch for you—color TV and ancient urn. And more surprises. When Watts had died, his remains had been shipped to a Zen Center in Northern California, except for three bone fragments which Jano had kept in that urn. And with it she had placed a curse, an ancient Tibetan curse on any who might defile those remains of a happy man. So the thief walked off with pleasure and pain in either hand, and which would triumph over him?

You can hear Alan Watts laughing all the way across the sunny slope of Mt. Tamalpais, and down into the serene and verdant Muir Woods.

INDEX

THE WORKS OF ALAN WATTS